Advance Praise for
Of Mud and Honey

"This is a heartbreaking tale of a happy family enveloped in tumultuous political currents completely beyond its control. The author's command of Aden's history as well as the region at large is remarkable, and she seamlessly weaves the political predicament into the personal story of the Barucha family. Trabulsi has composed a moving drama that illustrates the troubles of a city and nation in the microcosmic struggles of a family. A gripping and emotionally affecting political tale."

—*Kirkus Reviews*

"Roxana has created a masterpiece that had me enthralled until the very last page. The rich and detailed descriptions of beautiful Aden and its people, the bravery of Silloo, and the loyalty of Ahmed stood out amidst so many other amazing mini stories. I loved it."

—Divya Krishnan

"With fine-grained detail that gives her story the texture of memoir, Roxana Trabulsi evokes the bewilderment of expatriates whose lives are transformed by geopolitical events beyond their control. As their lives of beauty and abundance become a nightmare of intimidation and false imprisonment, Roxana carried me along with the fear and fury of her protagonists, who must discover their own reserves of resilience and ingenuity.

Their Parsi community — extending from Aden to Dubai, Bombay, Delhi, and London — mobilizes to support them, a sobering reminder of the essential role that our communities can play in times of crisis."

—Beth Barry

"Roxana is a gifted writer and storyteller. Her novel leaves me shaken. I am stirred to connect with her characters as they struggle against oppression and injustice. In the telling of this story, I move through time and space — through the old cities of Aden, Yemen and Bombay, India. I discover the young, vibrant city of Dubai in the '70s. Roxana's details are so precise, and the telling so rich that I can almost smell the nectar and taste the sweet tea under the searing Middle Eastern sun. It is a tale of family. It is a tale of tribe. She shows how these forces shape our collective history and define her family's saga. It is a gripping reminder of how quickly a country can turn against its members, condemn innocent people, and justify horror, all in the name of patriotism."

—Anita Luria

"I thought that I would be reading a love story when I picked up this book, and yet it turned out to be much more! Of Mud and Honey takes the reader on a journey through time, following the harrowing details of one family during the time of the British exit from Aden. I had never heard of the city of Aden, I certainly couldn't locate it on a map, and I had no idea that it was a Crown Colony. I love it when a book makes you think and challenges you to learn, all while being lost in the lives of the protagonists. The reader intimately witnesses the strength of character and moral fortitude of all the members of this family while feeling their daily struggles to survive. I was so immersed in their world that I had a hard time putting the book down. I needed to know that they were going to be okay, that they would survive this arduous time in their lives. Brava to Roxana Trabulsi for bringing this very personal story of the journey of these amazing people to life in such a beautiful and heartfelt way."

—Michelle Brockmann

"A beautiful and emotional book. The importance of showing love, loyalty, and kindness when all seems lost shines through. I especially enjoyed seeing how past kindnesses — shown naturally with no thought of return — helped even when in despair. A definite 'must read.' I loved reading this book. I may even have read it twice! It was gorgeous."

—Annie Adams

"Loved the book! Roxana Trabulsi captures the struggles and birth of an independent Yemen amidst the downfall of British colonialism. Her vivid narrative captures life's intimate details at a time when the characters struggle to survive. Yet through it all, this novel illustrates the importance of hope and, above all, love."

—Jennifer Sullivan

"What makes this book important and why it should be widely read is that throughout the world today — as well as yesterday and tomorrow — other families and individuals face the same tribulations as a result of coups, uprisings, revolutions, and changes of regime and policies; for example, in Yemen and Afghanistan today."

—Noel Brehony, Author of *Yemen Divided*

"I read this last month. Amazing. It is rare to find a nonfiction book that is a page-turner, but this is one of them. I can totally see this as a movie. The imagery is so evocative. You feel as though you are right there in Yemen. Congrats to Roxana Trabulsi on making the world a more beautiful, understandable place. Please write more!"

—David Luria

Of Mud & Honey

A Novel

Roxana Trabulsi

Ten|16
PRESS

www.ten16press.com - Waukesha, WI

For my parents, Rohin and Prochi, for teaching me
to look for beauty where there is ugliness, to find joy
through my sorrow, and to choose kindness, always.
This is your story. This is for you.

For Sarosh, Sohrab and Arnie. If I had to choose my
siblings again, I would choose you every time.
This is for you.

For David, my partner, my sounding board, the
calm steady balance in my life. Thank you for your
unwavering support and encouragement. This would
not be without you. This is for you.

For Max, Nylah and Shane, my greatest achievements.
For what would my life be, if I were not your mother?
You give me purpose. This is for you.

For myself, so I never forget that I can.
This is for me.

Author's Note

Historically, we have lived in a world that has inflicted tyranny, oppression, and misery on those who have been deemed weaker. Oppression, once seeded and rooted, will eventually stifle and choke the afflicted, who will either submit to or defy their oppressors. Freedom, a universal right, is denied to so many.

The Middle East has always struggled to find a clear path to freedom, entangled as it is in centuries of history and culture wrapped up in countries with resources so valuable to a Western world willing to sink to profound moral depths for access. The region is populated by cultures so similar in mindset, yet so distinctly opposed to one another—in some cases to the point of hatred. Aden, a small city close to the eastern approach of the Red Sea, has for generations been a magnetic hub, home to a multitude of cultures, a geographical location crucial to the West after the construction of the Suez Canal.

Some could argue that the catastrophic implosion that pulsed through Yemen in the 1960s and early 1970s was an inevitable result of the bubbling oppression that had been fermenting for generations. Yet others may argue that this story could have had a different outcome. I am just the storyteller, so I shall leave any such conclusions to you.

Part One

"There really can be no peace without justice.
There can be no justice without truth.
And there can be no truth, unless someone
rises up to tell you the truth."
—Louis Farrakhan

1

"Freedom, an innate right, denied to so many, must be taken—
the fight for which can be savage. Nobody can give you freedom.
Nobody can give you equality or justice or anything.
If you're a man, you take it."
—Malcolm X

November 2, 1967

A lot can happen in thirty minutes. If Harry had only known what the next half hour would mean in the grand scheme of things, he might have paid more attention. His mind was preoccupied, so much so that he had let his guard down.

His stride hastened through the sandy shopping streets of Steamer Point in the Yemeni city of Aden, crimson dust clouds trailing his every step along the uneven path. It wasn't even noon and the heat was relentless. Sweat trickled down his forehead and spine, soaking the white cotton button-down shirt now stuck to his back. The call to prayer began in one corner of the city and within seconds echoed through all the minarets dotted throughout the mountains. Reaching into his trouser pocket, he pulled out his handkerchief and dabbed the beads of perspiration from his brow. The taste of salt was heavy in the air, drifting in from the ocean just beyond the small garden he was passing, the lethargic waves barely audible as they climbed the shore. Years of brutal SAS military training had taught him how to manage the extreme weather of the Middle East. Even though his body automatically responded to the high temperatures, his mind wouldn't succumb, and for this he was grateful. He ignored the sweltering sun and damp heat pushing up against him from every direction, daring him to continue. Instead, his mind was distracted and consumed with disappointment—disappointment with the direction his government was moving in.

The decision had been made. The decision to pull out of Aden sooner than originally planned. A whole year earlier. Harry tried to ignore the pit in his stomach and instead focused his thoughts on the work he had done, all that he had accomplished with the local federation of sultans and the agreements that had been made, many of which Harry had negotiated himself. This wasn't the way to leave a country that had served them well until recently. Frustrated, he clenched his teeth. He had worked so hard to strengthen the relationships within the federation; his reputation was on the line. The last post of the British Empire and they were going to run with their tails between their legs. His brow furrowed as the pit in his stomach grew. Wasn't this exactly what his country was trying to avoid? History, he knew all too well, was infinitely wise and tried her best to warn us of the consequences of our actions. *Why do we continuously struggle with those lessons?* he thought. *Why do we always think that it will somehow be different this time around? Why is it that we never learn?* He quickened his pace while his eyebrows narrowed even more, creasing his forehead. The conversation replayed over and over again in his mind.

"It's not working, Harry," Lord Besick had said nonchalantly. "Tensions have risen. We're losing men, and it's clear that the insurgents want us out. It's hard to justify still being here, quite honestly."

"Sir, we told the federal rulers and sultans that we would stay, that our military base would remain permanently in the area, that we would help them with the handover. This isn't that. This is breaking every treaty we've signed with them. We're not keeping our word."

"Harry, there is no breach here." Now irritated, Lord Besick spoke slowly, enunciating each word. "The Crown is not responsible for any false hope or promises that Duncan Sandys may have made. That is preposterous."

"With all due respect, sir, you're saying that our government has made a unilateral decision that affects the future of Aden without even consulting the federation of sultans. When a British foreign minister, such as Mr. Sandys, makes promises that we then break, we stand to look like idiots. What about all those signed treaties? We *did* make promises to the sultans— promises to protect them from the nationalists. To maintain peace when we give them back their country and to help them with the transition. We're opening the door to chaos. They need us to ensure a proper handover. They trust us, sir."

"Treaties were not signed." Lord Besick raised his voice. "Might I remind you that the majority of your federal rulers are

illiterate thugs. A thumbprint is hardly a binding agreement."
He snorted in disgust. "Orders are orders. I'm not looking for a
conversation here, nor, quite frankly, your opinion. Are we clear?"

"But, sir—"

"Are we clear?!"

Silence slowly stretched and dragged itself between them as
Harry painfully brought himself to respond. "Yes, sir."

"Good, that's more like it. Let's talk tomorrow, shall we?
We'll need to discuss the logistics in detail. I want our troops
and civilians out as soon as possible."

Back on the sweltering streets of Aden, Harry's jaw began
to ache. He paused in front of a toy shop to massage away the
tension and let his thoughts flow. The dusty street housed a strip
of buildings with several shopfronts: Bhicajee Cowasjee, Star
Pharmacy, the Marina Hotel, and the boarded-up Universal
Bazaar, which had been owned and operated by a young Jewish
Yemeni, Benjamen Yahuda, until his departure in 1950. Harry
had not known him, but Yahuda's standing as a businessman was
legendary in Aden, his home until 1947 when the United Nations
passed a resolution that called for the partition of Palestine into
Arab and Jewish states. As news of the resolution spread, Arabs
across the Mid-East rioted, attacking and killing Jews for their
perceived role in the displacement of their Arab brothers. In
1950, Israeli Prime Minister Ben Gurion announced the Law of
Return, which granted any Jew the right to return to Israel.

Yahuda was one of fifty thousand Yemenite Jews evacuated in
Operation Magic Carpet, one of the most complex immigration

operations the state had ever known. Israeli, British, and American transport planes secretly flew them to their newly established home of Israel. Yemenite Jews made their way to Aden by foot from all corners of the country, desperate to avoid attacks from Arabs and arrive to safety. Harry remembered when Operation Magic Carpet was in every newspaper in London. He had been just a teenager then but followed every detail of the story, and ultimately it had inspired him to work for the British government—he was determined to be a part of something big and make a difference.

This ever-evolving country continued to awe Harry. To think that there had been fifty thousand Yemenite Jews here to begin with flabbergasted him. Yemen was so rich in culture, so steeped in history. These people had waited patiently to take their country back after more than a century of occupation. He felt for them.

His long legs scaled the large steps up to the veranda of Bhicajee Cowasjee, where he stopped for a moment at the tall stone pillars that guarded the shop. Placing his hand on one of the thick white columns, he expected it to be cool to the touch. But even this stoic sentry had succumbed to the sun's domination, and it felt warm and clammy, much to Harry's disappointment. Looking away, and feeling even more defeated, he was caught by a strange sense that someone was following him. Turning back to glance over his shoulder, he quickly scanned the street, but nothing struck him as out of the ordinary.

Inside the shop, the steady breeze from the overhead fans brought instant relief as he made his way toward the soda machine. Harry pulled out a drink from the icebox and lingered for a moment, reveling in the cooling air before using the attached opener to remove the jagged metal cap. Eagerly, he drew the bottle to his mouth. The sensation of the cold glass on his lips was heavenly. After gulping down the sweet, icy cola, he pressed the bottle up against his flushed and chiseled cheeks, taking sanctuary in the small pleasure.

Dara, the young Parsi man who owned the business along with his family, emerged from the back of the store and immediately began to shower his customer in a warm welcome. Harry had lived in Southern Arabia for close to fifteen years and was well versed in the many cultures that made Aden the haven that it was. He and his wife, Jane, were regulars at the shop, and they were also part of the larger social scene that Dara and his wife, Silloo, ran in. The warm weather and miles of beaches and mountain ranges meant an active life for most people who lived in Aden. Beach clubs, boating, water-skiing, dancing, and camp-outs along the shoreline were all a part of the everyday routine; through these activities, the small city fostered many friendships across its diverse communities.

"Harry, my friend, so nice to see you. How are you?"

"Ah, Dara, hello there. Forgive me for just helping myself," he said, holding up the empty Coke bottle and smiling sheepishly. "It's a hot one today, wouldn't you say?"

"Please, please, you are always welcome to help yourself. No need to apologize. Anything I can assist you with?"

Chapter 1

"I have a list somewhere," Harry replied, digging through his pockets for the folded piece of paper. "Jane asked for a few things. We are heading to a party tomorrow night in Ma'alla. A handful of officers and their wives, some of the secretaries. Apparently, there will be quite a spread. Jane wants to bring Yorkshire pudding... So, ah, here it is. Flour, eggs, milk, and vegetable oil."

"Jane was just here for flour last week. She must be baking up a storm!"

"Actually, she opened it up and there were a lot of little ants or something in the jar. That's why she wanted some more."

"Harry, that is just a little extra protein in this part of the world! Nothing to fret about." Dara chuckled, waving it off.

"Ha, that's true." Harry smiled knowingly at the shop owner. "But Jane was worried that the other guests might not be so understanding."

They both laughed while Dara leaned in. "Let me have someone pull your items for you. Can I get you anything else while you wait?"

"You are a good man, Dara. No, thank you. The drink was all I needed."

Dara rang up Harry's shopping list while they talked about their boats and wanting to get out for a good sail over the weekend. He then carried the bag of groceries and followed Harry out of the store, still chatting about the weather and the unusual increase in sharks of late. There was a definite need for more shark nets and better patrolling of the waters. Harry took the bag and then walked down the stairs, leaving Dara up by the pillars, still talking, both men equally engrossed in the topic. Harry's shoulders started to loosen; he was, at last, beginning to relax after his monumental day, no longer feeling quite so defeated.

A white 1958 Chevy pulled into a parking spot in front of Harry. He moved out of the way to give the driver some more space but remained preoccupied with his and Dara's conversation.

"Let's plan an evening at Shalimar with the missus," Harry suggested. "It's been a while since we had a night out. Maybe Pierre and Valerie can join us too."

"That's a great idea. You let me know when, and I'll make sure we have the best table!" said Dara.

A young Yemeni man emerged from behind the car in a scuffed-up blue collared shirt and beige cotton pants, his head wrapped in a checkered white-and-black scarf. He was chewing *khat*, his shoulders tense and his hands hanging oddly by his sides as he walked toward Harry, who was back to talking about sharks.

The man walked right up to Harry, his hands steady, his gaze penetrating as he looked him straight in the eyes, then lifted a P-64 pistol from his waistline and aimed it at Harry's forehead.

Stumbling backwards, Harry dropped his bag and put his hands up.

"*Shabab*, *Akhi*, brother. What are you doing? Let's talk," Harry pleaded.

Chapter 1

"*Skut, kalb Inglise*. Shut up, you British dog."

"Please… let's talk. I want to help you. I'm on your side."

The young man looked rabid, his eyes somewhere else—glassy, angry, hateful. He sucked in mucus from his nose and spat a ball of phlegm at Harry's feet.

Then he pulled the trigger.

⊗ ⊗ ⊗

The bullet tore through Harry's skin and muscle before it exploded into his cranial bones and prefrontal cortex. A cloud of gun smoke and the stench of burning flesh permeated the air. Dara watched in shock and horror as his friend crumpled to the ground like a bloody rag doll—Harry's face instantly gone.

The shooter tossed a piece of paper onto Harry's blood-splattered chest, his body splayed out. Without hesitation—his hand perfectly steady, his eyes cold and empty—the young man pointed the gun at Dara. Gesturing to his mouth with his free hand, he used the gun to mimic slitting his throat. His message was clear: keep your mouth shut or you're next. And then, as swiftly as he had emerged, he was gone.

Dara flew down the steps toward Harry, yelling hysterically for help, for the police, ambulance, anyone. He ripped off his shirt, revealing his crisp white *sudreh*, trying desperately to stop the bleeding, but there was no place to start. Harry's face was unrecognizable. Blood was everywhere.

As Dara continued screaming, a crowd started to form and people began running and calling for help. Then sirens. He could barely hear them over the dull ringing in his ears, startled by the muffled sound and vibration of his own yelling.

He watched as the ambulance finally arrived and the paramedics poured out, moving quickly, ready to take action as though there was something they could do, but there was no hope. Harry had died the instant that bullet made contact.

Dara sat in the growing pool of blood as it mixed with dirt and sand. The medics covered Harry's body with a sheet and carried his friend away. Only the blood remained, inching its way out, away from him, tainting the ground forever. What was happening? He wiped the sweat from his brow, realizing that he too was drenched in blood, dust, and tears. He picked himself up, blinded and choked by the piercing sunlight and insidious heat. He dragged himself home.

2

"The only paradise is paradise lost."
—Marcel Proust

October 20, 1967

The catastrophic implosion that was about to pulse through Aden remained hidden, bubbling and fermenting under the tranquil waters of the Red Sea, unbeknownst to Dara. A warm breeze whipped through his dark hair as he guided his speedboat swiftly through the temperate waves. The turbo-powered engine sucked in water through a grill, then rapidly shot it out the back at forty-five gallons per second, propelling and jerking the boat forward. Even through squinted eyes, the sheer beauty of the Aden shore was unobscured. About halfway between the club and Elephant Bay, he leaned smoothly into the throttle. The boat lifted its nose obediently and sped off toward the horizon. Approaching an inlet, he released the throttle, shut the engine off, and pulled out a bottle of Beck's from the army-green Coleman cooler. The ocean lapped gently at his boat, lulling him softly from side to side. Leaning back in his captain's seat, he took a slow, deliberate gulp of his beer and admired the picturesque coast that surrounded him.

His eyes followed the range of shades from cobalt to turquoise shimmering up through the ocean floor to the line of posts that connected the shark nets around the swimming area, meticulously aligned to keep swimmers safe. The fine red sand that powdered the beach glistened in the distance. He turned to gaze at the silhouette of the elephant head, its trunk naturally sculpted out of the mountains, looking regal and all-knowing. From where he sat, the sky was a striking shade of aqua, empty of clouds or anything else, just a vast expanse of cerulean. The sun caressed his nose and cheeks with a searing heat that penetrated his golden skin. In the distance, he could just make out the blurred outline of the Gold Mohor Beach Club on the horizon. It looked tiny in contrast to the mountains of Crater, which sat immense and unyielding, anchored and proud behind it. The paved roads were barely visible on the steep rocks that clung to the hillside. Houses and apartment buildings in a range of whites and beiges huddled together to house the city's population.

Dara finished the last of his beer and started the engine. He decided to take one more loop around the harbor, passing the Officers Union and the Italian Club before heading back toward the dock at the Gold Mohor. At this point he was already late. A few more minutes would make no difference. The boat bounced excitedly between waves as he sped back to the shore with the wind in his hair. As he glided back into the harbor, he recognized a muffled Paul Rich under the hum of the engine and whistled along to the song coming from the speakers on the club patio.

Hassan was there waiting for him, wading in the water at the dock ramp and saluting as he entered the harbor. As the club watchman, he ran a security patrol for all the boats docked; conducted beach safety patrol for the sailors, swimmers, and boaters; maintained the shark nets; and made sure that the sandy beaches were always clean and pristine. Hassan had sharp, dark eyes and olive skin, weathered by the extreme Yemeni sun. He was well acquainted with the ocean, with keen senses and an ability to react quickly. A few years earlier, a young British woman had been swimming in the ocean just beyond the protective nets. A shark had made its way into the shallower water and attacked her. Hassan heard her screams and managed to find her in seconds with nothing but his small patrol boat and an oar. He beat the shark relentlessly on its head with the oar until it begrudgingly let go of the woman and swam away, then he pulled her into his patrol boat with what was left of her right leg. His speed and fearlessness had saved her life. Her husband was so indebted to Hassan that he tried to pay him hundreds of pounds to thank him. Hassan flatly refused the money, saying that he had done only what in his heart he knew was right. He had an uncanny way of getting to where he needed to be, or to where someone else needed him to be, at exactly the right time; this, in his mind, was nothing special, just his fate.

"*Sayid, keef al-bahr?* Did she sing to you today?" Hassan asked, his eyes smiling.

"*Dayimaan ya*-Hassan, always! You know, she is my first love—but please don't tell my wife!" Dara turned his head up at Hassan, eyes wide as he curled his tongue between his teeth mockingly. Hassan laughed, shaking his head from side to side.

They joked back and forth about Dara's love affair with the ocean as they secured the boat to the stand.

Dara adored this country and its people. It was the men and women like Hassan who added to its rugged beauty. The heart and warmth of the nation was unparalleled. In Yemen, a native would always welcome you, invite you into his home, and offer you tea—and even the shirt off his back. They wanted to know your story and were always willing to share theirs. Adenis were kind, genuine, and fiercely loyal.

The youngest of ten, Dara had spent most of his childhood at boarding schools in India. His family still had close ties in Bombay, which was a second home to them all. It was routine for India-based families to travel between India and Aden. Dara traveled back to Aden at every opportunity and each time would play shopkeeper at the family business for as long as he was allowed to stay. After secondary school, he enrolled in mandatory military service in India but was discharged early because of his imperfect sight. Dara returned to Aden in 1953—a young, motivated, and spirited bachelor—to help run the business with his older brothers. He had watched the family business grow throughout his childhood and had longed for his turn to join in his grandfather's and father's legacy. A natural extrovert, he thrived in the expatriate community. He was often found socializing with foreigners and locals alike. Dara's expat friends enjoyed his company, his stories, and his tremendous skill on his speedboat. He was a man who reveled in the splendor of life.

Chapter 2

Dara, now even more late to meet his wife, Silloo, and their children in the clubhouse, could not tear himself away from his casual conversation with Hassan. He guessed that he would likely pay for it later, but these real, raw relationships fueled him. He could spend hours and hours talking with Hassan about anything and everything, from the size of the waves to the price of gold. More importantly, he never wanted to rush his conversation and make Hassan feel that he was not worthy of his time. It was why men like Hassan held Dara in high esteem: Dara was the type of man who cared about people and treated everyone equally. He would stop, make eye contact, shake hands, hold an elbow, read expressions, and genuinely engage with people Even though they lived in a society where class distinctions existed so blatantly, Dara did not believe that he was better or superior. He had a sincere interest in every person he met and showed it. His intent came across in his interactions. For people of a country that had been bound and colonized for centuries, that level of respect went a very long way.

Dara eventually sauntered into the clubhouse, running his hand through his hair, his golden tan warm and glowing in the dust-filled beams of sunlight filtering in through the large window. He found Silloo sitting at a table with their son, Aram, who was sleeping soundly in his mother's arms. Silloo was in the middle of telling their older son, Rustom, and Dara's brother Zaal an animated story that she had made up. She tipped her head back, and they all laughed boisterously. Aram's little body rose and fell with his mother's, yet he remained in an intoxicated slumber, mouth agape and cheeks flushed.

"Dara, Dara, come, come, Silloo is telling a funny story!" Zaal belly-laughed. "Funny story," he repeated.

Zaal was twelve years older than Dara, the oldest of his mother's children. He had been born with multiple neurological disorders that affected his nervous system, hampering his speech and communication, compounded by severe epilepsy. Yet Zaal persevered and was sweet, kind, gentle, and forever smiling. He loved collecting stamps and postcards and would not hesitate to ask every person he met to send him one from their travels. He would meticulously remove the stamps from letters and mount them in a black leather-bound book. Each time Zaal would receive a new postcard, he would lay the collection out on the floor and organize them by continent, reciting the name of where each one had come from as he held it in his hands, smiling triumphantly to himself as he placed it in its appropriate spot. Zaal was a simple man; his many epileptic fits had left him quiet, but never short of affection. He lived with his mother in the apartment below Dara and Silloo. Silloo adored her brother-in-law, and he adored her as much, if not more, in return. Zaal would often come up to play with the boys, sometimes stopping in for lunch, always bearing gifts for his beloved nephews, and Silloo always had a special sweet treat waiting for him.

Dara and Silloo had met as young teens at a mutual family gathering. They had caught each other's eye, but it wasn't until Silloo moved to Aden in the late 1950s that they began courting.

Chapter 2

They married in July 1961. Together they shared a love of music and dancing, sunning on the golden shores of the Gold Mohor and Italian beach clubs, and riding the waves in Dara's sleek imported Norwegian speedboat. They balanced each other. He was mesmerized by her beauty, a slave to her every wish, while her level-headed practicality kept Dara's unpredictable personality in check. They would often ride the waves with friends to secluded beaches on the opposite side of Crater, the city named after the dormant volcano that sat at its center, areas that were only accessible by boat. There, they would camp, cook, drink, and spend nights playing cards and laughing into the early hours of the morning. They socialized frequently and enjoyed spending weekend evenings at their establishment, Shalimar—a restaurant and nightclub that the family owned alongside their cinema, Shenaz. Their life in Aden was idyllic, and they had no doubt that it was here in Yemen where they would raise their family and grow old together in this, their paradise.

Dara looked over at Silloo, catching his breath. His wife had large, almond-shaped brown eyes, high cheekbones, delicate lips, and hair down to her hips that she styled in a perfectly coiffed updo. Her white cat's-eye sunglasses sat on top of her head, purposefully placed where her hair turned up. She looked marvelously chic for an ordinary day lounging at the beach. Their eyes met, and she raised a playful eyebrow. *Look who's here!* she gestured to Rustom, the whole while keeping her eyes fixed on Dara's. Dara raced over to his son and flipped him upside down and over his shoulders. Rustom, only two years old, squealed in delight. Aram remained asleep, undisturbed on his mother's bosom.

The club was busy that night. As the sun set and the warm ocean breeze moved in, everyone shifted onto the patio to drink their Double Diamonds and Pimm's and lemonades, socializing well into the evening as the large speakers infused the atmosphere with all their favorites: the likes of Hal Munro rocking the "Jailhouse Rock" and Bobby Stevens crooning "Johnny Remember Me." They lingered into the night, feasting on kebabs and French fries, talking to friends and playing with their children until the children and Zaal were so exhausted that Dara and Silloo piled them into the jeep and made their way through the mountain roads to their apartment building in Steamer Point. After parking behind the building, Dara carefully lifted a sleeping Rustom over his shoulder. The two-year-old wrapped his arms around his father's neck, resting his head on Dara's broad shoulder without opening his eyes.

Dara exchanged pleasantries with the doorman, who remained seated in his folding chair outside the entrance of the building, chewing *khat* and playing with his worry beads in one hand while holding the other to his head in greeting as he watched them make their way into the building.

"Mohammed, all good with you?" Dara said, looking at the watchman. Mohammed nodded his head, but then called out to Dara just as they were about to climb the stairs to their apartment. "*Sayid*, there was a man here tonight. Asking many questions about your family and who lives on what floor."

"Really? Did he tell you his name or where he was from?"

"No, no, nothing. And I told him if he was so interested, he should go ask you."

Dara smiled, starting to feel the weight of his child on his shoulder and back. "Thank you, Mohammed."

"*Aiwa, Sayid, aiwa.*"

Zaal headed to his mother's apartment, whispering his goodnights and waving to his nephews. As Dara and Silloo and the boys approached their place, Ahmed, more family member than servant, was waiting at the threshold with the door open. Adjusting his white skullcap, he took their bags and helped them put the boys into their beds before saluting them and heading home for the night.

3

"The difference between fiction and reality?
Fiction has to make sense."
—Tom Clancy

November 2, 1967

Dara climbed the four flights of stairs to his apartment, with blood stains on his skin and soaked through his clothes. Leaning into the doorframe, his legs giving way, he pounded his fist on the entryway. Silloo, startled, rushed to unlatch and open the door, and there in the egress stood the solemn figure of her husband, barely recognizable, the remnants of his white *sudreh* and pants covered in blood and dirt, tears streaming down his bloody face. She gasped and fell backwards, convinced that the blood he wore was his own.

"Oh my God, Dara, what happened? Where are you hurt? *Ahmed!*"

Together they helped Dara into the apartment. His eyes were cold as he looked at his beautiful bride, tears welling in her eyes and begging for some explanation. His hearing was still dull, confusion and horror overwhelming him. Searching for his voice, he finally spoke slowly and deliberately.

"I am okay. It's not my blood. Harry was shot. In front of

the shop, in front of me. We were talking, and then…it just happened…so fast."

Silloo looked at him blankly. "Harry? *Con nu* Harry? *Apro* Harry? Which Harry? Our Harry?" She flipped back and forth between English and Gujarati.

"*Haa*, yes," said Dara.

Silloo clasped her mouth with both hands in disbelief.

"It was an NLF guy, a young kid." Dara closed his eyes, trying to fight back the tears that were desperate to escape. "I tried to save him, Silloo, but it was too late… He is gone. The man shot Harry in his face." Dara rubbed his temples with his thumb and forefinger, choking back the tears, the image crystal clear in his mind. "It was horrific."

Ahmed slid his hand under Dara's elbow, ushering him toward the bathroom, whispering, "*Sayid*" as he looked toward the living room door, from where they could hear Rustom talking to his nanny, Fatima. He guided Dara into the bathroom, taking his clothes and running the shower for him.

Dara took a long, hot shower, desperate to scrub the image of what had just happened from his mind. He had never witnessed anything like this before, and in the past few years of unrest and skirmishes, nothing this violent had happened so close to home. This was the start of something terrible. The fight between the National Liberation Front and the British had been ongoing, but had he not paid enough attention? He searched his mind for something he may have missed. The hot water stung as it ran down his body, the steam stretching through the air, filling his lungs with warm vapor and misting the bathroom so much he could barely see. He stayed in the bathroom for a long time, understanding that the moment he stepped out, he would be stepping out into a new reality. He could no longer be complacent; the world as he knew it, his world, was forever changed.

"I need to go back to work," Dara said to Silloo as he stepped out of the bathroom with a towel wrapped around his waist, steam clinging to his body and following him into the room, his tone somber.

"What? Back to work…now? Dara, can we talk first? Can you tell me what happened?" she asked. Her voice was calm and metered, her distress cleverly hidden behind a brave façade. Yet he knew her too well. He could feel her anguish.

"Now is not the time. I need to get back to the shop, and I think I will stop at Harry and Jane's. I was the last person to see him. I told you what happened. We were talking about going out for dinner and sailing and the ocean, he bought groceries for Jane, and not even five minutes later he was dead. Shot in broad daylight, on the street. I need to go talk to her."

Silloo watched him dress himself, his hands trembling. "Are you sure it's wise to go alone? I can come with you."

"No, Silloo, please, just stay here with the boys." Silloo flinched, clearly stung by his abrasiveness. He swallowed back the lump in his throat, immediately regretting his tone.

"What if someone comes after you? What if they are following you? And they see you go to Jane's? We have a family!

Chapter 3

You can't take a risk like this! I-I won't allow it." Her voice began to shake.

"Silloo!" he said firmly, which startled her. "They are not going to come after me. If they were going to shoot me, they could have done it then and there. I have to go check on the staff and the shop. I will be back soon, I promise." His voice softened, and the corners of his mouth rose to a barely discernible smile.

"Stay home with the boys and call me at the shop if you need anything. I will stop at Harry and Jane's and then go straight to the shop. Okay? Please, trust me."

He kissed her forehead and walked out of the room, heading straight out of the apartment as though it were any other day. As if he had not collapsed in the doorway covered in blood only an hour before. His footsteps sounded on the hard, cold tile, the sound softening as he walked farther and farther away. Silloo sank into her bed, her body trembling.

✧ ✧ ✧

Lying in the expanse of a dormant volcano, the ancient port city of Aden sits proudly by the eastern entrance of the Red Sea, across from Djibouti and the northern tip of Somalia. In 1839, in an effort to prevent pirate attacks on the Red Sea en route to India, the British East India Company landed in Aden and secured the territory. Then in 1860, it was declared a free port and began to thrive as a regular stopover for seamen. At that time, a handful of Parsi Zoroastrians moved from India to take advantage of the port city's booming trade. Dara's grandfather was among the first Parsis who made their way to Aden to seek a new life, making the port city home for his family and the generations that followed. The growth and development of the shipping port was attributable to a handful of Parsi families that transformed the port into one that could handle steamer traffic between Europe and India. The Parsis had the wealth to expand into other areas of trade, and families like Dara's were instrumental in boosting the economy.

Even though the city was surrounded by rugged mountains and barren deserts, its port had made it a strategic intersection for Middle Eastern and African trade routes for centuries. With the completion of the Suez Canal in 1869, Aden, a natural stopover for ships on their way to India and the Far East, became increasingly important to the British. The city thrived well into the 1950s and early 1960s. It became the second-busiest port in the world after New York City, bringing prosperity, wealth, and a robust economy to its citizens. The country's rich history—bejeweled with an array of cultures, religions, and indoctrinations—seeded the Yemeni soil. It grew from an integral stop on the ancient incense routes to the primary fueling station from west to east. From myrrh and frankincense to Judaism, Islam, and Communism, there was little that the sands and soil of Yemen had not born witness to.

The current unrest was not new. Dara had always stayed on top of the news, reading the paper every day and listening to the nightly BBC radio broadcasts. It was no secret that dissatisfaction from the surrounding protectorate had been percolating for some time, in large part because of radicalization by Egyptian President Gamal Abdel Nasser's anti-colonization messages. He was stoking animosity toward British rule in Aden. By the 1950s, Britain had begun pulling out of many of its occupied territories around the globe, an impact of the Second World War. While North Yemen was slowly being radicalized by the Egyptians, the USSR was simultaneously instigating a quiet socialist movement across the region. The Soviet Union had a vested interest in Aden's natural harbor and Socotra Island, where, it was rumored, they had built a submarine base not far from it.

Most elite Adenites, including Dara and his family, were happy to have the British stay, but the pressure from the north became far too great and violence began hurtling out of control. The National Liberation Front (NLF), a group of mostly young, uneducated men from North Yemen and the protectorate, partnered with the Front for Liberation of Occupied South Yemen (FLOSY), a smaller, more educated group, to fight and kill British soldiers in a quest for independence. On the other side of the conflict, a federation of sultans and sheikhs had worked closely with the British in an effort to gradually take control of Aden upon the scheduled British exit. The plan was to have a true handoff, with some remaining British military presence. One hand in while the other was out, so to speak. The British government had agreed to a peaceful transition and, in turn, to help by staying and maintaining law and order after the handover.

For Dara and other Adenites, this was the best outcome they could have imagined.

Daily, the papers talked of Prime Minister Harold Wilson's Labour Party, newly established in the UK and facing a dire situation with a devalued sterling, soaring oil prices from the closure of the Suez, and a surge in anti-British uprisings throughout the world, causing priorities to change. There had been a stretch of time where the nationalist groups were capturing British soldiers and beheading them, then leaving their heads on stakes out in the desert. Pictures made their way into the British newspapers, so it was no wonder why, in desperation, the administration had decided to pull out of Aden by January—the announcement was pushing the city into a fight for control. Although the NLF and FLOSY had once fought together against the British, now with the news of the British occupation's impending departure, they turned on each other: vicious rivals in an increasingly violent and bloody civil war, one that had now touched Dara directly.

❖ ❖ ❖

The vision of Harry's assassination continued to plague Dara's mind. Their friendship had been relatively new; they had been just starting to get to know each other better, still acquaintances on their way to becoming friends and part of an extended social group. Many Indian foreigners in Aden, like Dara and his family, had opted for British subject status, which had been offered to them under British rule. They all mostly kept their line of work to themselves, unless it was already publicly known, like Dara's ownership of Bhicajee Cowasjee. It was not unusual to befriend a spy and be none the wiser. Dara never asked too many questions about anyone's work. The less you asked and knew, the better. He would often speculate about the foreigners' jobs, as some were more obvious than others. It was apparent to him now that Harry had been involved in something big, and most likely with the British government—why else would an NLF guerrilla want to assassinate him? The NLF were staking a claim, making a point. To them, Harry meant nothing; his life and family, his wife were of no consequence.

Dara kept replaying the scene over and over in his head, the killer's face etched in his mind. He knew that boy, had watched him grow up, playing soccer in the streets, had handed him countless ice creams and sodas over the years. The boy had struck him as shy and well mannered, self-conscious, even quiet. Now that seemingly pleasant young man was a cold-blooded murderer. He squeezed his eyes shut, once again trying to erase the picture from his mind.

Alone in his office, Dara picked up the phone and dialed his friends Pierre and Valerie, who had recently moved to Aden from Brittany in northern France. Pierre had been offered a job at the French embassy in Aden, and he and Valerie jumped at the opportunity. Although a few years younger, the newlyweds had become close to Dara and Silloo. The two couples often spent weekends at the Gold Mohor or the Italian Club. Most

Thursday nights, the start of the weekend in Aden, they would go out for dinner and dancing at Shalimar. This time, however, the purpose of Dara's call wasn't social.

"*Allo*," said the voice on the other end of the line.

"Hi, Valerie. Dara here."

"Dara, my dear, 'ow are you? 'Ow is my Silloo?" Valerie chirped in her French accent.

"We are all good, Valerie. Is Pierre available? Please, may I speak with him?"

"Ah, yes, of course."

Dara waited a few moments before his friend picked up the phone.

"Dara, *mon ami, comment vas-tu?*" Pierre asked.

"*Pas bon, mon ami.* Pierre, did you hear about Harry?"

"'Arry. 'Arry Mason?"

"Yes, Harry Mason," said Dara.

"*Non, que s'est-il passe?* What 'appened?" asked Pierre.

"He was shot today. Right in front of me—the NLF. Outside my shop, we were just talking—" Dara could taste the bile rising in his throat. His heart pounded in his chest.

"What!? *Oh mon Dieu! Non, non, non.* Dara, we did not 'ear about any of this. They must be keeping it quiet. Let me make some phone calls and try to find out if anyone knows who is responsible. 'Ave you spoken to Jane? Oh, *non, non.*"

"Yes, the military police arrived at their place right after I did. Thank God at least I was able to be with her when she found out. I didn't think I could witness anything worse than watching Harry be executed in front of me, but then I held Jane as they told her. Ah, I just don't know what to say." Dara rubbed his forehead, tears rising again. His chest tightening even more.

"*Oh mon Dieu.* I can't believe it. This is just terrible. I will try to see what I can find out."

They ended the call, and Dara leaned forward on his desk, his head in his hands, trying to make sense of everything. For many years, Adenites had thought themselves largely removed from the trials and tribulations of the rest of the country and for the most part wanted to remain a British colony. But the escalation and frequency of the violence was making it difficult to chalk up these uprisings as inconsequential and controlled.

Dara thought back to the first major incident he could remember, which in hindsight should have broken the spell of denial most of the citizenry still seemed to be under. In December 1964, a well-known Yemeni, Fadli Khalil, had been on a routine visit to the *khat* market in Crater. A British informant, Fadli would stroll through the busy streets, looking for gossip and information, bantering back and forth with merchants and locals. On this fateful day, NLF terrorists barreled through the market in military jeeps, faces covered and armed with machine guns. They annihilated Fadli with several bursts of machine gun fire, then finished the job by tossing a smoke bomb over his body before peeling out of the market in a swift getaway. It was all over the news, and everyone was talking about it everywhere. There were rumors that Fadli had escaped, but the truth was that the terrorists had left no part of him recognizable. This was the beginning of their terrorism campaign in Aden; the nationalists were determined to wipe out the British intelligence network and instill fear with violent public killings. With every assassination, they would leave a note on or near the body that read "executed by the NLF." Once they had executed most of the Arab officers, they began targeting senior British officers, Harry now among them.

Dara and Silloo sat at their dining table and listened to the BBC radio broadcast that evening. Independence was imminent. The January 9 handover was being moved forward to the end of November. The British wouldn't stay in any capacity. Which was a one-hundred-eighty-degree turn from what had been announced. They were supposed to maintain a presence in Aden and help the sultans with a transition to a fair and just government. Now all nonessential personnel were being evacuated from Aden posthaste. Dara and Silloo had heard from their friends in the foreign embassies that a lot of the expats had twenty-four to forty-eight hours to pack up and leave. Planes lined up on the tarmac at Khormaksar Airport, no time for goodbyes, take what you can and go. Meanwhile, the fighting in the streets was ramping up, so if you weren't on an evacuation list, you were sheltering in place.

"Dara, this is scary. All the violence. I have a really bad feeling about it. Shouldn't we be leaving like everyone else? Is it really safe to be here now with two young children?" Silloo said, walking over to the balcony and watching the streets. Dara had started to polish silver decanters at the dining table.

"Well, I think we just have to wait and see. It should all settle. These NLF guys want the British out, so once the British leave, things might just go back to being quiet. Nobody wants violence," Dara said thoughtfully. "I do wonder how long this Communist push will last, though. Yemenis are Muslim, first and foremost, not Communist." He shook his head. "Hopefully they'll realize that sooner rather than later. I suppose we will just have to be very careful for now and watch closely."

The call to prayer began. Silloo loved how it would start with one muezzin and then, like dominos collapsing, other mosques would follow suit almost immediately. The same each time, five times a day. It was predictable and comforting. She closed her eyes, took a deep breath, and allowed her neck and back to loosen.

Dara's grandfather had taken a chance on change when he moved from Bombay in the 1800s. He came to Aden as a young man on his own and started a tailoring business, which grew along with the city, as did his family. When his son, Dara's father, was old enough, he joined the tailoring business, and together father and son developed it into a profitable trading company unlike any other in the city. They relied largely on the expanding British military presence, which had multiplied after the completion of the Suez Canal in 1869, bringing with it an influx of expats.

Of Mud and Honey

Aden's potential was just beginning to be realized. Hundreds of jobs were created between the port, refinery, and merchant businesses to support the needs of the new immigrants. Dara's family business continued to prosper alongside the city's thriving economy. Aden flourished through trade to the passengers coming in and out of the city on ships. The streets and shopfronts were a colorful scene to the many tourists that flocked the city. All the shops looked similar, with narrow open fronts screened by blinds or hanging merchandise. The streets were filled with peddlers selling water, nuts, and lentils, or perfume merchants who would mix a concoction to the buyer's liking. Toy stalls were often tucked into the corners of buildings or on their steps and were run by young Yemeni children in their dusty clothes and torn sandals. Letter writers were often found on the pavement sitting on a chair at a small desk, ever ready to help those who could not fill forms or write letters. With portable typewriters, they were prepared to handle anything in Arabic, Hindi, or English. Today, Bhicajee Cowasjee sold almost everything a local might need. It was easily classified as a bodega, supermarket, ice cream parlor, toy shop, and high-quality department store (importing the finest European products) all in one—essentially one of the largest retailers in Aden.

Along with Dara and Silloo and Dara's mother and brother, three other brothers lived in their building; together, his family occupied five of the eight apartments. Jamshed, Zarir, Dara, and Homi occupied an apartment on each floor. The oldest brother, Bhicajee, lived in a different building with his family. Two of the siblings, their sister Maki and brother Behram, lived in India with their families. With increasing tensions in the area in the 1960s and the threat of the British departure, Dara's family had decided to expand their business interests to other developing gulf countries, such as the small and promising city of Dubai in the United Arab Emirates. Dara, Silloo, and Dara's older brother Jamshed planned to stay in Aden and continue the family business. The hope was that the unrest would ease, the canal would reopen, and they would be able to return to enjoying their life in Aden as they always had. During the uncertain times leading up to the departure of the British, Dara was paying the NLF twelve hundred dinars a month, a stipend to protect his family and the business, a common practice for merchants in Aden to prevent looting and attacks on their establishments.

"Dara, come to the balcony, quick. The sunset is spectacular!" Silloo called out, her words tumbling over each other, her waist bent over the handrail as she stood on the tips of her toes.

The vista was unparalleled. The sun, a huge fiery ball, was slowly slipping into the ocean. The sky was ablaze with shades of crimson, orange, and yellow. Dara leaned into his wife, handing her a glass of Martini Rosso, her favorite, slipping his arm around her slim waist and running his thumb on her bare arm. He sipped on his scotch, the ice cubes clinking against the sides of the tumbler.

"Maybe everything will be okay, *maro jan*. Look at that sky." She inhaled a deep breath, in awe of nature's beauty. He smiled at the mere thought.

"Listen, listen, do you hear the fireworks?" Dara said as he looked down at the street and saw a group of young men running. At first, it looked like a celebration, people running in the street with sparklers, but Dara quickly saw what was happening and his heart thumped. Behind the men was actually another mob chasing them with guns and grenades. In a split second, he realized that the little red sparks were a hand bomb, thrown a mere eighty feet away in front of their building. The crystal tumbler in Dara's hand fell to the ground and shattered. He grabbed his wife, covering her head with one arm while they both dove into the apartment, falling hard and fast onto the tile. They felt the blast. The building shook, shattering the glass on all the street-facing windows. Their ears pulsed from the explosion while the air became thick with smoke and a pungent smell of burning fuel. The blast was a signal of what the country was enduring: the NLF and FLOSY were fighting for control of the city.

"Silloo, are you okay?" Dara yelled. Adrenaline pulsed through his body.

"Yes, yes, I'm fine. I landed on my hip, but I'm fine."

Ahmed charged into the living room. "*Sayid, Sayidati.*"

Coughing, Dara waved his hand, signaling for Ahmed to help him. Together, they raised Silloo up from the floor. Shards of glass were embedded in her arms and legs. Dara pulled off his shirt and held it to her face to shield her from the smoke as they stumbled out of the room to tend to her wounds. The instability in the city was becoming unnerving. Their apartment building faced the main street in Steamer Point; it was here that a lot of fighting was taking place. They were not safe anywhere, not even in their own home.

Over the next few days, the situation on the streets only got worse. News of the accelerated British withdrawal led to many heightened clashes all around them. Attacks on British troops coupled with rival NLF and FLOSY fights were developing into a days-long bloody civil war as both parties attempted to run for the finish line and take the reins from Britain. The UK was in a quandary; the original plan was evolving and changing minute by minute, and it was becoming clear that the British would inevitably hand over control to the very forces they had been trying to squash. Eventually, the NLF succeeded in overthrowing FLOSY, and nine days after the announcement that the British would be leaving by the end of November, the NLF telegrammed the UK, informing them of their victory. Transition negotiations took place in Geneva over the next few weeks, and thus negotiations for independence, for the first time in more than 128 years, were on their way. The fighting finally ceased, and it felt as though the worst just might be over. The NLF, only a few thousand men, had pushed out the most powerful colonial power in the world, and the British went from fighting the NLF for control of Aden to passing it over with open hands.

4

"Take the first step in faith. You don't have to see the whole staircase, just take the first step."
—Martin Luther King, Jr.

December 1, 1967

Dara sipped his coffee while scanning the Friday edition of *The Aden Chronicle*. He held a piece of toast in one hand, meticulously spreading a thin layer of butter on it followed by an equally thin layer of strawberry jam. Then he carefully peeled and sliced a banana, placing each perfect disc on top. As he bit into his crunchy toast, he read the lead headline:

> *High Commissioner Sir Humphrey Trevelyan reflects on Britain's exit from Aden: "So we left without glory but without disaster... Nor was it humiliation. For our withdrawal was the result not of military or political pressure but our decision, right or wrong, to leave."*

Dara closed his eyes and shook his head, pursing his lips in disdain as he moved on to another article. The past month had been a whirlwind of events and insecurity. It had begun with Harry's assassination, but the incidents that followed were almost as baffling, not only to Dara, but to other Adenites. The fighting had finally stopped, even if that meant the NLF was now the ruling party in Aden. Only a day before, the British gunnery post that had been set up on the roof of their building for months had been dismantled, and the roof was now quiet and empty. Silloo had allowed Rustom, now three years old, to go up for the last time and give the British soldiers a cookie and some cold soda to say a bittersweet goodbye. Many of Dara and Silloo's expat friends had already left Aden. Embassies had evacuated a majority of foreign nationals in light of the British withdrawal and increased fighting. The city was eerily quiet.

He continued scanning the front page.

The National Liberation Front is to drop Liberation from their name and will be identified as the National Front henceforth. Under the auspices of their new name, the Front was committing to some substantial changes in the local economy, along with land reform. Among their highest priorities was the removal of the former rulers and sheikhs. That made sense to Dara, since they were thought of as British puppets, but the question of what that truly meant made him shudder. Nationalization of foreign-owned companies would commence, and they would witness the end of Aden's free port status (which the economy had relied upon since the middle of the nineteenth century). The goal was to pursue a policy of "positive neutralism," an attempt to keep everyone happy. The Front promised to protect foreign nationals and communities. Dara was unsure how this would all play out and what nationalization might mean for his father's legacy, but he trusted the Yemeni people, so he decided that he would be cautiously optimistic. After all, his family had served the Adeni community for over a hundred years; they were well respected. He could not imagine that they would do anything but work with his family. It was in everyone's best interest, and if that did not promote a policy of "positive neutralism," then he did not know what would.

"Silloo," Dara called down the hallway. "Come on, get the boys, let's go to the club!"

December 24, 1967

As the new NF government worked to pull a functioning government together and boost the economy while also pursuing negotiations for aid from Britain, life for those living in Aden had calmed down somewhat, and normalcy was slowly returning. Fighting in the streets had completely stopped. The new government had been accepted and embraced. Local businesses were back up and running. The beach clubs were busy, and although life was a little quieter and fewer people were in the streets, there was a sense of peace again. After six weeks of uncertainty, Dara and Silloo got back to more normal activities: taking the boat out with their children and friends, and camping on the local island beaches. More typical social interactions had resumed, like sing-alongs by the campfire, and after the fire was long burned out. On nights when the moon was taking a break from the sky, they would take walks along the beach and delight in the bioluminescent algae glowing green with every step into the wet sand along the shore.

The new administration seemed to be moderate, only nationalizing some of the local businesses. Dara and the family had to give up Shalimar. The National Front closed the restaurant/nightclub down and changed its name to The Casino, although it was anything but a casino in any true sense of the word. Locals and expats still made their way there to eat, drink, and dance. Best of all, George Pacheko and his Italian wife, Lillian, and their band had decided to stay on as the club's entertainment, continuing to belt out their sensational melodies.

Sad to lose Shalimar, Dara's family still considered themselves fortunate to have managed to keep Bhicajee Cowasjee unscathed and within the family. The energy of the city was slower, but Dara and Silloo had, at the very least, started to feel safe again. No longer worrying for their own safety, things were settling. It was, in their opinion, a good outcome.

Now that life was more normal again, Dara's mother and Zaal returned to Aden from Bombay, where they had been waiting things out. The family was back together and slowly embracing the long-awaited calm. December passed quickly, and after the tumult of the autumn, they decided that they wanted to celebrate Christmas Eve the way they had in past years. After everything the Baruchas had been through, it seemed appropriate and earned. They planned a night of festivities at The Casino for dinner and dancing.

Dara's family built Shalimar restaurant and nightclub and Shenaz open-air cinema in the early 1960s, between little Aden and Crater. The two buildings sat at the foot of the Aden Pass, flanked by mountains, and were icons of modernism in the city—the buildings had become beacons of eclectic architecture. Under nationalization, not much had changed. The interior of the Shalimar remained as it had been, adorned with pillars and lush fabrics. The serene, expansive outdoor terrace was furnished with oversized plush red velvet chairs. Yet it was the view from the terrace that was always the showstopper. Vast breathtaking panoramas of the mountain pass formed the backdrop to the warmth of the furnishings. A parquet dance floor positioned in the middle of the outdoor seating area was accustomed to the tips of the locals' shoes while they danced the evening away to the live music played by George Pacheko and his band. They would sit on the terrace against the backdrop of the mountains, chatting and socializing into the early hours of the morning.

Dara's older brother Jamshed and his wife dominated the dance floor that night. Nazneen was a stunning woman, with peach-colored skin, a delicate round face, large dark eyes, and long black hair. She stood tall, dressed in the latest Bombay fashions, always with her own added twist—a beacon of style, fashion, and finesse. A beauty in every sense of the word and the envy of men and women alike. She twirled gracefully on the dance floor, her gaze fixed on her husband, whom she adored. Zaal, their oldest brother, sat in a big armchair watching his brothers and their wives jiving and twisting; he chuckled and clapped along. Every so often, one of them would lean over and pretend to grab him, which would make his whole portly body vibrate and convulse in fits of giggles.

Things almost felt normal. That evening, they all let go, living in the moment and enjoying each other's company, allowing their fears and tensions to melt away. The night ended with a sense of contentment for each of them and hope that a new year would only bring with it a renewed sense of good fortune. The political climate had changed so dramatically from what they had originally anticipated. If the British had maintained their presence, as was originally planned, nothing would have changed. With the takeover, there was a time when they could have lost it all, everything that three generations had worked to build. Losing Shalimar had stung, but it had been the price they had to pay to keep their family legacy. The main business was still theirs, and they all appreciated that. It was, they understood, a part of living as an expatriate in another country.

Back at home, Dara clambered into his bed. Even though the stress of the past few weeks had dissipated somewhat, he still felt physically and mentally drained. His mind drifted in and out of an unrestful slumber. In his sleepy haze, he kept seeing Harry's murder, his body crumpling to the ground. But in this dream, Harry would get right back up, just to be shot again, falling to the ground once more. The vision kept playing over and over again, like a stuck movie reel that Dara could not get out of. It was the oddest thing. He could hear the sirens from the ambulance, but the ambulance never arrived, even though it sounded as if it was right next to him.

"Dara, Dara, *ooto*, wake up. The phone," Silloo said, shaking his arm.

He opened his eyes, startled by the blinding light. It couldn't possibly be morning yet. He could have sworn that he had only been asleep for a few short minutes. The phone rang with what sounded like desperate urgency.

"Hello?"

"Dara, *jaldi aawo*, come now, quickly. It's Zaal. He's having an attack. *Jaldi, jaldi*, Dara!" His mother's shrill screams vibrated through the phone.

Dara jumped out of bed and ran out of the apartment, down two flights of stairs, and through his mother's door, Silloo following right behind him. He flew into the kitchen and grabbed a spoon before making his way to Zaal on the living room floor. His brother's eyes were blinking rapidly, his knees were slightly bent and stacked over each other, his hands bent inwards at the wrists up by his chest, his fingers splayed and spread out, his body convulsing.

Silloo ran to him and tried talking to him as his stiff body jerked and spasmed. Dara grabbed his chin and tried to force his mouth open to shove the spoon in. He struggled with the utensil in one hand and Zaal's head in the other.

"Silloo, quick, hold his head as straight as you can." It took a few attempts, but he finally managed to get the spoon into his brother's mouth. He held it there to prevent Zaal from choking on his tongue until the seizure subsided. His voice remained steady, his gaze focused.

Mamma was a small woman always dressed in a plain chiffon sari worn exclusively the Parsi way, with the *pallu* worn from the back to the front and over her head, showing the border of her embroidered *sudreh*. She was a pious Zoroastrian, praying five *Gehs* every day and following the practices of her beloved religion to a fault. She was a quiet and solemn woman for the most part. Always in deep thought or prayer, poised and graceful. Her paramount focus on the family business after her husband passed away had earned her the devotion and respect of all her children and the community at large.

"Mamma, what happened?" Dara asked, almost shouting, although he didn't mean it to come out that way.

She winced. "I just went to get his breakfast, *Dikra*, and then I heard him yell and then a loud thump on the floor. I came running and saw him like this, and then I called you," she sobbed.

"It's okay, Mamma," Silloo said, stepping forward and taking the small frame of her mother-in-law into her arms. "We are here now. It's okay."

Dara interrupted, "Silloo, we should call the ambulance. This one, this one is different." It was taking a long time for Zaal to make it through this seizure. Dara continued to hold the spoon in his brother's mouth with one hand while supporting his body in the other. Zaal stared up at the ceiling, emptiness in his eyes. The only sound in the room was Dara's voice praying softly under his breath, "*Ashem Vohu, Vahishtem asti Ushta asti, Ushta ahmai, Hyat ashai Vahishtai ashem,*" over and over again into Zaal's ear. His brother's body eventually relaxed as his breathing began to steady.

Dara's father had been married twice. He had three children with his first wife, and after she died unexpectedly, he married Dara's mother. They had seven children together, of which Dara was the youngest and Zaal the oldest. In the 1950s and 1960s, most parents throughout the Middle East who valued education sent their children to boarding schools in India. Most Parsi families would send their sons to the Parsi School and their daughters to St. Joseph's Convent in the hill stations of Panchgani, India. The hill stations were made a popular vacation spot by the British during the British Raj. With elevated lookouts of scenic views and luscious green valleys, it was a pristine location for hiking, biking, and strawberry picking. Exuberant bright-green hills gave way to breathtaking lake vistas.

School had been hard for Zaal both socially and academically. Mamma had sent him to the Parsi School, but he had struggled, and after one incident in particular, she pulled him out. She would take the details of that with her to the grave. All Dara knew was that Zaal had been targeted by a group of boys who had bullied and picked on him for his disabilities and simple nature. Mamma never shared the story with anyone, but Zaal sometimes alluded to being burned by the boys, whom he remembered were laughing. Whenever he saw matches, he would pick them up, look at them quizzically, and then ask whoever was there why they were funny.

Zaal was on the heavier side, not very tall but not noticeably short either. He had a sweet round face and small eyes, deep-set and close together. His mouth was also small and slightly pursed when closed. He spoke simply and, most of the time, only when spoken to. Once Mamma decided to bring Zaal home to Aden, he never left her side again. Dara was five when Zaal returned from his short stay at boarding school. His mother had hired a tutor for Dara, Master Gadabhay, who would come to the apartment to tutor Dara in English and math. Zaal would often sit with them, repeating everything that Dara had to say. Master Gadabhay never seemed to mind and would often give Zaal "projects" or "homework" to complete as well. The brothers and their wives took great care of Zaal. They understood him, and his limitations, which made them love and protect him ferociously.

By the time the ambulance arrived, Zaal's attack had passed and he was stable. The paramedics helped Dara get Zaal into his bed, checked his vitals, and monitored him for a short while before leaving. This was routine for his attacks, and although this one had seemed stronger than the others, there was little that they could do for him. Dara and Silloo stayed by Zaal's side for a long while. His eyes were now open and somewhat alert. The color was slowly reappearing in his face. Silloo tried to tell him one of her stories that he loved to hear and usually had him laughing in seconds, but apart from looking at her and blinking, he didn't respond.

"Dara, he is not coming back the way he usually does." Her concern was clear on her face.

"Hmm, I know. Maybe he just needs to rest. Maybe we should let him sleep a little. Let's go up and check on the boys and change. *Chaal*, you rest, Zaalu. I will be back in a little while."

An hour later, Dara returned to Zaal's bedroom. He was lying on his stomach, asleep. Dara sat on the bed and started to stroke his brother's head. Zaal's eyes were open.

"Zaal?" Dara said. "How are you feeling? It's Christmas Day, your favorite day. Just think how much fun we're going to have with all the kids opening presents. Silloo is making your favorite, *Sali Margi*, and she made extra *Sali* for you! *Chalo*, Zaal, maybe you should have something to drink now. Do you want some water?"

Zaal would often retreat after an attack. It was hard for him to understand why his body was doing what it was. Dara persisted, but his brother remained unresponsive.

"Zaal, *ooto*, come on."

Dara carefully turned his brother onto his back. Zaal's head drooped to one side, and his eyes remained fixed and cold. Saliva trickled out of the corner of his mouth, down the side of his face, and onto the pillow.

"Zaal!" Dara felt the blood rush to his face. "No, no, no. Come on, ZAAL! Wake up!"

Tears welled in Dara's eyes as his chest constricted and his head began to pound. He pulled his brother's limp body into his own, wrapping his arms tightly around his wide back and quietly sobbing into his shoulder. Zaal was gone.

⟡ ⟡ ⟡

Mamma's shrill cries echoed through the apartment and into the hall throughout the day. She was completely devastated by Zaal's unexpected death. He had become her faithful companion, and as all her children had grown and embarked on their own lives, he had remained. At forty-six, Zaal had spent much of his life with Mamma. She had been his primary caretaker, a huge responsibility, yet she leaned on his presence, which had continued to bring her joy and purpose. He was her firstborn child, the one who had bestowed upon her the gift of motherhood. He had epitomized unconditional love. In that moment, learning of his death, her heart hurt so intensely that she couldn't fathom how she would ever make it through a day without him.

Dara spent the next few hours of Christmas Day making funeral arrangements with his older brothers while Silloo tended to his mother and explained to the boys what had happened, the festive mood in the apartment quickly becoming one of sadness. Although the boys were too young to fully understand, the oldest, Rustom, knew that the adults were upset, so he played quietly with Aram, staying out of the way of their mother and grandmother as they tackled their grief.

Dara contacted Mr. Mardden, the director of the *agiary*, the fire temple, to request his services. Aden was one of the only cities outside of India and Iran to have a Zoroastrian house of worship. According to the ancient Persian religion, as soon as a person has taken their last breath, the body becomes impure. Instead of burying their dead, Zoroastrians lay the dead body out in a *dakhma*, or tower of silence, to be stripped of its flesh by vultures and disintegrated by the heat of the sun over time. The philosophy holds that you come into this world with nothing and should leave in the same way. This funeral ritual, although somewhat extreme, prevents contamination of the earth through burial and maintains respect of the sacred fire. It was his mother's wish that Zaal be attended to accordingly.

Shortly after receiving Dara's call, Mr. Mardden visited him at his apartment. "Dara *Saab*, I am so sorry for your loss," the director said in his thick Indian accent. He pressed his palms together in front of his heart and dipped his head.

Dara saw a flash of Mr. Mardden's hand-embroidered *topi* as he bowed. He nodded back in gratitude.

"I am sorry, but I have some bad news that I know you will not be happy to hear," said Mr. Mardden. "You see, Zaal *Saab* will not be able to go to the *dakhma*."

"What do you mean?" Dara snapped. "Why not? My mother will never accept that. Zaal must have a traditional Zoroastrian burial." He felt the heat rising through his chest. His body suddenly felt very heavy. "Mr. Mardden, you know that! My brother must have a proper funeral. How can you even suggest anything different?"

"Dara *Saab*," Mr. Mardden said apologetically, his palm

held up in an effort to calm Dara. "There are just not enough Zoroastrians here in Aden to carry the body to the *dakhma*. As you know, we need at least sixteen men. The distance from the *agiary* is, well... it is very far." He rubbed his palms together as he spoke. "Four men to carry from the *agiary* to the *dakhma* gates, then four men to carry to the first stop, then we need four men to carry inside the *dakhma*, then, lastly, four men to carry the body to its final resting place inside the *dakhma*. Eh, we just don't have sixteen Parsi men in Aden right now, and the distance up the hill is simply too far for just four men to carry the whole way." The director looked down at his feet. "I am very sorry, Dara *Saab*."

Dara closed his eyes. "I understand the problem. Mamma would not want a non-Zoroastrian to touch Zaal. Will we be able to carry out the other rituals as we normally do?"

"Yes, of course, *Saab*," replied Mr. Mardden eagerly.

"But then where does his body go?" Dara asked.

"We will take him to the cemetery behind the *agiary*, *Saab*." Mr. Mardden was looking at his shoes again. He understood how painful this was for Dara to hear, and even though he had nothing to do with this outcome, he somehow felt responsible. He waited silently, head bowed.

"Also, *Saab*, there is one more thing."

Dara took a deep breath, wondering what else could possibly go wrong.

"Since you are always the one who volunteers to bring our deceased Parsi brothers and sisters to the *agiary* in your station wagon car, I-I am sorry to have to ask you, but can you transport your brother's body?" Mr. Mardden lifted his gaze, determined not to seem cowardly.

"Oh yes, yes, of course I will, Mr. Mardden. I would not want anyone else to take Zaal. I will be there within the hour."

"Yes, Dara *Saab*, thank you. We will be ready for Zaal *Saab*. No problem, just take your time."

❀ ❀ ❀

Jamshed helped Dara remove Zaal's body from the apartment to the car. Silloo and Nazneen flagged Mamma on each side, arms locked, and held her up. She continued to sob uncontrollably as they followed the men to the station wagon. Silent tears fell to the ground as the men loaded their brother into the car and drove away. The drive to the *agiary* was quiet, each man lost in his thoughts of his eldest brother. Once at the fire temple, they moved Zaal to a small, clean bungalow surrounded by tranquil gardens, winding paths, and reflection pools. The brothers silently worked alongside the priest to wash Zaal's body and then wrap it in a traditional white muslin cloth.

A while later, the family filed into the space for the prayers. A dog was brought in, in accordance with Zoroastrian tradition, to confirm that the body was in actuality deceased. Mr. Mardden walked him over to the body that lay on three square wooden boards symbolic of the tenants of the religion: good words, good thoughts, and good deeds. The dog walked around the body with no reaction, "official" confirmation that Zaal's soul had in fact departed. The priest chanted the last funeral prayers while placing sandalwood on a fire burning in an urn. The bungalow was filled with the scent while layers of light white smoke sat gently atop one another, ebbing and flowing through the room.

After the prayers, Zaal's body was carried outside and laid out on a rectangular stone. Each family member took their turn to approach the body and pay their last respects, speaking their goodbyes to their beloved Zaal. The two priests, Mr. Mardden, and one of the Parsi employees from Bhicajee Cowasjee carried the body a quarter of a mile to the cemetery. The family followed, the evening sun fierce in the sky. They walked in procession to the sound of sand crunching under their feet and Mamma's intermittent sobbing reverberating through all of them.

5

*"When life is too easy for us, we must beware or we may
not be ready to meet the blows which sooner or
later come to everyone, rich or poor."*
—Eleanor Roosevelt

February 1968

Zaal's death came as a hard blow to the whole family, and the
notion of life going back to normal, which they all had embraced,
was now suspended by grief. New Year's passed quietly. The
family busied themselves with life and work. Dara and Jamshed
focused on the business, which was beginning to suffer from
the declining expat population in Aden. The closure of the
Suez Canal and the elimination of the Armed Forces Institute
(NAFFI), which had been the largest sources of income for so
long, now caused them to be stuck with stock they could not sell
and a dwindling customer base. Dara and Jamshed were hard-
pressed to find new and creative solutions for their business.

Silloo and Nazneen were focused on keeping Mamma busy
and surrounded as much as possible by her grandchildren as
both women themselves dealt with their own grief. The days
stumbled into each other as the family worked to find their new
rhythm amid so much change.

Chapter 5

In the winter of 1968, the family opened a new department store in Dubai. Dara's brother Zarir had made his way to the developing port city to explore expansion opportunities. Dara, still struggling with the loss of his brother and the brutal murder of Harry, decided to fly out to visit his brother and find out more about the up-and-coming city.

Dubai was a small emirate in the United Arab Emirates, formerly a British protectorate. The ruler, a progressive Bedouin and visionary, Sheikh Rashid, wanted to see his city's infrastructure boom and was determined to build it into a flourishing trading hub. Fortunately for the sheikh, oil was discovered in the late 1960s, which kick-started the economy.

Dara's family was one of the first immigrant merchants to move to Dubai and start a business. They began with a restaurant much like Shalimar in Aden but called it The Sahara. Owning and running a restaurant in Dubai created the need for fresh imported foods. They began importing cheese and milk from Australia and New Zealand, which in turn created a need for cold storage. Within a short period of time, they expanded and were running multiple businesses in the city, partnering with locals and contributing to the growing economy.

Arriving in Dubai, Dara was awestruck by its twinkling lights, clean roads, and desert expanses with a smattering of beige, white, and brown buildings. In some ways, it was reminiscent of Aden, but younger, newer, fresher. A taxi took him from the airport to his brother Zarir's apartment building, driving around a large roundabout with a huge clock tower at the center. It reminded him of Trafalgar Square in London—large and stately, alone in the wide expanse of the city, but on a much smaller scale. Zarir had an apartment in one of the tallest buildings in the city, and the view from his balcony was spectacular. It looked out on a slim body of water, about a half a mile in width and, ironically, called the Creek. Dara looked on as the busyness of the Creek moved at a rapid pace. The cool breeze felt heavenly as it swept across his face.

The Creek had a sensational history serving as a port for *dhows*, traditional sailing boats coming from India and East Africa. In the early part of the century, it had been the base of Dubai's booming pearling industry, along with trade and fishing. The Creek separated the city into two parts and in 1961 was widened to accommodate the growing trade. This small port was filled with *dhows* that rocked and bobbed in the water. Square pallets piled high lined the dock. Dara watched the men below and could almost hear them mocking and jostling one another, playful yet working hard. It felt like he was watching an anthill with the streams of people working in all directions.

The brothers spent their evening reminiscing about Zaal and getting caught up on all the family news, then they were up early the next day to walk to the shop. Dara was eager to immerse himself in all the hustle and bustle and feel the energy he had observed from the balcony up close. They walked among the pallets, dodging the seagulls that swooped in and sailed up to find a mast to rest on. The smell of salt from the sea permeated the air. Dara was soaking in all the action when he noticed and was suddenly taken aback by stacks of gold bars on pallets sitting openly on the ledge that ran alongside the Creek.

"Is that really what I think it is?" Dara asked.

"Gold bars," Zarir said, sweeping his hand over the pallets. "Can you believe how many you see, little brother?" He chuckled. "You know how the Indians like their gold, and the Indian government is now trying to control the sale of gold. Even owning it in India now is not so easy."

"Yes, I read that they are struggling with a high volume of gold imports, devaluing the rupee, which creates a lot of other problems too," Dara said thoughtfully. "Is this legal? It doesn't look like anyone is trying to hide these bars, or even steal them for that matter."

"No, no one is trying to hide them. There is no need. Here in Dubai, this is legal," Zarir explained. "Re-exporting is a business tool here. The gold comes here from Africa and is then shipped into India. No taxes are imposed, so it is a very efficient and financially viable way of getting the gold to India. However, I have heard rumors that India is going to ban ownership of gold bars and even limit what goldsmiths can hold. They are trying to control the illegal imports of gold into India, I think maybe sometime this year."

"Hmm, so that will just encourage a whole smuggling industry around gold."

"Most likely. Indians will always find a way to get it!"

The brothers continued to the new storefront farther on. With all of the people, *dhows*, water taxis, and whatever else was hidden on those boats, along with the pearl-diving and fishing, there was no shortage of activity here. It was magnificent to see up close.

"Zarir, I have an idea. Let's commission one of those *dhows* to bring all the inventory we have sitting in storage in Aden. It will take us years to sell those things there. Especially now with NAFFI gone, our business is just not the same." Dara's excitement was building. "We are overrun with old orders from NAFFI that were never fulfilled. We should send all the surplus inventory here. Maybe I will even jump on the *dhow!*" He smirked. "The *dhow* can dock right here on the Creek, and think of how easy it will be to unload it. I will have to do a lot of paperwork to release the goods from Aden, but so what? That inventory will just sit there doing nothing for who knows how long, so it makes sense for it to come here."

"That's a great idea, Dara. Actually…I've been thinking…" Zarir hesitated. "Maybe we should move the whole family here." He paused, searching for Dara's reaction. "With everything that's been happening in Aden, who knows what the future there will be like? It could be a new beginning. I have met many of the locals here. They are wonderful people, and there is so much opportunity in Dubai. No threat of a Communist regime takeover either. Sheikh Rashid is a kind and smart man. I have met him, you know, a few times now. His vision for this country is limitless. He wants people like us to be part of that growth. It would be such a great opportunity." Zarir's gaze drifted off, his turn to be excited.

"What? Move from Aden? That's crazy!" Dara said. "Things in Aden are going to be just fine. This new government is moderate. Things are settling down, and they are supporting us. I was worried for a while there, you know…after my friend was assassinated, but I think that it is actually going to be all right. They just need some time to learn. They are young, that is all. Aden is our home. Why would I ever leave?" He brushed away Zarir's comments. "You should stay here and continue to build on what has been started. We can expand Papa's business into the gulf. You are the perfect person to do this, but I have no intention of leaving Aden, not now anyway."

"Just think about it, Dara—we could all be here. When I spoke to Jamshed last, he said that Nazneen was taking the kids to India and enrolling them in school there. Doesn't it make more sense for us all to be together? Aden is not stable anymore. How long will he live away from his wife and children?"

"Aden will be fine, Zarir. I can't think about leaving right now. Jamshed's boys are older. They need the schooling that India can offer. My situation is different."

Dara stared out at the Creek, daydreaming, determining how to commission a *dhow* and bring his excess inventory to Dubai. He was only half listening to his brother. Dubai certainly seemed like an incredible place, but he was not ready to entertain any ideas of leaving Aden yet.

Dara returned to Aden with a renewed excitement and a long list of things to do. Arriving home from the Khormaksar airport, he walked into the apartment to find his wife listening to music and reading on the sofa. He dropped his bags at the door, poured himself a scotch, and joined her.

"Oh, honey, you wouldn't believe the trip I've just had. You should see this city. It's really something. Our new shop faces the Dubai Creek, which is just..." Dara was talking a mile a minute. Silloo listened intently, her inside vibrating with her own excitement, waiting for a pause so she could jump in with news of her own.

"That's great, *maro jan*, my love. I'm happy that you had such a successful trip. It sounds like Zarir has really settled in there, and you seem very excited about...this Dubai."

"Yes, yes, he has. He was trying to convince me to move there." Dara laughed. "Can you imagine? I mean, I can see why he is so enthralled with it. It's magical."

"Really? Are you thinking of a move for us? What with all the upheaval here, maybe that is something to consider?"

"*Nahre Nai!* I already told him, nothing doing! I am not ready to leave Aden."

They sat quietly for a few minutes. Silloo played with the fabric of her skirt impatiently, her pulse quickening.

"Darling, I have something I need to tell you," she said, interrupting the silence. Her gaze slipped down to her lap. She looked so beautiful draped on their couch.

"Is everything okay? You seem so serious." He lifted her chin with his finger and met her sparkling eyes. She placed her hand on his cheek.

"Dara, my *jan*." She smiled. "I'm pregnant." Her whole

face lit up. "I know the timing is crazy. Aram is still so young, but I am just so happy to have something to be happy about. It's a blessing."

"Oh Silloo, wow, really?" Tears pooled in Dara's eyes. She nodded. "This is great news! This is just what we need—a new beginning." Dara was beaming from ear to ear. They sat quietly in each other's arms for a long time, imagining their future.

"I was thinking about having this baby in London. I could take the boys and have the baby there. I can stay with my mum. She will be there to help."

"Okay, yes, of course. Whatever you want, you should do that. Silloo…I love you." Dara took his wife's hand and pulled her up from the couch into his arms. "Quizás, Quizás, Quizás" started playing on the reel-to-reel tape player. He pulled her close, one hand around her tiny waist, hers up at his shoulder. Hand in hand they swayed. He nuzzled into her ear and sang to her. Things were only going to get better.

6

"The only way around is through."
—Robert Frost

March 1968

Everyone knew that the newly established Adeni government was facing internal struggles, and the new leader, Qahtan Al'Sha'abi, was ignoring the rebellions brewing within his own party. The Front had positioned itself as a party based on scientific socialism, but within the group, there were factions developing with strong left ideals, many of them not even realizing that they were Communists until well after the party took over. Communist groups outside of Aden, ready and willing to support with arms and aid, pushed the new government to embrace stronger socialist ideals.

"*Sayid, Sayidati,*" Ahmed said, hurrying in from the kitchen with a transistor radio in his hand. "There is something big happening in the streets."

Dara jumped out of his seat and rushed over to listen alongside Ahmed to the Arabic newscast.

"What is it?" Silloo questioned, wrapping her hands around her hot teacup.

"The army and police have launched a de facto coup," Dara

relayed quickly. "They are trying to encourage the government to change direction and become more unified." He paused and listened intently. "They say they did this to save the country from Communism."

"But isn't the new government Communist? I am confused," Silloo said, taking a cautious sip from her cup.

"It *is* a Communist government, but there is a group within the government that does not feel that it is Communist enough. The average Yemeni following their rhetoric does not understand that the principles of this ideology is Communist. It is very confusing."

They all hovered around the small radio for the rest of the day, listening as the news trickled in. Over the hours that followed, they learned that Qahtan Al'Sha'abi's house was surrounded and demands were being made to change the government and policies. That night, they slept restlessly, anxious for what might come next. Over the course of the next few days, demonstrations erupted throughout the streets. The news reported of divisions rising within the army—with more officers declaring their loyalty to the Communist left. Dara and Silloo followed the news arduously, building up rations and staying at home. Miraculously, again, everything seemed to settle and resolve itself within a few days. Relieved, they chalked it up to a new government ironing out the kinks.

As the days progressed, the news reports came in on how President Qahtan Al'Sha'abi had persuaded the military leaders to stand down and that, in return for their compliance, he would not retaliate against them. He was bringing in his cousin, Faysil al-Shaabi, as secretary general to reorganize the NF and bring the two sides together. Over the next few months, Faysil desperately tried to do this. The rumors, however, were that the military had not been properly purged of the more radical elements, and Faysil and Qahtan's attempts to strengthen the NF's position were never truly realized. Although many of the individuals who had plotted and planned the de facto coup had been expelled or pushed out, some still remained in their positions, biding their time until they could oust Qahtan. In his arrogance, Qahtan yet again failed to acknowledge the threat.

May 1968

"Your Excellency," Salmin said, entering the president's office.

"Salmin, *ya-raab*, please, please, come sit. Have tea," said the president, a cigarette between his teeth. Salmin, one of Qahtan's key advisers and an NLF leader, could barely make out the president's dark, heavy face and characteristic mustache through the thick layers of smoke floating in the dimly lit office. The president was in his mid-forties, which made him considerably older than most of the other Front members. He sat behind an imposing desk wearing a white shirt, gray tie, and gray suit pants.

"Thank you, Your Excellency," Salmin said. He continued, his voice hushed, "Mr. President, there is talk that there may be another coup on the horizon."

"Coup? On who?"

"Eh, you, sir," said Salmin. "You see, the extreme left is getting frustrated. They want you to enforce stricter socialist policies here in Aden. They're saying that it's taking too long. They want to see more progress—quickly. It is not a bad idea."

"Salmin, please. I am the NF leader. Without my leadership, there is no Front. Ha! Let them talk all they want and let the army launch another coup. I would like to see them try." Qahtan leaned forward, the cigarette squeezed between his fingers, the long, arching ash about to drop. He was beaming from ear to ear. "I will crush them." He made a fist, choking the cigarette between his tobacco-stained fingers, the ash disintegrating on the desk. "The same way I did last time. I will not be told how to run my country. The left is weak, powerless. They can talk all they want, but they cannot beat me." He leaned back in his black leather chair and smiled again.

"Sir, they're calling for a national democratic revolution. They want to give power to the soldiers, peasants, and workers. They want to form a people's militia. They're calling for true nationalization of all foreign banks and trade—and to close the port here in Aden," Salmin explained.

"*Sadiqi*, they're crazy! It will never happen. No one wants that. Don't worry, I will control them all, ah? I will get the aid from Britain. Trust me. You will see. Okay. *Yalla*. I don't want to hear any more of this nonsense talk. Go now, no more of this."

Salmin left the meeting feeling disdain and disgust. Outside, he met back up with Abd al-Fattah Ismail. He leaned against the wall next to him, and Abd offered him a handful of *khat*. Salmin carefully placed the leaves into his mouth, pushed them into place with his tongue, and chewed. The release came immediately. He felt calmer, even if it was imagined.

"So, what did the donkey say?"

"We just need to keep doing what we're doing—keep making him weaker from the inside. The left needs more prominent leadership and unity in the armed forces. We cannot afford to lose loyalty, but he has no idea what's coming." Salmin smiled.

"What did he say about the money? The assistance he promised he would squeeze out of those British bastards? The money they promised us when they left? Did he say anything about that?"

"He said he will get it."

Abd laughed. "They aren't giving him anything. We'll get the Soviets to help. They just need a little push."

"*Akhi*, brother, we need to be patient. Our plan is working. We will continue working with him. Let him think that he's bringing us together. Then we'll force him out and make you prime minister."

"And you, *ya-raab*, you are the one we'll soon be calling 'Your Excellency!'" said Abd.

"*Insha'allah, ya-*Abd, *Insha'allah.*"

Chapter 6

June 22, 1969

Quiet opposition against Qahtan continued to build within the Front. Abd and Salmin became two of Qahtan's most trusted advisers, as per their plan. Salmin encouraged Abd to separate himself from his own allies, further alienating himself. Pushing out Qahtan's legitimate supporters paved the way for the left to make their move and take over. On June 22, it all came to a grinding halt.

Despite the tumultuous political situation, Dara attempted to maintain some sense of routine for the family's sake, if not his own. They tried to go about their lives as normally as possible, but the one thing he worked to keep separate was his combing over the newspapers for any signs of change within the government, any sliver of detail that could help ease his growing anxiety. Over the past few weeks, he had read about some disturbing developments. What was more concerning was what he was hearing from friends. It seemed that Qahtan wanted to see his former ally, Muhammad Ali Haitham, a man with strong military ties, removed as the minister of interior. Then in an incredible turn of events and in an attempt to throw a curveball at their opponents, Qahtan and Faysil offered to resign. Much to their dismay, the resignations were accepted. Among the party, Qahtan had come to be viewed more as a dictator than a socialist leader and was placed under house arrest, and Faysil was arrested. The more conservative left had eventually succeeded in infiltrating the army and either turning loyalty away from Qahtan or purging the Front of any right-wingers. Salmin emerged as the new chairman of the presidential council, sharing responsibility with Haitham and Abd al-Fattah. The newly established government had close ties to the Communist regimes of the USSR and China and were committed to instilling the ideals of a Communist government in South Yemen. Salmin refused Faysil's requests for clemency and threw him in a detention camp.

Dara was unsure what to make of all of it; it had become a waiting game. Even with the upheaval in the government, their lives seemed to carry on without much disruption. Things were different, life wasn't as idyllic as it had been before, but at least the political turmoil had been removed from their lives. They plowed on and tried to live their lives as normally as they could.

July 21, 1969

Dara's excitement was unmistakable. He had been watching the clock all night in anticipation of the moon landing. The mere thought of men walking on the moon gave him chills— the concept alone was sublime—and he felt that the only way he could adequately honor such an occasion was to invite his closest friends over to watch it happen in real time. Pierre and Valerie joined them very early that morning for a full American champagne breakfast, which seemed like an appropriate tribute.

"Silloo, come on, come on—you're going to miss it!" Dara called down the hall.

"I'm coming," Silloo answered. "The baby woke up. I will be there in a few minutes."

Dara bobbed around the room, handing out champagne glasses before finding his seat on the sofa.

"Come on, boys!" he urged his sons. "Come and watch! Will the Americans land on the moon today? Let's see!"

The tired boys climbed up on their father's lap, unsure of why they had been woken from a deep slumber to sit in front of the television. As *Apollo 11* started its descent, the four adults and two children huddled around the television to watch the grainy black-and-white images, almost indiscernible, and listen to the crackling audio as Houston spoke to the spacecraft's crew.

Running critically low on fuel, the astronauts had just one shot to land. Neil Armstrong had disabled the autopilot and was directing the spacecraft on his own to a safer landing spot. Everyone in the living room, along with the rest of the world, sat on the edge of their seats. And then they heard Armstrong announce what would become a quintessential statement of American achievement: "Houston, Tranquility Base here. The Eagle has landed."

Dara and Pierre jumped up and screamed, Dara placing his fingers in his mouth to whistle over and over again. What a triumph! He looked at Pierre with tears in his eyes and said, "There is a man on the moon—how incredible is this?"

Pierre, also teary, reached out and hugged his friend. "Think of the possibilities. Just think, my friend. What a world we live in!"

March 1970

Dara poured himself a scotch and set up his reel-to-reel player, queuing up his African reel. Miriam Makeba crooned to hard melodic drumbeats. It was a cool night for March. A steady breeze filtered in from the balcony window, and he watched as the moonlight bounced off the ripples on the ocean. Silloo and the children were in Bombay visiting family, so he had the whole apartment to himself and was enjoying the unfamiliar solitude.

A loud knock at the door interrupted his thoughts. He opened it to find three young men standing there uncomfortably.

"Dara Barucha?" one of the men asked.

"Yes, can I help you?"

"We come from the prime minister's office with instructions to put your family business under custodianship," said the youngest-looking of the three.

"What do you mean? What is custodianship?" Dara asked.

"We will be doing some investigating. You do not need to go to your office tomorrow. Please just stay here. We will call you when we want you to come. Okay?" said one of the other men politely.

"Okay, but why is—"

"We will explain all details tomorrow."

The men left as quickly as they had arrived. Dara, perplexed, picked up the phone. Bhicajee, Dara's oldest brother, was their father's second child from his first wife. Almost twenty years older than Dara, Bhicajee had been sent to London to pursue an education in accounting after concluding his secondary schooling in India. It was quite an honor to have been bestowed with an elite British education, and because of their father's early passing, he was the only one of his siblings to be afforded this privilege. With the onset of the Second World War, he returned to India to join the navy and serve his country but was able to go back to London to finish his degree after the war. Bhicajee was sophisticated and worldly.

His time in London had given him an appreciation for the finer things, and he had easily adopted some British traditions like dressing in three-piece suits and proudly carrying a pocket watch. He had returned from England with innovative ideas and an expansive knowledge of products and luxuries that the British elites living in Aden, as well as those traveling through, liked to indulge in. Knowledge that he had imparted on his very eager younger brother Dara. Together, they built up their retail dynasty in Aden, unmatched by any other merchant in the region. Dara trusted Bhicajee and always looked to him for counsel.

"Dara, *kem*, is everything okay?"

"I'm not sure. Three men were just here. They told me that they are taking our business under custodianship. I am not to go to work tomorrow. I was told that they will call me when they want me to go in, but—"

"Dara, hold on. Someone is at my door, probably the same men. Let me call you back."

Dara dialed Jamshed's phone, but there was no answer. A few minutes later, Bhicajee called back and confirmed that the same message had been delivered to him.

"It's hard to say what this is all about," said Bhicajee thoughtfully. "This may be the first step to nationalization."

"Should we be worried?" Dara asked.

"I don't think so, not yet anyway. These men were polite and respectful. Let's see what they say tomorrow, but I do suspect this is step one in the nationalization effort. We knew it would come eventually. It was to be expected. By the way, where is Jamshed? Have you spoken to him?"

"No, I just called him, but there was no answer. I will wait a little and then try again. Don't worry, I will find him and tell him what is going on."

The next morning, the three brothers gathered and waited impatiently to be called in to Bhicajee Cowasjee. It was noon before the call finally came. The three young men were waiting for them in the office above the store, in *their* office and at *their* desks. They were dressed in monotone gray pants and shirts and stood awkwardly around paperwork scattered about the desks.

"Mr. Bhicajee, Mr. Jamshed, Mr. Dara, we have reason to believe that there has been illegal activity conducted through your business."

Jamshed, offended by this accusation, looked directly into the young man's eyes. "What are you talking about? What illegal activity?"

Chapter 6

"We understand that a *dhow* was commissioned to Dubai at the end of 1968. We have been looking at the bank activity of Bhicajee Cowasjee, and we have reason to believe that you smuggled something into Dubai and have moved money elsewhere."

"Now you listen here, that is just not true. We have all the paperwork that shows exactly what we sent to Dubai. That *dhow* was filled with goods and items that we owned and could not sell here in Aden, so we transferred them to our new shop in Dubai," Dara said. Bhicajee stood with one arm folded across his chest and the other resting on his chin, nodding his head in calm agreement.

"We have been instructed by the prime minister's office to investigate this issue, and in the interim, we will take over operations of Bhicajee Cowasjee. You will not be permitted into the shop or office while the investigation is ongoing."

"What? How long will that take? How are we supposed to live? We have families to feed! My father and his father started this business over one hundred years ago. Our family has an excellent reputation in this city. What kind of nonsense is this? How dare you treat us like common criminals. We are respected, honest businessmen," Jamshed objected.

"Please, calm down. You will still receive your salary and any dues, but you will not be allowed to come to the office unless we instruct you to do so. And if, as you say, you have done nothing wrong, then you will be allowed to come back."

Bhicajee took a step closer to the men, signaling to his

brothers to stay calm, and said, "Okay, we will wait until we hear from you, and please remember that we are willing to cooperate with you regarding this investigation. We have nothing to hide. So please do not hesitate to ask us any questions that you may have." Bhicajee turned to Dara and Jamshed. "Brothers, it is time for us to take our leave." Both of them looked at him defiantly. "Come on now, there is nothing left here for us to do."

They stepped out onto the veranda flanked by the massive stoic pillars and stood for a moment, scanning one another's faces.

"Let's walk," Bhicajee said. The brothers crossed the street to the gardens and down toward the ocean. "We should go sailing this afternoon."

Dara looked at his brother in disbelief. "Sailing? Shouldn't we do something about those men in our father's shop?"

"Boys, there is nothing we can do right now," Bhicajee reasoned. "Let them do whatever it is they think they need to do. Did you see the expressions on their faces? They don't even know what an account ledger looks like. We are now living in a Communist country. Things are different, and we need to adjust to this new way of doing things. It's very likely that they are going to nationalize us, which really should not come as a surprise. They are not taking our salary, or detaining us, so let's just see what they do. You both know as well as I do that they won't be able to keep the business running. They will ask us to come back. We just need to be patient. Now, let's go sailing!"

Chapter 6

During the many months of the custodianship, Dara's days were spent mostly at the Gold Mohor Beach Club with Silloo and the children. The prime minister's men desperately tried to find some illegal activity that they could accuse the brothers of. They would call them into the office several times a week to try to understand how to manage the day-to-day operations. Bhicajee had been correct. The men had no idea how to manage the shop, and they began losing money. It destroyed the brothers to witness the demise of their business empire, but they patiently allowed the situation to play out as it would.

"Dara, I just heard from our bank. There has been some activity at the company." Bhicajee sat down next to Dara on a beach towel. Both men stared out into the horizon, the sun beginning its descent. The Beach Club was still operating as it always had. It almost felt as if nothing had changed when they were within the confines of the club.

"What kind of activity?" Dara asked, his eyes fixed on the horizon.

"Well, you know that all the banks have now been nationalized, correct?"

"Yes, that just happened a few weeks ago."

"So, it seems the prime minister's men asked the bank for a substantial loan to cover the debt that they have run themselves into, but a simple loan would never be enough to make up for their ineptitude. The shelves are apparently bare, and the shop is running at a loss." Dara shook his head and looked down at the sand beneath him. "The bank manager suggested that the prime minister's office bring us back and allow us to fix the ailing business." Bhicajee smiled, now looking at his brother.

"They did what?" Dara stared back in disbelief.

"You heard me correctly. With no proof of foul play and a dwindling store that they are running into major debt, the prime minister's office has made an offer for us to return. There is the issue of the loan that they requested and who will pay it back, but these are details that we can work through, I think."

"Bhicajee, this is great news." Dara, feeling triumphant and motivated, started making plans to save their business.

Eight months after the custodianship had begun, Bhicajee Cowasjee—empty, dilapidated, and tired—was returned to Dara and his brothers. Eager and ready to get their lives back on track, and confident that at least for now they would be left alone to manage their century-old business, Dara and his staff stripped the walls, changed out carpets, cleaned, and organized. Within two weeks, the shop was fresh and ready to reopen.

Part Two

"Choose a woman who is committed to finding the depth within her own soul. You might confuse her for a goddess, and who could blame you, she has within her the forces of earth, air, fire, water and ether. She is the container for the whole Universe. She can create life. And together, the life you can create will be beautiful."
—Ramdesh Kaur

7

"There's always another storm. It's the way the world works.
Snowstorms, rainstorms, windstorms, sandstorms, and firestorms.
Some are fierce and others are small. You have to deal with
each one separately, but you need to keep an eye on
what's brewing for tomorrow."
—Maria V. Snyder

Silloo was born in Bombay on August 11, 1937. She spent her childhood as a military nomad, moving from post to post throughout India and then Pakistan after the Partition. Her father served in the British Indian Army and had worked his way up to the rank of colonel. He was her hero and idol, a strict and stern man, but also incredibly loving and gentle, with an insatiable sense of adventure. Throughout her life, she referred to herself as "the colonel's daughter" with tremendous pride. She attributed her ability to handle anything thrown her way to this simple fact, which her mother had ingrained in her early on. One day, after Silloo collapsed into a fit of tears in anticipation of something she was afraid to do (something so inconsequential that it had escaped her memory), her mother had brought her over to a mirror, clasped both hands firmly on her daughter's seven-year-old shoulders, looked at her through their reflection in the mirror, and said, "*You* are the colonel's daughter. *Always* remember that. There is *nothing* you cannot do. Look in your eyes and tell yourself that with pride every day."

Silloo's mother, Arnavaz, was a tall and somewhat intimidating woman. Progressive for her age, she wore her hair short, much to the chagrin of the elders in the community, and wore trousers with button-down shirts tied at her waist. A rebellious modern woman, a concept uncommon in 1940s India. However, as much as she was consumed by, and completely and utterly devoted to, her three young children, she remained undeterred from her favorite pastime: hunting tigers. A fearless rebel in her own right, she took up this pastime to save babies from the perils of wild tigers in local villages that liked to steal them.

When Silloo was six years old, a middle-aged man had come to visit her parents. One night, when the scotch was flowing, he mockingly brought up her mother's tiger hunting.

"My, my, what is this? A woman who hunts tigers? *Va, va!* I don't believe it! You know I have hunted tigers before. This is not a woman's work. *Sahib*, how do you allow your wife to do this? Does she really hunt tigers?" He winked at the colonel.

"Mr. Gupta, I am sure my wife would be happy to take you out on a hunt. Especially since you are already an experienced hunter, as you say. Arnavaz, what do you think? Shall we go tomorrow? We can take the children too," the colonel said.

"Oh, no, no, *Sahib*! I am sure that there is so much planning to be done. I can't expect you to make such a great effort on my behalf at such short notice." Droplets of sweat were now clearly visible on Mr. Gupta's balding head.

"Nonsense, Mr. Gupta! It is no trouble at all. We can set out before dusk tomorrow. We have the whole day to prepare. It would be my privilege to show you how a *woman* hunts a tiger," Silloo's mother said, smiling.

"Oh...yes, thank you, thank you. But is it safe to bring the children? How about we just stay in your lovely home tomorrow night. Please do not make any bother for me." His head bounced from side to side, searching desperately for agreement.

"We leave tomorrow afternoon. Now, you should get some sleep! You will be up most of the night tomorrow, waiting for a beautiful Indian tiger to greet you." The colonel got up and escorted Mr. Gupta to his room.

The following day was spent organizing the hunt. They left at precisely 5:00 p.m., giving them enough time to make it to the hunting post and set up. The hunting posts were like small tree houses built between sprawling branches. They were made of wooden boards and had guard rails. The rails had slits so that the hunter could sit low to the post floor and balance their shot gun on the slats. Silloo, her brother, and her sister were well versed with their mother's work and perched on a blanket amid the treetop. Silloo and her brother flanked their father, their little sister in his lap. Their mother set up her shotgun. Serious, attentive, focused, and in complete control. With sweat dripping off his face, leaving wet spots on his safari jacket, Mr. Gupta spoke incessantly about anything that came into his mind, his fear clearly apparent.

"Mr. Gupta," her mother finally said, "if you don't stop

talking, the tiger will climb this tree and have us all for dinner."
She winked at her children. Mr. Gupta fell silent.

"Excuse me, but how often do you actually see tigers here?
Every time you come or only sometimes?" he asked in a hushed
voice.

"Shush, Mr. Gupta. Look, look, down there," she whispered.
Mr. Gupta gulped.

A tiger was sauntering its way through the brush. It was
massive, its coat hanging loosely off its bony structure. She
fired the first shot, then two more echoed through the woods,
followed by the sound of Mr. Gupta's urine falling through the
wooden slats of the post down into the leaves of the trees. Silloo
recalled the disgusted look on her mother's face as she glared
at him.

"I do not enjoy taking the life of an animal, Mr. Gupta,"
she said disdainfully. "However, there are many tigers in these
woods, and they are notorious for stealing babies from the local
villages. There are few men in this area who are willing, or quite
honestly even capable, of dealing with the problem, and so I
must do my part. I do this to keep the tigers in control." Silloo's
mother was a force to behold.

From a very young age, Silloo had come to understand and
accept hardship in its most basic and unrelenting form. With the
realization that life was not always fair, she had taught herself
to never take the good times for granted. Tragedy had already
devoured her and spat her back out multiple times before her
tenth birthday. At eight years old, she lost her younger sister

to typhoid, only to lose her beloved mother six months later to a burst appendix. In the months after her mother's sudden death, she clung to her father and younger brother in her insurmountable grief and flooded them with love and affection.

Even though tragedy ebbed and flowed through her life, miraculously she still grew into a loving and affectionate woman. She had inherited her mother's tenacity, fierceness, and fearlessness. Through the challenges of her younger years, she had learned to hold on to hope, a trait that sustained her throughout her life. Ultimately, it was within her family that she found refuge and happiness.

Silloo's father, Soli, often referred to as "the colonel," remarried soon after Silloo's mother died. Her stepmother, Shirin, and the colonel had courted in their youth, but family dynamics had forced them apart. He had, in fact, been the love of her life, and when things didn't work out for them, she swore to never marry another man. In a chance encounter after Arnavaz had passed away, the couple reconnected and quickly rekindled their romance. Within six months, they were married.

Shirin was not a typical stepmother. Her love for Soli was so deep and pure that it propelled her to fall in love with his two children also, thinking of them as her own. She was honored to be a stepmother to them and made it abundantly clear to Silloo and her brother that she would never try to replace their mother. She understood their pain and was committed to easing it. Shirin became Silloo's best friend and confidante, the woman whom she would affectionately call "Mum" for the rest of her life.

Of Mud and Honey

The partition of India and Pakistan marked itself solidly and in perpetuity in Silloo's mind. In those few days after the British left India, at just ten years old, she had vivid memories of being ushered into a tufted red leather bench seat in the general's compartment of a passenger train and traveling from India to Pakistan. All the other passenger compartments were jammed—men, women, and children so crammed that some hung off the sides or clung on to the roof of the train, all in hopes of a new life.

Fourteen and a half million people crossed the borders to be in the country of their religious majority during this time. A line determined by Sir Cyril Radcliffe, "the working boundary," became the somewhat arbitrary border between the two countries. A desperate need to get to the right side caused a disorderly mass migration of Muslims to Pakistan and Hindus to India. The chaos went unmanaged, resulting in the deaths of close to two million people. Embedded in Silloo's memory was the horrific image of a baby falling out of its mother's arms from atop the moving train. The train and life kept barreling forward. Everyone watched in horror, paralyzed by the inability to do anything else. The sickening image was followed by hours and hours of the mother's inconsolable wailing. The memory haunted Silloo throughout her life. Watching the baby fall from its mother's embrace reminded her of the loss of her own mother—the complete and utter despair that she felt being ripped away from the person who had given her life. In that moment, she promised herself that someday when she had children of her own, she would hold on to them with every fiber of her being and never let them go, no matter how fast things moved around her.

⟡ ⟡ ⟡

Soli moved his family from Pakistan to Aden in 1958 after retiring from the army. There he joined his sister Ava and her sons in running part of their family business. Ava's husband had been deceased for many years but had left her with a profitable enterprise. Soli was tasked with designing, building, and running a cinema and a restaurant, the first in the country. The buildings were contemporary in design and distinct among the Aden skyline.

The colonel was so taken by the breathtaking views of their natural surroundings that he asked Shirin what she thought of living somewhere where they could enjoy a view of the city on one side and the ocean horizon on the other. She asked him how they would ever do that. At that time, he wasn't quite sure but promised her he would find a way. One morning while taking his morning walk on the pier, he watched a retired barge being pulled into the dock. He had an idea and started up a conversation with an old Yemeni man that happened to be working on the dock, securing the boats. Soli was curious what they would do with the barge.

"That old thing?" the man replied. "It will be stripped and destroyed. It's no good now. It's old like me." He laughed. "No use for us old things."

"What if I wanted to buy it? Who would I talk to about that?"

The old man threw his head back in amusement. "You, you want to buy it?" he asked, pointing his finger back at Soli. "What will you do with that old piece of junk?"

"Yes, I want to buy it, and I'll show you what I'll do with it." Soli smiled.

Still laughing, the old man gestured to the dock office. "You can speak to Ismail. He can tell you who to talk to. But be careful, you will end up paying a lot of money for a piece of garbage."

"Thank you, sir. I am not worried about that barge's age. Think of the stories it could tell."

The retired barge was his answer. It was the perfect solution to his desire to live on the water and have a view of the city and the horizon at the same time. Soli did indeed buy the old barge, turning it into a magnificent houseboat. It had a kitchen, dining room, two bedrooms, and stairs that led to a spacious top deck where Silloo would lie out on cushions and read for hours. A small slice of paradise.

November 8, 1971

Dara leaned back in his office chair, his hands pressed together as if in prayer, framing his face. He looked up at

Jamshed, his uncle Burjor, and Darius, one of his employees. They were discussing options for each of the branches of the business that they still had control over.

"There is no point then in keeping a space for Melody Corner," Jamshed said.

"No, I don't think so," Dara replied. "We sent all the inventory to Dubai. I don't think we can run a music shop here in addition to the department store. There just aren't enough customers. We could create a small music department, but we don't need anything more than that."

"No, it doesn't make any sense to keep it. You're right, there just aren't enough people in Aden anymore," Jamshed lamented.

They could hear a commotion outside, but the men thought nothing of it. It was not anything out of the ordinary. Most likely some men cajoling in the street below.

"How would you like to move to Dubai and run the music shop, Darius?" Dara asked.

"I hadn't really thought about a move. I would have to talk to Hufrish and see what she thinks, but I suppose I'm open to the idea."

"Let's talk to Zarir," Dara said, turning to Jamshed. "We need a better understanding of what the clientele in Dubai is like. Let's see how those music systems we sent sell there."

The voices were now rising from the shop and getting more boisterous, finally catching the men's attention. A thunder of footsteps barreled up the stairs, the office door flew open, and eight men armed with machine guns burst in.

"What the hell is going on?" Dara jumped up and out of his chair, adrenaline surging through his veins. "Who are you? What do you think you're doing?"

The cacophony of voices made it hard to understand what was being said. Dara zeroed in on two men in the back of the group—two of his employees. He was shocked and confused.

"You are out, you and your brothers. You are all under arrest," a small, portly, greasy-looking man barked, his machine gun resting uncomfortably on his solid, round belly.

"Under arrest for what?" Dara barked back. "The prime minister's office gave us the business back. We haven't done anything wrong."

The man's head was wrapped in a white scarf. He had an unusually circular face, a thick mustache, and dense stubble along his sagging jawline. The man grabbed Dara by the shirt and pinned him to the wall. The gun dangling awkwardly between them, he shoved the barrel into Dara's chest, snarling and spitting out his words mixed with *khat*.

"The office of President Salmin Rubaya Ali is taking over this business. You and your brothers are going to jail. You understand now, *y'ahmar?*"

Dara pushed him back, but three more men came from behind, forcing him back up against the wall. Darius and Jamshed rushed forward, but they too were grabbed by the arms and shoved into the wall.

Silloo kissed each of the kids on the top of their head. "Fatima, I will be back in a couple of hours. Please make sure that Ana takes a nap after her lunch."

Fatima, a plump Somali woman, had come to work as a nanny for Dara and Silloo after Rustom was born. She was a sweet, quiet woman who doted on the children. She had Ana perched on her hip as she smiled her big, warm smile and grabbed the little girl's hand to wave goodbye to her mother.

Silloo blew the children another kiss before she left. She looked stunning in her white A-line dress, a red scarf draped elegantly around her head and tied in a loose knot under her chin, and the ensemble stylishly completed with her signature white cat's-eye sunglasses. She was on her way to help Dara plan for the annual sale at the shop, and then they were going to head to the club for a quick lunch date.

Once at the shop, she heard arguing from the office upstairs. *How odd,* she thought, pausing for a moment on the steps.

"Mrs. Silloo, no, no, no, don't go up there," the cashier, Yazdi, said nervously. "There is a problem upstairs. I don't know what."

Silloo looked up the stairwell, debating whether or not she should proceed. "Yazdi, please call Dara *Saab* on the intercom. Just tell him I am here."

"Yes, yes, of course, madam."

The intercom buzzed but with no answer. He hit the button again, holding it down for longer this time, and Dara picked it up.

"Sir, I-I am sorry to disturb, but Mrs. Silloo is here."

"Quickly, let me speak to her," Dara said. Yazdi handed her the receiver. "Silloo. Listen, there is a problem here. You need to go home, go straight home, and do not leave the children or Mamma."

"Dara, what's going on? You're scaring me."

"Silloo, go home *now!*" he shouted. The line cut. She could hear more shouting from the office now. She turned and ran home.

✤ ✤ ✤

The short, stubbly man grabbed the intercom receiver from Dara's hand and smacked it back down on the cradle. Dara went for him. "You bastard, you let me talk to my wife!" he yelled.

"Don't worry." The man smirked. "I will take care of your wife after I finish with you."

"You son of a bitch! You touch my family and I will kill you, you understand? *Ha?* Do you hear me?" Dara yelled. The man just looked at him and laughed.

"Please, sir, let us just make a few phone calls, *Ha?*" Jamshed tried to reason with him. "Come on now. There is no need for all this. We can show that this is all a big mistake." He reached for the phone. "I will simply call the prime minister's office, and we can have this sorted out in a few minutes."

The man grabbed the receiver from Jamshed's hand and threw it across the desk. "You will call nobody! You will come with us now."

"We are not going anywhere!" Dara yelled back. His body was heated, his breath heavy.

"You do not own this business anymore. It belongs to the people."

"What are you talking about? We signed a contract with the prime minister." Dara was fuming. *Who the hell does this guy think he is?*

The man pointed his machine gun at Dara. "Shut your mouth, or I will finish you right now."

"Shoot me then, you coward. You don't scare me. Go ahead, hide behind your gun." Dara's vein pulsed at his temple.

The man lifted his gun, staring down the barrel at Dara. Dara met his gaze; he would not back down.

"Call the police inspector. *Please*, just call him now," Jamshed interjected. He looked over at Dara, trying to get his attention and calm him down. The man lowered his gun and wiped his sweaty palms on his shirt.

"You want the police inspector, okay, okay. I will call him, and then you will see."

Dara looked over at one of the men standing quietly in the back, one of his employees.

"Ali Nagi, what are you doing with these men? Why? Why are you doing this? Do you agree with these thugs? You know what kind of men we are. Why are you not helping us? How can you just stand there?"

Ali could not look Dara in the eye. He stood just staring at his feet.

✥ ✥ ✥

Silloo got home to find that her phone line and Mamma's had been cut. She did not want to scare Mamma and played off the cut phone lines as an outage. She needed Ahmed. She found him cooking in the kitchen.

"Ahmed, there is something bad happening at the shop with *Sayid*," she said softly. "I need you to find out what is happening. Please go. There was shouting, and it sounded like there were a lot of people in his office. I have never heard him shout like that. But, Ahmed, do not go to the shop, it might not be safe."

"Of course, of course, *Sayidati*, I will go find out. You stay calm. I will be back soon." Ahmed readjusted his skullcap and left.

Ahmed was only a few years younger than Silloo. He had been just fourteen when Silloo's stepmother had spotted him at the market. He was the second of thirteen children from a poor Yemeni family. Ahmed was a hemophiliac, and his father found it a huge inconvenience to care for his sickly child. His mother had died when he was very young, and his father's second wife did not care for him. "A sick child is a useless child," she would say before she beat him with a stick and chased him out of the house. With nowhere else to go, he would roam the streets of Crater and Steamer Point, selling fruit and chatting with the foreigners in broken English.

His hemophilia had made it very difficult to help his father. Ahmed's father had been a master mud builder, one of those Yemeni craftsmen who had learned to build with special attention to the geography, climate, and materials of the country. His family had come to Aden from Sayyun, a town famous for its mud buildings. He had worked tirelessly in the fields near the *wadi*, mixing mud and straw with his bare hands. He would then use framed molds to lay out and smooth the mud. Once it had baked hard in the sun, he would pull up the bricks and place them in piles. The bricks were used to construct houses and buildings throughout the northern part of the country. The mud structures had thick walls, along with windows that were strategically placed away from direct sunlight and made small to keep the interior cool. The buildings were placed very close together to provide shade and protect the interior from the insidious heat. Often, intricate carvings would adorn the frames of the windows.

Moving to Aden had not been the opportunity that Ahmed's father had hoped it would become, and money was always an issue. The construction of mud buildings was not as prevalent in Aden as it was throughout the north and he struggled to find work. In moving to Aden, his father had hoped to bring his trade, teach a younger generation his skill, and lead a more affluent lifestyle. However, that had not been the case, and he could only find work on the docks.

Unfortunately, Ahmed's hemophilia made it hard for him to do any hard labor or join his father on the docks. Which is why he was relegated to roaming the market and aggravating his stepmother even more. Although a rambunctious and sweet fourteen-year-old he despised his inability to contribute to his family's income. After all, that was his duty as his father's son.

Shirin had seen Ahmed many times in the marketplace and took a liking to the spirited boy. He was thin and gaunt, with slightly sunken cheeks, mischievous deep-black eyes, and a smile that would melt a thousand hearts. She would purchase fruit from him, disregarding the bruises and mold they bore. Ahmed's father noticed Shirin's soft spot for his son. Seeing an opportunity, he took a chance.

"*Sayidati*, this boy of mine, he is useless to me, but maybe you have work for a young boy in your home, yes?"

"Are you looking to give away your son, sir?"

"Oh, no, no. It is just that he has many medical bills, and he simply does not make me enough money to keep my wife happy. She does not like him, says that his mother haunts her through his eyes. What am I to do?" He shrugged his shoulders, threw his hands in the air, and looked at her eagerly.

She smiled. She had never had children of her own, for fear of alienating Silloo and her brother Sohrab, and how could she resist the boy's kind eyes? There was something about him that she had been drawn to from the very first time she saw him.

"Okay," she said, and with that Ahmed happily came to live with the colonel and Shirin. He helped with chores around the house and with Shirin's catering business in the afternoons. And with every passing day, they saved each other's souls.

Ahmed felt a strong sense of loyalty to Silloo's family. Silloo's Arabic was not perfect, and Ahmed's Hindi and English were minimal, yet the two understood each other to perfection. They would muster up every word they could, in every language they knew, and mesh them together to form their own unique dialogue. They managed the most meaningful conversations despite not sharing one common language. To Ahmed, Silloo was an older sister and mother rolled into one. She and her stepmother had saved his life. His loyalty and adoration were unwavering. When the colonel and Shirin retired to London, it was decided that Ahmed would go to work for Silloo. There had always been an understanding, an unspoken vow, that Shirin would take care of Ahmed, and in turn he would take care of her and, by extension, those whom she loved.

⬥ ⬥ ⬥

Inspector Mohammed Ghanem arrived from the police station looking perplexed. He took statements and then hurriedly excused himself to make some phone calls, returning an hour later.

"Dara, Jamshed, what these men are saying is true. They have come from the president's office. The prime minister's office cannot and will not help you. I am afraid that whatever you agreed with them means nothing to these people. Nothing good will come from you standing your ground here. I recommend that you come to the police station, and I will be able to let you make phone calls from there. I am worried that if you stay here, this will not end well."

"Inspector Ghanem, what is this? This is crazy." Dara was confused, angry, and tired.

"Dara, trust me, just come to the police station. They will kill you if they have to. Please, just come."

"Dara, *chalo*, let's go," said Jamshed. "Come on, we haven't done anything wrong. We should listen to the inspector. There is no time to be bullish, *chalo*."

The mob of men from the president's office—followed by the inspector, Dara, Jamshed, Uncle Burjor, and Darius—all walked awkwardly to the police station, a few doors down from Bhicajee Cowasjee. The portly ringleader with the machine gun started up with the inspector.

"I want you to throw this garbage in a cell where they can rot."

"I am sorry, *akhi*, but they are not guilty of any crime." The inspector leaned in and spoke quietly. "They are a well-respected family in the community. I am not sure that what you are doing is wise."

"How dare you! I represent the president. It is on his orders that I am throwing this scum in jail." He was vociferous, his arms gesticulating everywhere, his machine gun still draped around his neck and seesawing across his potbelly. Inspector Ghanem, who knew the Barucha family well, allowed the man to talk.

"Well, we do not have a cell for them. I need to keep my cells for real criminals, and since these men are no threat to anyone... I am sure you understand my predicament." He paused. "This is what I can do. I will have them stay in the office space upstairs."

The man begrudgingly agreed, then turned and walked outside to inform the other men.

"Inspector, what are we being held for?" Jamshed asked.

"They are sending someone to talk with you tomorrow morning." Inspector Ghanem looked unsure. "This is an *intifada*. The government has been taking companies, like yours, under custodianship. They are trying to protect workers and the national economy from foul play. You know, smuggling and cheating the systems. They have found a few foreign companies that have illegally sent money out of the country in anticipation of nationalization, robbing the Yemeni people from what is rightfully theirs."

"But we were already under custodianship. They found nothing, and in fact, they put our company in debt, then asked us to come back and fix it. We even offered to honor their debt by taking on their overdraft from the bank. They have no grounds to do this."

"Do you think they need anything to base it on, Mr. Jamshed? Let me ask you this, did they hire locals to work at your store during the custodianship?"

"Yes, they did. Why?"

"Do those people still work there?"

"Well, yes, there are a few, but honestly they are not good at all, and our plan has been to let them go—"

The inspector interrupted and spoke over Jamshed. "They were put there for a reason, maybe to watch what you were doing and to try to catch you doing something you were not supposed to do."

"That's preposterous!" scoffed Jamshed. "They can plant whomever they want. They won't find anything because there is nothing to find."

"Well, fortunately they have agreed to my terms in detaining you, and they must think that they do have something on you and your brothers. Look, for now you are here and you are safe. You can get food sent from your house. We do not have the means to feed you, but they are leaving two of their men to guard the door at the police station. They say no visitors right now, but I think I might be able to work around that and at the very least let one of your family members come and see you. Tomorrow they will send someone to talk to you, and then I think maybe they will let you go. Mr. Jamshed, these men are not all Adenites, who know and respect your family. These men have been ravaged by the occupation. They have nothing. Most of them are from the protectorate. They are angry, hurt, and poor. They do not see you as good men who care for them or their country. I suggest that you listen to them and do as they say. They are not afraid and are ultimately backed by the president's office," Inspector Ghanem warned.

Chapter 7

Dressed in a traditional *futa*, a short-sleeved gray collared shirt and a white crocheted prayer cap, Ahmed walked through the back alleys of the city, listening for any talk on the streets of Steamer Point that might help him understand what was happening in his city. He was on his way to see his cousin Mazin, who would likely have a good idea of what was really going on. Mazin was well connected, an old man who had lost his sight as a child but was now legendary in the city. Locals trusted him and would bring him offerings, telling him their deepest secrets, hoping for any insights he could share. Many locals believed that *Allah* had taken Mazin's vision but given him the gift of seeing into men's souls. Ahmed knew that even if Mazin was not aware of what was happening, he would be able to advise him. The smartest thing to do was to go to his cousin.

Turning into one of the side alleys, Ahmed entered his cousin's house through a small metal gate. Mazin was sitting in his *majlis*, legs crossed, torso rocking back and forth, hands at his knees, facing the sky in offering as he spoke to God under his breath. Ahmed approached and waited quietly until Mazin was done.

"*Shaqiq*, I need to talk with you."

Mazin became still.

"Cousin, is that you, *ya*-Ahmed?"

"*Aiwa*, it is me."

"Come, come sit." Mazin patted the cushion next to him on the floor, his gaze fixed ahead. He called out for a tea and then took his cousin's hand as he sat down.

"*Shou al'akbar?* Tell me, cousin, your heart is beating fast. What is troubling you?"

Ahmed took a deep breath. "Something happened at my family's shop today. I need to find out what it is. *Sayidati*, she is scared and worried. *Sayid* had men in his office shouting when she went there. *Sayid* sounded scared and told her to go home and stay there. I promised her I would find out what happened. I am coming to you first. I don't know what to do."

Mazin's brow furrowed. He patted Ahmed's hand, still in his, with his other hand. "The new government is taking over some local businesses this week, but I am surprised that they would come to your family. Your family has been here for a long time. They are respected. They are no threat." He looked perplexed.

"Mazin, I cannot let anything happen to any of them. *Wallahi*, if I have to give my life for either of them, I will do it."

"I know, I know." Mazin patted Ahmed's hand again. "Go back to *Sayidati*, stay close to her, wait at her building downstairs. I will have Amer get some information and bring it to you. I will need a little time, maybe an hour or more. For now, you stay close to your *Sayidati*."

"Thank you, *ya*-Mazin, I will do as you say." Ahmed took his cousin's hand in his and kissed it before rising to leave.

"Ahmed, *Allah ma'ak*, be careful. Keep close to her. This new government, some of them, they are not like us. They are angry and scared and very dangerous."

Chapter 7

⟡ ⟡ ⟡

Ahmed waited downstairs at the entrance of Silloo's apartment building for what felt like a very long time before Amer arrived. Amer was tall and slim, wearing a black suit jacket over his *futa* and collared shirt, and a white turban. A traditional Yemeni *khanjar* sat around his waist.

"*Hala, hala*, Ahmed."

"*Shou akbar?* What is the news?"

"I am sorry it took some time to find out what happened today. Your people are in the police station, four of them—your *Sayidati's* husband, his brother, and two others, I don't know who they are. They were taken in the name of *intifada*. An uprising. Workers' revolution. Their employees arrested them."

"They are in jail? Their employees? *Yaani*, the staff from the shop?"

"They are in the office on the second floor. Looks like the police are not so convinced they should be there, but they have to follow the orders of the president's office. The employees accused them of doing some illegal things, but it seems the employees were planted there. You can try to speak to your *Sayid*. Go to the alley between the police station and Star Pharmacy. You can call to them from the alley, but wait until later, for night. There is a lot of activity there right now. Be careful, brother. If they find you are helping them…well, you know, just be careful."

Ahmed shook Amer's hand and pulled him into a one-armed hug. He would not tell Silloo anything yet. He would wait until after his visit to the police station.

✧ ✧ ✧

Silloo had Mamma come up to their apartment but hadn't told her about the incident at the shop—she didn't really know what to say at this point. She was hoping that Dara would just walk through the door and explain everything.

They set up a tea party with the children. Ana, at three years old, played hostess, setting cups and saucers around the table as she chatted to herself and her grandmother. Silloo watched her mother-in-law study her granddaughter, Mamma's hands continuously folding and unfolding a handkerchief. It always surprised Silloo how lonely Mamma looked. For a woman with such a large family, with so many children and grandchildren, she always seemed guarded. Even more so since Zaal had passed away.

The doorbell rang. Startled and unsure of what to do, Silloo stared toward the hallway.

"*Areh, Dikri*, aren't you going to answer the door? What is wrong with you?" Mamma sounded annoyed.

"Um, yes, Mamma, I am. I will." She walked slowly toward the entry hall and opened the door just slightly. Ali Nagi, one of the Yemeni employees from the shop, stood, head hanging, in the doorway. "Ali Nagi, what are you doing here? Is everything okay? Do you know what is going on?" She turned to see where Mamma was before continuing. "There was something happening at the shop. Can you tell me anything?" Ali was a relatively new employee at Bhicajee Cowasjee, but he had an agreeable nature and was likable, or so it had seemed.

"Mrs. Dara, I am very sorry for what happened today."

"What *is* happening? Can you tell me what is going on? Are you part of this?"

Ali could not look at her. He stared at his feet, shifting from one foot to the other. "I am sorry, but this, this had to happen. It was very necessary. I promise you, they will not be hurt. They will be okay, I-I promise you. If you need anything, you tell me, and I will help you, okay?"

"What are you talking about, Ali? What *has* happened? And what do you mean they will not be hurt? I want to know where my husband is." Silloo kept her voice down, trying to shield Mamma from overhearing. "Why have our phones been cut? What is going on? Please, can you tell me?"

"I am sorry, Mrs. Dara. The men are at the police station in Steamer Point. The police have given permission for you to go and see them this evening. There are some questions about the business. It is nothing to concern you. Everything will be fine." Ali apologized over and over again, rambling on about the whole thing being nothing to worry about until he abruptly turned and left.

Dara was not coming home. Silloo had an overwhelming feeling that this situation was much worse than she knew. It was time to tell Mamma.

Ahmed waited until the streets were relatively quiet, then made his way to the police station. He walked past the shop, dark and silent, and then the Marina Hotel, ducking in and out from under the arches of the buildings to stay out of sight. He stopped in front of Star Pharmacy and picked up a few small rocks, looking around to make sure that no one could see him as he slipped into the alley. Cautiously, he threw the first rock up at the second-story balcony and waited. Nothing. He hoped that Amer was right about this. He closed his eyes and chanted quietly to himself, *"Fee Aman il'ah."* He knew that Mazin would never lead him astray. He threw the second, then a third rock at the balcony, hoping that it was in fact Dara behind that window. There was some shuffling from behind the glass. A head poked through the window. Ahmed hid in the shadows, watching intently.

"Is someone there?" He recognized Dara's hushed whisper.

"Sayid, it's me, Ahmed."

"Ahmed! Where are you? Oh, thank God! Are Silloo and the children okay?"

"Yes, they are fine. Don't worry. I will take care of them. Are you okay? What is happening?"

"The president's office has taken the company this time. They are detaining us. I will know more tomorrow. Tell Silloo we are fine. Go now and come back again tomorrow at the same time."

"Okay, okay. *Allah ma'ak sayid.*"

"*Shukran, ya*-Ahmed."

❖ ❖ ❖

Silloo settled the children with Mamma before slipping out of the apartment to make her way to the police station. She walked past the shop, which was eerily quiet, then continued on her journey. She caught her breath outside the station doors before entering. Seething with adrenaline and filled with anguish, she approached the inspector. "I am here to see my husband."

The officer looked at her sympathetically and excused himself to find the chief.

"*Sayidati*," the chief said, entering the small waiting area. He was tall and slim with friendly eyes. "Please, follow me."

Upstairs, a young man sat outside the closed door, his head wrapped with a white scarf and a machine gun lying in his lap. The police chief exchanged words with him, and the man opened the door. The men were sitting at a conference table, Jamshed with his head in his hands. Dara stood as the door opened.

Silloo ran into her husband's arms. The emotion was too much to bear. She buried her head in his chest and sobbed silently. "*Maro jan*, my love," she said over and over again.

"Silloo, are you okay? The kids, Mamma, are they all right?" Dara pulled her away to look at her face.

"Yes, we are all okay," she said, wiping her eyes, straightening her shirt, trying to gather herself. "What is happening?"

"It's an *intifada*, workers' revolution. They have a problem with us, but what exactly that problem is I don't know. The police chief said they will keep us here for now. There are no charges yet."

"So why do you have to stay here? Why can't you come home?"

"We are being detained. It will just be a few nights probably."

"Okay," she said, trying to sound as though she really was.

"I will need you to send us some things if we're going to be here for a few days."

"But, Dara, why is this happening?" As much as she tried to hold back, tears started to fall from her eyes.

"I don't know, my love. Look at me." He clasped her face in his hands and wiped her tears with his thumbs. "We will be okay."

Silloo pulled herself up and cleared her throat.

"You will need to send Ahmed back with what we need. They said that we must have food sent from home. Can you also check on Freny? Bhicajee is still traveling, and she is all alone."

"Yes, of course." Silloo looked around at the bare office space. It was large and open, with tall white walls and a terrazzo tile floor. An oversized table sat in one corner with six chairs scattered around it. The balcony looked out onto the main street of Steamer Point and the street garden. It was sparse and hollow, and made her heart feel heavy.

"We will also need something to sleep on and something to eat out of. Send Ahmed with those supplies and any messages you have for us. If we can talk to him, we will."

"All right, sleeping things, eating and drinking utensils, food. What about clothes?"

"Yes, yes, good idea, clothes, and, my love, please stay home, do what they say, and try to call the British and Indian embassies—we will need their help. And Freny, please check on Freny."

"Okay, but Dara…they have cut our phone lines."

"What?" Anger percolated inside him, but he tried to stay calm. "Okay, well, the chief said he would let us make some calls tomorrow. But if you can make a call, then the embassies first, then Zarir in Dubai. And Freny."

"I am sorry, but *Sayidati* has to leave now," the police chief interrupted.

Silloo and Dara wrapped their arms around each other as tightly as they could.

"I love you," she whispered.

"I love you too," he said into her ear, kissing her head.

8

*"Courage is not the absence of fear, but rather the judgment that
something else is more important than fear."*
—Ambrose Redmoon

Silloo watched the water spill out of the plastic jug and into
the bathtub as Ana splashed around, soaking the bathroom
floor. She smiled, envious of her daughter's obliviousness,
wishing she could absorb some of that unscathed innocence in
this moment. Her legs felt weak, and she sat with her shoulders
hunched. Overwhelmed, scared, and anxious, Silloo hoped that
this whole situation was just some grand misunderstanding
that would blow over, that it was all a terrible mistake. Her
boys buzzed around her with toy airplanes, smelling of talcum
powder, their hair still wet from their baths. She inhaled a
deep breath, soaking in their sweetness.

Her moment was interrupted by an abrupt pounding at the
front door. Her heart raced; her body was paralyzed. The taste
of sour vomit bubbled up in her throat while beads of sweat
formed on the back of her neck.

"Who's there?" she called through the door, Fatima and the
children behind her.

"Open the door now!" a man's voice snarled.

"Why should I open the door? Who are you? And by what

authority do you come here?" she called out, holding her breath. She could hear other menacing voices in the hall.

"We come from the president's office. Open this door."

Ana, wrapped in a towel, started crying in Fatima's arms, and the boys clung to Silloo's legs. As she opened the door, she was hit by the foul odor of sweat and cigarettes from the man at the front. It was Ahmed Kazim, an employee from the shop. He pushed the door open, knocking her off balance and into the wall.

"What do you think you're doing?" she yelled.

There were fifteen or twenty men crowded in the hallway, clambering their way into her apartment. She recognized some of them, also employees from the shop—locals. So this is what an *intifada* looked like. Ahmed Kazim was the leader of the mob. He had been hired during the custodianship and had always made her uncomfortable.

"Where are your authorizations? Show me some warrant that permits you to come into my home."

"I will do as I want, and you will be better off to keep quiet, woman. Understand?"

The boys hid behind their mother. Fatima stood dumbfounded in the hallway, holding Ana.

"Fatima, take the kids into the other room," Silloo said calmly, maintaining her composure.

Ahmed Kazim and four other men walked through the apartment, looking around, picking things up and tossing them carelessly back. They used their machine guns to sweep her small crystal figurines off the table, sending two of them to the floor in pieces. Kazim pointed to two daggers hanging on the wall, and one of the other men started taking them down.

"What do you think you're doing?" Silloo asked.

"I told you to be quiet!" he bellowed at her.

Kazim swept his hand across the room and stopped just past Silloo's waist. "All this is mine now, to do with as I please," he said, eyeing her from head to toe.

"Watch yourself, Ahmed Kazim." She spat her words at him.

Kazim leered at her, smirking, and sauntered out the door. The other men filed out behind him, carrying with them Dara's daggers and a spear that he had brought back from their honeymoon in Africa.

"Where do you think you're taking those things? They belong to my husband."

"Your husband is a criminal, and everything now belongs to the people! You understand?" Ahmed Kazim said in low, calm voice.

She stared at him, unable to speak, unable to move, unable to understand why this unfathomable horror was taking place.

He turned to her from the hallway, still smirking. "And you, you are no longer allowed to leave this apartment." His smile grew long and wide. "You, the old women, and those children are under house arrest."

Silloo could taste the acid climbing up her throat as she shut and locked the door behind them, sinking to the floor, her head in her hands, her whole body trembling.

Chapter 8

November 9, 1971

The sand crunching under Ahmed's sandals was the only sound in the dark, quiet streets of Steamer Point. He crept along, checking periodically to make sure no one was following him. As promised, he had first walked to check on Dara's sister-in-law Freny. She had been visited by Ahmed Kazim and his men earlier in the day. They had told her that she was not to leave her apartment as well. Ahmed was overwhelmed by his need to protect his employer, his family. His fists curled up tight at his sides as he approached the police station and hid in the shadows, pausing a long while before aiming his rock for the second-floor window.

Dara had been standing by the window of the conference room at the police station, eagerly waiting for Ahmed's signal. He called out to Ahmed as soon as he saw him in the street, his face clear in the light of the streetlamp. They exchanged quick pleasantries before Ahmed launched into events of the previous evening.

"Last night, Ahmed Kazim came to the house with a group of men from the shop, ah, your workers. They took some things off the walls, had loud words with *Sayidati*, and then left. Today they came back and were making lists of all the things in your home."

The men had ransacked the house. Tipping things over, dropping things to the floor, pulling pictures and wall hangings off the walls. Ahmed chose his words carefully. He wanted to tell Dara what had happened without painting too clear a picture. The truth was that when Ahmed had seen the mess that they had left, it had shaken him.

"Lists, took things off the wall—what do you mean?"

"*Sayid,* they were going through your house and making a list of all your things. You know, your music, glasses, plates, everything…everything."

"Did they take anything?"

"Only last night—they took your daggers off the wall. Today, no. They told *Sayidati* that she must stay in the house. She is not allowed to leave or see anyone. But they will let Fatima and me come and go. I went to see Mrs. Freny before coming here. She is in the same situation in her apartment in Steamer Point, but her maid is staying with her all the time. They also went there and made lists."

"And what about Mamma?"

"Also the same. But they are allowing your mother and *Sayidati* to be together."

Dara's eyes narrowed. He was not accustomed to feeling so helpless. The vein at his temple pulsated. The sensation was becoming all too familiar.

"Ahmed, how is *Sayidati?*"

"She is very strong, *Sayid.* She is taking care of everyone."

"Take care of her, Ahmed. Please."

"*Aiwa, Sayid.* Of course."

"Be careful."

"Ehh…*Sayid.*" He hesitated.

"Yes, Ahmed."

"Please take care of yourself."

Dara turned, facing the other men in the conference room. Jamshed sat in a chair, his arms crossed, staring at the ground. Dara began recounting his conversation with Ahmed to them when Jamshed stood. "I know. We heard. This is worse than we think."

"Jamshed, don't panic."

The conference room door opened. A tall, clean-shaven police officer stood in the doorway, fiddling with the beret in his hands. "Good evening. I have spoken to the president's office, and they have informed us that there is an official investigation into your business here in Aden." He shifted his feet and remained in the door stoop. "We have been instructed to detain you until they complete the investigation."

Dara moved in closer. "Detain us? Did they say for what? Or for how long?"

"They did not give us details. Just that we are to keep you here at the police station until further notification." He looked at his feet, embarrassed. "Well, I will let you know if we are informed of anything else."

⬧ ⬧ ⬧

The men kept coming and going, sometimes taking things with them as they left. Silloo was worried about Mamma. There was so much happening, so much to process, all of it scary and incomprehensible and happening to all of them. She wasn't sure how well Mamma was coping. She wasn't exactly sure that she herself understood what was happening. Mamma seemed like a very stern woman on the outside, but there was a soft side to her, a warmth, and that was more and more apparent to Silloo these past few days.

"*Dikri*, do you think they will take the money in Jamshed's apartment? I have money in mine too." Mamma had a habit of hiding money all around the house. Born in a different era, she believed in keeping her money close and out of sight.

"How much money, Mamma?"

"There is quite an amount in the apartment, I think. For emergencies, you know..."

Silloo thought for a moment. "I think we should collect it all and hide it. Do you know where Jamshed has put it?"

Mamma placed her slender fingers on the keys tucked into her sari petticoat, patting them. "I have the keys to his Godrej right here, *Dikri*. I know where the money is," she said, smiling softly. "But it is already hidden."

"*Chalo*, Mamma, we can't keep it in the Godrej, that is the first place they will look. Let's go quickly, before it gets dark and while none of those thugs are here."

Up in Jamshed's apartment, the women unlocked the steel Godrej cupboard and tapped on the hidden drawer. The drawer magically opened, and Mamma pulled out three stacks of pounds sterling.

"Mamma, wait. They will be suspicious if they search and

find no cash at all—everyone has cash in their homes. We should leave some here so they don't suspect we moved it."

"*Areh, Dikri*, but what if they take it?"

"Listen to me. You have to trust me, *Apo Gee*. Give me the money. We need to leave some here, and we will hide the rest." Silloo held her hand out, and Mamma stared at her, her eyes filled with tears.

"*Chalo*, Mamma," Silloo said softly. "We will get through this together. I will take care of you, I promise. *Apo Gee*. Please."

Mamma reluctantly handed the wads of cash to Silloo. The evening sky was slipping in; slivers of orange and gold highlighted the horizon. Silloo knew that they must move quickly before they needed lights and could be placed in Jamshed's apartment. She had no idea who was watching or how intently. She placed some of the cash back in the cupboard, trying to make it look hidden. The women closed everything up and headed to Mamma's apartment to do the same. Mamma reached in between her clothing, her hands knowingly finding each wad, systematically pulling out small bundles of cash hidden between the layers of fabric on the shelves. She then made her way to the mattress, where she pulled out more parcels.

They went back to Silloo's, calmer now that they were where they were allowed to be. Silloo locked the front door and instructed Fatima to keep the children busy. They laid out the stacks of cash on the table and sipped tea while staring at it all, trying to think of where it could be safely hidden. Silloo inhaled the mint and lemongrass in her tea, and the aroma comforted her.

"Mamma, I think I might know what to do." Silloo jumped up and hurried into the kitchen. She returned a few minutes later with a screwdriver and grabbed as many wads of cash as she could. The evening call to prayer echoed through the mountains.

"Mamma, *chalo*, bring the rest of the money."

"Where are we going?"

Silloo had too many things swirling in her head and simply turned and walked away. Mamma followed her into the bathroom with her arms full. Silloo pulled out three plastic bags from her waistband and handed them to Mamma. "Start putting the money in these bags. Then wrap them with masking tape and give them to me. Make sure they are sealed so no water can get into them."

"But, *Dikri*, why are you doing this? We will need some money."

"If they find this money, they will take it. This is all we have left. We need to keep it safe. In the meantime, they must feed us and provide us with the basics. They can't just leave us here to rot like old fruit." She paused, hoping that this was in fact true. "So hopefully we will not need this money anytime soon. They *will* take whatever they find so we need to make sure that they do not find this. Please just help me, *chalo*."

Mamma dutifully followed her daughter-in-law's instructions without further argument. Silloo analyzed the wooden panel on the front of the bathtub, trying to decide the best way to remove it, and started unscrewing the four screws that secured it. Pulling the panel off, she scanned the space around the tub.

"Here, this is the spot." She pointed to the back corner. "Okay, Mamma, you give me one at a time. I am going to hide them around the back. Even if someone opens this, they will never see them back there. Those monsters will never think a woman would even know what a screwdriver is, let alone be able to use one, nor would they think us smart enough to hide the money in the first place." She smiled triumphantly.

Mamma looked like she might cry. They finished placing the bags of money behind the tub and then screwed the panel back on.

"Thank you. I'm grateful that you are here with me," Mamma said, reaching out for Silloo's hand with her long fingers. Silloo gently squeezed her mother-in-law's delicate hand.

"Thank you, Mamma, and I'm grateful to have you with me. *Chalo*, let's have a little more tea. It will all be okay." Silloo was not sure she believed what she had just told her mother-in-law, but she desperately wanted to, and she was saying it as much for herself as for Mamma. They walked hand in hand back into the living room.

November 11, 1971

It was Aram's fifth birthday, and Silloo tried to think up ways to make the day special, ignoring her worry and fears, but every piece of it was a struggle. How was she to explain to him why his father was not there, or why his party had been sabotaged by a group of scary men ransacking their home? There was no cake, no balloons, no friends, and to make it worse, she was running out of food. She had begged Kazim for supplies, but he had mocked her.

"Drink water—that is what we do in the villages when there is no food. You people think you are big and powerful, but you can't survive one day without all your luxuries."

She begged him for milk for the children and some bread. They could survive on that, but he just brushed her off.

"We can't get you anything today. Maybe tomorrow."

"Okay, my brother-in-law has powdered milk in his apartment upstairs. Can we take that for now?" she pleaded.

"You think I am stupid? You will not leave this apartment—do you understand? There is a guard at the door now. That apartment and everything in it belongs to me. You will not have anything from there!"

Silloo's continuous pleas fell on deaf ears. That night, they scraped together what they could for food. The children were hungry and disagreeable, but there was no other choice. She paced her living room, trying not to panic, trying to stay calm.

Chapter 8

She would ask Fatima and Ahmed for help. How awkward, to be in a position where she had to go to the people who worked for her and ask for help. There was no other choice.

It was in the dark hours of the evening and late at night on those first few days, when she lay alone in her bed, that she found herself the most frightened of what might happen to her, Mamma, and the children. Any of those men could break into her apartment at any time and do whatever they wanted, and she feared that they just might. They had already begun taking what they wanted. What was to stop them from adding her to the list? She shuddered at the thought.

There was still no contact from Freny. All she knew from Ahmed was that Freny was in her apartment with her maid going through this same ordeal with no news or access to the outside world. They were all jailed, prisoners in their own homes, caught up in a battle that they should have had nothing to do with. Regretful that they had not left Aden when so many others had. Resentful of Dara's complacency, wishing she had pushed him more on the move to Dubai. She stopped herself. She could not imagine how this might end. She could not go down the rabbit hole of blaming him. With the daily ransacking, and in an effort to keep track of what had been done and what needed to be done to get out of this mess, she decided to start writing a diary. Later that evening, Kazim returned.

"Your brother, he said there is money in his house that we can use for you for food."

"My brother-in-law, you mean. Jamshed." Her heart began

to *thump, thump, thump*. "Oh, that's good news, so now maybe can you get me some bread and milk?"

Silloo and Mamma realized how lucky they were that Silloo had thought to leave some money behind. Jamshed had told the men about it in an attempt to have the money used to feed the women and children. Unfortunately, Kazim and his men took the decoy money that had been left in Jamshed's Godrej cupboard and left Silloo with nothing but a bare pantry. The children were unhappy. Ana cried and cried for her bedtime bottle. While she wailed, Silloo, too, cried silently as she desperately tried to console her young daughter and soothe her to sleep.

She now had to lean on Ahmed completely. Tomorrow she would have him check on Freny again, and get some food for her. Relying on Ahmed to buy food for them was more than she could bear, but she would pay him back, every penny, and she would ask him to stay with her as much as possible. Her mind raced continuously. She needed to get out of the house, get access to a phone, access to anything and anyone so she could get help. It was becoming clear to her that she needed to start doing something to change their situation.

"*Sayidati*," Fatima whispered. She had slipped into the room without Silloo noticing.

"Fatima, yes."

"*Sayidati*, I saw Dr. Khoureshi's maid on the street just now when I was coming into the building. She said to tell you to turn off the lights and go to the balcony at 8:30 p.m. Sit low and out of sight, next to Dr. Khoureshi's balcony."

Chapter 8

Dr. Khoureshi lived in the next building on the same floor as Dara and Silloo. The buildings were about four feet apart, with the balconies lined up side by side.

Silloo looked down at her wristwatch. She had ten minutes.

"Did she say why?"

"No, *Sayidati*. But she is very trustworthy. She would not trap you."

"Okay, help me, let's turn off all the lights and put some music on, not loud, just enough to distract."

The women worked quickly and quietly, and at 8:30, Silloo slipped out onto the balcony. She had no idea what she was waiting for. What if this *was* a trap? How could it be? The doctor and his wife were good people, and after all, she was only sitting on her balcony. She had to feel hopeful. She squatted low and started to pray an *Ashem vohu* under her breath.

A ship blew its horn in the harbor, startling her, and she thought about how many times she had heard that sound, thinking nothing of it. How she wished she could sound a horn right now—but who would hear it? And if someone did hear it, would they hear within it her desperation and fear?

She heard movement, some rustling, but all the lights at the Khoureshis' were also off. She sat frozen, waiting, listening, her heart pounding so loud she thought for sure someone would be able to hear it, if it didn't jump out of her chest.

"Silloo, 'ar you there?" the familiar voice whispered on the other side of the balcony.

Tears rushed to Silloo's eyes, a lump forming in her throat. Relief vibrated through her whole body. "Valerie," she choked out her friend's name. "Oh, Valerie." She sobbed quietly into her fist.

"Oh, *mon ami,* 'ar you okay? What is 'appening? 'Ow can I 'elp you? Tell me. 'Ere, can you reach my hand?" Valerie reached over the half-wall of the balcony and slipped her hand into Silloo's.

Silloo lowered herself all the way to the ground, her knees to her chest. The words poured out with hushed urgency as she told Valerie every single detail. In turn, Valerie told Silloo that Dr. Khoureshi's wife, Noor, had heard the commotion and shouting in Silloo's apartment. She had listened at the window and then sent her maid to investigate. As soon as she had found out what had been going on, she called Valerie *tout de suite.*

Silloo and Valerie stayed on their respective balconies for a couple of hours, talking and sharing, ignoring the concrete half-walls that separated them, losing themselves in the comfort of each other's voices. They made a plan for Valerie to return in three days. After her friend went back inside, Silloo remained on the balcony floor, quietly sobbing into her hands.

❖ ❖ ❖

The days bled into one another. With each morning, Silloo's fears intensified. The "mongrels," as Silloo referred to them, led by Ahmed Kazim, came to the house every day to rifle through all her personal belongings and had begun taking more and more: crystal, porcelain, jewelry, cash, anything they could get their hands on. More than once, she had seen the men stuff her things into their pockets. There was no list or inventory of what was being taken, and a part of her knew that she would never see those possessions again. She shifted her thoughts back to the tasks at hand and away from how violated and vulnerable she felt. Ahmed's daily meetings with Dara were what kept her breathing. She knew that her husband was still alive, and she knew that she had to take care of her children and Mamma. There was no time to fall apart, no time to show fear, and no time to focus on things beyond her control. *They were still alive*, that she knew, and her goal now was to make sure they all *stayed* alive. So, she watched as the soulless men invaded her home, smiling and laughing, bantering in Arabic about the size of her breasts and her smooth skin, violating every aspect of her being with their words and hands, touching everything and stuffing their pockets with her precious memories as though all of it, including her, was theirs.

It became clear in those first few days that they would take whatever they could, so Silloo and Mamma began hiding anything of value.

"Mamma, I think we need to hide the jewelry in a better place. I have an idea." They collected all the jewelry that they could between their apartments and hid it in their Godrej steel cupboard. The cupboard's secret drawer was a lifesaver.

Valerie continued to visit two or three times a week. Silloo looked forward to her evening conversations. They made her feel hopeful and less isolated.

"Valerie, what is it like in the rest of the city?" Silloo asked. "Are other people in this same situation?"

"Ah, *non, mon ami*. It seems there are only a few families like you. Pierre and I have had no problems. It is as if none of this is 'appening if you do not know people in these circumstances, but we are with the French embassy. It is the merchants of the city that are being targeted. Families like yours. I am so sorry."

Silloo was quiet for a moment, brooding over her next question. She hated to ask for help but realized now the gravity of her situation. "Valerie, I need help." Silloo cringed, grateful that she did not have to look at Valerie while asking.

"Of course. Anything," Valerie responded.

"Would you help me contact the embassies? I am completely cut off from the world here. They will not let us talk to anyone."

"Yes, of course, Silloo." Valerie didn't hesitate. "I will ask Pierre to talk to the French embassy and see how to reach the others. We will get you 'elp. I promise."

When Silloo shared with her how their belongings were being taken, Valerie offered to take what she could and hide it. Silloo would pass a few things over the balcony to Valerie, their fingers gently touching each time. This exchange continued for the next few visits. It was never anything big, but Silloo managed to pass a few small meaningful items, like her wedding album and some baby pictures of the children. Valerie carefully carried away what she could.

The routine in the apartment continued, and each day brought more of the same. The mongrels would show up midmorning and turn the house upside down for the next eight hours.

Ahmed Kazim had suspected that there was more of value in the apartment. He spent two hours one day trying to break the Godrej cupboard. Silloo and Mamma stood, holding their breath as he kicked, hit, and yelled, trying to find the hidden drawer. He must have knocked every inch of the cupboard except the one spot that would have popped the top of it open. After that close call, Silloo would get up at 5:00 a.m. every day to meticulously tape the jewelry to her body. It was, in her mind, the safest and only place they had not yet touched.

November 13, 1971

The phone lines were finally reconnected, and still Kazim and his men continued to chip away at the women. They removed the physical phones from each apartment, leaving open phone lines without the mechanism to make a call, continuously inflicting mental torture on them. They allowed one phone, which was left for them to use, in Silloo's apartment. The first phone call she made was to Freny.

"Silloo, it's been terrible, just terrible, I tell you. Are you okay? And Mamma?"

"We are trying to stay calm. How are you managing?"

"They are taking everything—all my jewelry, gold coins, and money, more than three thousand shillings. Even Bhicajee's mother's jewelry, and they broke my Godrej, shattering the mirror all over the floor. I have tried to keep a list, but these men are so threatening. They shout if I write anything down." Freny, usually even-tempered and soft-spoken, was panicked.

"Oh Freny, I wish you were here in the building with Mamma and me."

"That would have been much easier. They're saying that all our things are *haram*, forbidden. What am I to do?" She clicked her tongue on the roof of her mouth.

"Freny, they've taken Dara, Jamshed, Uncle Burjor, and Darius to jail. They've been held there since Monday. They are doing the same things here, looting our homes."

"But why? Oh no. They put them in jail? What is the reason for all of this? They're saying crazy things about my Bhicajee, accusing him of being a spy and whatnot, all nonsense. When I tried to make a list of my own jewelry that Kazim was taking, he shouted at me to step away or he would take *me* to jail. *Areh*, Silloo, what is happening?"

"I don't know. I just don't know. Is your maid still with you at least?"

"Khinsi? Yes, yes, she is staying with me. She has witnessed all of this also. I've asked her not to leave me at all. I just don't understand this."

"Good, that's a good idea. As soon as we can leave, I will come to you, or you can come and stay with me."

"Yes, dear, that would be nice. Be safe, Silloo."

"You too, Freny. Now that our phones are working, you can call me anytime, anytime at all. Okay?"

November 24, 1971

Each day fell clumsily into the next as they adjusted to the morning swarm of parasites ransacking and pillaging their homes. With the phone now reconnected, Silloo was relieved to have access to the outside world again. She immediately called the embassies and Yemeni officials in an effort to get the men released.

Silloo began to settle into her uncomfortable reality. Her skin was red and sore with welts from the adhesive of the thick, heavy tape that she used to adhere her jewelry to her body and the weight of it pulling at her skin. Ahmed Kazim and his group of growling mongrels had gone beyond stealing valuables. Silloo had watched them haul out all of her photo albums and the 8mm movies of her children.

Dara had always loved new technology and was one of the first to buy a movie camera. It had quickly become his favorite hobby. He bought his first 8mm movie camera, a Nikon Super

Zoom-8, just before their honeymoon. He loved saying its name to anyone who cared to listen. *Nikon Super Zoom-8*. He would let the word *zoom* linger at his lips just a little longer than necessary, and was often seen with one eye to the camera, capturing memories of Silloo and the kids at the beach club, at home, or at birthday parties. Their friends joked that the children would have a perfect record of their lives when they grew up because Dara had not missed a moment. And now these men, with one sweep of their arms into a cardboard box, were tainting and stealing all her memories, her moments, every happy minute of her life, destroying every physical thing that represented her being, erasing her entire existence.

"What could you possibly want with those? Those are movies of my children, my memories, you animal!" she tore into Ahmed Kazim.

"This is evidence, my lady. We are taking it to conduct our investigation."

"I am not your lady, and you are a liar—what investigation? There is no such thing. You are a liar and a thief," she snarled.

Ahmed Kazim glared at her, fixing his gaze at her wrist. He stared at her Favre-Leuba wristwatch, a wedding gift from her husband, who was always notoriously late. Silloo, the colonel's daughter, raised on military time, hated Dara's tardiness with every fiber of her being; even when she tried to have a sense of humor about it, it bothered her. Dara had set the watch thirty minutes behind when he first gave it to her. When she asked him why her watch was slow, he told her it was not slow at all, but set to Dara standard time, so *he* would always be on time. They had laughed when recounting that story, and every subsequent time that Dara was late, he would tell her that it was her fault for adjusting her watch to the correct time.

"Give me that," Ahmed Kazim said, pointing to it.

"Give you what?"

"That on your wrist."

"What do you need my watch for?"

"I want it. Give it to me now. If you know what's good for your husband, you will give it to me!" he shouted.

"Your pathetic threats don't scare me. You aren't even half the man my husband is, you pig."

Ahmed Kazim grabbed her wrist, twisting it behind her back and slamming her into the wall. Her head spun from the impact, and he leaned into her with all his weight, pressing his groin into her behind. She could feel his hot, stale breath on her face and his bulge pushing himself harder into her.

"Give me the watch now or I will take it myself, and anything else that I want." He leaned in even closer and harder.

His spit landed on her face. Silloo mustered all the strength she could to push him off and away from her. Trembling and nauseous, she undid the leather strap. Again unable to understand why this was happening, her anger prevailed, suppressing her vulnerability. She was not weak and would not be broken. *I am the colonel's daughter,* she said to herself.

Ahmed Kazim snatched the watch from her hand. He inspected it, pulled it up to his face, and took a long inhale of the strap while staring at her. "If you would just cooperate with me, this would be much easier for you," he said softly.

"I would rather die."

December 1, 1971

The days turned into weeks, and before Silloo knew it, it was December. Ahmed Kazim refused to release any money for food or for Ahmed and Fatima's salaries, so she pulled out some cash from its hiding place and gave it to Ahmed for daily rations. They kept the quantities very small so as to go unnoticed—just enough to get by.

Silloo became even slimmer than before, her bones beginning to show through her smooth peach skin. Dark circles had formed under her eyes, yet she still stood tall and continued to carry herself with grace and dignity. The ransacking of their homes had mostly stopped. There was nothing left for the men to take, almost everything was gone now except for a few necessities. The men showed up more sporadically and only to heckle.

Freny was finally allowed to leave her apartment, and the first place she and Khinsi went was to see Silloo and Mamma. Freny was a delicate, small woman. At fifty, she looked much younger, with the most beautiful translucent skin. Soft-spoken and gentle. She struggled with her vision, but when she sat at her piano and closed her eyes, the music that emanated was pure magic. Freny would spend hours lost in Bach and Beethoven, drifting effortlessly in the melodies. Her skill on her piano was well known throughout the community. Her two teenage daughters were thankfully away at boarding school in India, and her husband, Bhicajee, was now stuck in India and unable to return to Aden. So Freny managed alone with Khinsi.

Even during an *intifada* and being under house arrest, she would never dream of arriving at Silloo's apartment empty-handed. She bought along the way a small packet of glucose biscuits, her favorite, and a bag of cheese puffs for the children. Freny loved to sit in Silloo's rattan swing chair and bounce ever so gently as they talked and sipped on hot Lipton tea infused with lemongrass and mint.

"That Kazim fellow took it all, Silloo. He took everything. Bhicajee's mother's jewelry that was meant for my girls. Gone."

Silloo listened intently, unsure of what to say. Feeling the same sense of loss.

"You know, my Bhicajee had an iron box filled with treasures inherited from his mother. A long time back he had shown me the box." Freny smiled at the memory. "Inside was some old, thick gold jewelry, you know, the heavy Indian kind. Beautiful pieces. When he showed me, he was so excited to be able to give those pieces to the girls on their eighteenth birthdays." She teared up. "I haven't got the heart to write to him and tell him they are gone, taken, like everything else."

"Were you able to make a list of everything they took? Maybe you will get it back." Silloo smiled weakly, knowing that was highly unlikely.

"I tried, but like I told you before, they threatened to take me to jail if I made a list or tried to protest. So, when they left, Khinsi and I would make a list from memory. I'm sure I missed some things, but many of these pieces I will never forget. Never. They just walked into rooms and took whatever they wanted. It was hard to keep track, there were just so many of them. I made him sign my lists, that Kazim."

"You did? How did you do that? Didn't he threaten you not to make lists?"

"Oh, I would not let it go. He would not let me make a list while he was taking things away. I made the lists from my memory, and then when Mr. Das Gupta came—you know, from the Indian embassy—I made him ask. He said he would do it at the office, but still, he didn't. Then the next time Mr. Gupta came, that's when I made him do it. He didn't dare give me his lip with Mr. Gupta there. He is afraid of any political official seeing what he is really up to."

"He is a snake, that man."

"Yes. You know, the day they broke Bhicajee's Godrej, I watched in tears. Why would anyone want to do this to another human being? He turned to me and said, 'Why are you crying? Why don't you smile and laugh?'" Tears welled in Freny's eyes, that moment still so raw for her. "That other one, Ali Makhtari, he is the one that was stopping people from visiting me and bringing me food. Can you imagine?"

"What did he do? Who did he stop?"

"My friend Mehra. She brought me some rations, you

know, bread, milk, rice, and when she arrived in the lift, he got up and pushed her back in!"

"He pushed Miss Pallonjee-Patel into the lift? Was she hurt?"

"No, thank God. Can you imagine? But she is a tough woman. She went straight to the police station and came back with an inspector and reported that thug."

"I don't know what is wrong with these people. They are soulless."

"He even made Mr. Gupta climb all six floors of my building."

"Why?"

"He wouldn't allow anyone in the lift to see me. He threatened the liftman. You know Mr. Gupta has a heart condition?"

"Oh Freny. Here, let me pour you some more tea."

They drank in silence as the call to prayer erupted throughout the city, then talked for a while more before Freny and Khinsi made their way back to their apartment.

After Kazim's many advances on Silloo, Ahmed would linger in the apartment until Kazim and his goons were done for the day. Once Ahmed left, Silloo could lock and bolt the door. Fatima also continued to stay with Silloo, taking care of the children, working hard to convince the men to allow the kids to go outside and play, even if only in the parking lot. After three weeks of confinement, the children were finally allowed outside. Silloo spent her days making phone calls to embassies, officials, anyone who would talk to her, begging for help.

Finally, in the first week of December, the First Secretary at the British embassy was allowed to visit her. It was the first time anyone, other than her employees and Freny, had been allowed up to the apartment since November 8th. When he first arrived, the guard downstairs refused him access, but John Goodwin was a tall, muscular man, and the small Yemeni man wielding a machine gun was no deterrent for him. He shoved the man back onto his wooden stool and made his way up to Silloo's apartment.

"Mrs. Barucha, I'm so sorry that it has taken me so long to get here. Dara did call us at the embassy last week, but these men haven't been an easy bunch to deal with, as I'm sure you know." He wore a pained look on his face.

Silloo knew John Goodwin a little from the beach club; their children were close in age. He listened and took notes as she recounted what had been happening in the month prior. John was horrified and desperate to help her and Dara. Silloo, now somewhat accustomed to this hell, was simply glad to see a familiar face and have someone she trusted to talk to.

"I'm committed to helping you, Silloo, but I do have some news that may concern you. We're being recommissioned back to London. I will be leaving in a few days." He paused, reading the despair on her face. They had just allowed him in—how long would it take a new person to gain access, and would someone she didn't know have any inclination to help her? "I will brief my replacement on this case. It will be the first thing that I do. I promise. I promise that we'll do everything we can to help. We're applying pressure on the Yemeni government. It will take time, but even from London I'll make sure that pressure stays on them."

Silloo stared at John, her body numb. Her fears were unrelenting. She had to stop hoping that someone else would help her. It was becoming clearer and clearer to her that she needed to do more and be the person she relied on most.

9

*"The smallest act of kindness is worth more
than the greatest intention."*
—Khalil Gibran

December 22, 1971

The lieutenant stood wearily in the doorway. He was close
to Silloo in age, likely in his early thirties, clean-shaven, with
sun-kissed Yemeni skin. He wore a traditional police uniform—
khaki shorts and a collared khaki shirt, with badges of accolades
on his right chest. He held his red beret in his hand as he entered
her home.

"Good morning, *Sayidati*. I am Lieutenant Fuad Hizam."
As he announced himself, he stood slightly taller.

"Good morning." Silloo stiffened. She wasn't sure why
this man was here. The police hadn't had much of a presence
in the past six weeks, apart from holding Dara and the rest of
the men. She crossed her arms in front of her chest, feeling
her insides tighten. He looked almost as uncomfortable as she
felt but spoke softly and respectfully. He didn't seem like the
others.

"Would you like some tea? I have no milk, but I can give
you *Sulamani chai*."

"Oh, I almost forgot, I brought something for you." He reached into his satchel, the strap draped across his chest, and pulled out a small jar. "My family is originally from the Wadi Do'an in the Hadramout. They have been beekeepers for many generations." He smiled widely.

"Isn't that where those beautiful trees grow? With the flowers?" Silloo asked.

He smiled and nodded his head. "Yes, the Sidr trees grow in abundance in the Hadramout."

Silloo had heard about the Sidr trees. They had bright yellow flowers with a very strong and captivating aroma. Locals believed that Sidr honey had magical properties because of its aromatic nectar. Many natives throughout Yemen used it exclusively for its medicinal properties. She had had it before, but it was hard to come by and quite expensive.

"Perhaps my family's honey will go well with your tea?" He smiled, interrupting her thoughts.

"Thank you," she said, accepting his gift.

Hizam shuffled awkwardly as sand from his heavy boots scraped the terrazzo tile. He took a deep breath as she headed into the kitchen to fetch a tray with two cups and a large pot of tea. She placed the honey jar ceremoniously on the tray with a delicate spoon by its side.

"*Sayidati*, I just came from talking to your husband."

She gripped her biceps with her fingers, bracing herself for what might come next. "Is he okay? Did they do something to him?"

"Oh yes. I mean, no, *Sayidati*. He is okay, I mean. I'm so sorry, I didn't mean to scare you. *Sayidati*, this is somewhat of a long story, but please bear with me. Eh, shall we sit?" He gestured to the dining table.

"So, you see, my *Baba*, he knew your father-in-law. *Baba* came to Aden as a boy. His father had hoped to be a beekeeper here, but it was too dry in the city to grow healthy Sidr trees. He tried for many years, but the Sidr trees wanted nothing to do with the city." He smiled warmly. He had kind eyes. "So he went into the milk business. It was not nearly as profitable as honey, but *Baba* grew his business and, in fact, he delivered milk to your husband's family for many, many years. *Baba*, he was a very hard worker, and he wanted more for his children than he had, you know?" He gestured with his hand, and Silloo nodded in agreement. The discomfort in his voice was beginning to ease. "Your husband's father was a very kind man, a good man. Every morning, he would wait for *Baba* to deliver milk to his house, and then he would spend time talking to him, sometimes even walking with him while he made his deliveries." She could hear the awe in his voice. "Some days he even tried helping him, but *Baba* wouldn't allow that." His forehead furrowed, and he shook his head slowly as he brushed away the unthinkable image.

"My *Baba* was a very simple man, *Rahimah Allah*. He couldn't read or write, but he was very clever and was intrigued by the British and their lifestyle. He had questions, and your husband's father would always have answers for him—or discussions, shall we say," he said.

Chapter 9

Silloo was not sure where this conversation was going or why this seemingly sweet young man was sitting at her dining table.

"They became friends, and *Baba* told your father-in-law of his dreams for me when I was first born. You see, I was, am, his only son and the youngest of ten—I have nine sisters. *Baba's* deepest regret was that he never had the opportunity for an education. He questioned everything and loved to discuss ideas. He desperately wanted more for me. *Baba* told me that your father-in-law once told him that any man's future was fifty percent hard work and fifty percent luck." His eyes fell to floor as he smiled at his father's memory. "A few years later, after their friendship had evolved, he told my father that someone who worked so hard deserved some luck and offered to pay for my education."

Silloo's eyes widened. She wasn't surprised by her father-in-law's gesture but was shocked that she hadn't heard this story before. She shifted in her seat, straightening her back. They both paused to sip from their teacups.

"Of course, my *Baba* protested, but your father-in-law insisted, saying if the roles were reversed, he was sure my *Baba* would do the same. *Baba* could not argue with that. He asked *Baba* only to promise to remain his friend and continue their walks and discussions as long as they both could. Unlike any other Yemenis in the village that I come from, I received the same education as many of the expatriates here in Aden." The lieutenant swirled the contents of his teacup as he searched for his next words.

Hence his high command of the English language, Silloo thought.

"*Sayidati*, when your father-in-law died a few years later, I was still very young. But your father-in-law had made the arrangements for my education when I was just a baby, and I was educated through his generosity and kindness, and my father's hard work and…good luck." He smiled again.

"My education allowed me to join the police academy, and I have been working my way up through the ranks. I now work at Central Intelligence. Your husband's family gave me opportunities that I would never have had. Your father-in-law chose a milkman to befriend and to make his one dream come true. It was a small gesture from your father-in-law, but my family from that moment forward was offered a different path. *Baba* talked of this man's honor until the day he died." The lieutenant paused, looking down at his beret. "He would cry when he spoke of him and the conversations they had. He would say in disbelief that he was merely an illiterate milkman, but while they walked together, side by side, he was a respected, intelligent man with interesting thoughts and ideas." The lieutenant took another moment to gather himself. "You see, your father-in-law not only gave me the gift of education, but he gave my father the gift of respect and honor."

After another pause, he continued, "I have just come to learn of what has happened to you and your family, and I'm very sorry that this situation occurred. This is not what we Yemenis are. I want you to know that I will help you and your husband. I know that your family is honest—and innocent—and I will prove it. You see, I was just made the chief investigator on this case."

Silloo stared in disbelief, digging her nails into her arm to make sure she wasn't dreaming.

"I am working with the police station on arranging a visit for you."

She gasped and fought the tears that sprang to her eyes. She wanted to jump from her chair and hug this man.

"But, please, you must be patient. These men who are doing this, they are not part of our justice system. They represent the president's office, and we must tread carefully. Although they come in the president's name, he is likely unaware of what they're doing. There is a long history that is empowering them, and, in their hearts, they believe they are honorable and doing what is best for their country."

"I don't understand how they think that it is all right to treat people this way."

"*Sayidati*, when the British came to Aden in the 1800s, there was nothing here. The port had been neglected, and our country had been torn apart by one irresponsible ruler after another."

"Yes, and it was families like mine that came here from India and spurned the revival of Aden. We turned the economy around. Well, along with the British. Our company with all the products that we sold helped build the port and the trade that has gone through it. Think of all the big companies that were here and thriving. Not just Bhicajee Cowasjee, but Palanjee Dinshaw, Luke Thomas, Peninsular, emm, what was the other one? Oriental, Michael Cotts, and Cory Brothers. All these businesses made this city what it was, and these men claiming to be socialists have destroyed it. Aden has been a city of educated Adenis who have enjoyed the lifestyle here. I do not understand this."

"*Sayidati*, the people of the protectorate surrounding Aden had little involvement in any of those economic developments."

"Yes, Lieutenant, but the rulers felt trade was beneath them, and they were happy to pass on the responsibility to expatriates like us. It was a win-win situation."

"But it resulted in a lack of development and education for the protectorate, which led to resentment among the more rural Yemenis. The men who are empowered by the president's office are those men. They did not enjoy the luxuries and modernism that we have in Aden."

She had not thought about that, how different things were just a short distance away in the protectorate.

"Under the British rule, there have been many expatriates settling in Aden, and the Yemenis from the protectorate do not like that. They see their country being taken over by Indians, Somalis, and whoever else. They resent how sophisticated and international Aden is becoming, and they really do not like all these other communities moving into the city and making it their own."

"What does this have to do with me? Why am I being targeted by these men? Being harassed in this way? And why can't the police do more to help me?"

"*Sayidati*, the existing police force is made up of many Adenis who have risen within the British-led boom of the city. They have been and are content with the way things were under British rule, and, quite honestly, they want life to remain unchanged. This revolution was fueled mostly by the men from North Yemen and the protectorate, men who have watched their countrymen prosper while they have remained behind because of the stubbornness and ignorance of their sheikhs and rulers. These decades-old sentiments run deep. These are the men who are doing this. I promise you that I will help you, just as your family helped me. I will do everything in my power to straighten this out and maintain the honor of your husband's family. In the meantime, please keep me informed of what is happening. My job is to investigate this case and prove whether or not your husband and his brother have done something illegal."

"And what about the men who keep coming here, holding me hostage and taking our things? Can you stop them from tormenting us?" She looked at him earnestly.

"Like I told you, they are not official in any capacity, you understand, but they have been recruited by the president's office to officiate under the order of the president. The police do not have any jurisdiction over them, which is why the police station had no choice but to take your husband into custody. The order of the president overrules all of us. So, I don't have any power to stop them, but I am hoping that by proving your husband's innocence, we can move forward and end this situation."

Tears slowly rolled down Silloo's cheeks. She thanked him and, for the first time in six weeks, felt a little hopeful.

"Are you able to document everything that has been happening here? I think it would be a good idea to have that."

"Well, yes, I have been writing a journal every night that details what happened that day."

"Let me see if I can get you a typewriter so you can type it out. It may be useful for our case."

She nodded in agreement.

"Your family is like my family, *Sayidati*. Your honor is my honor. It is my family's turn to help you." Fuad Hizam smiled warmly. He adjusted his beret back onto his head, saluted Silloo, and walked out of the apartment.

Silloo rushed to the other end of the apartment in search of Mamma.

"Mamma, Mamma, *tamune ka che*? Where are you?"

"*Areh, Dikri*, I am in the bathroom, just one minute." Mamma emerged, adjusting her *kasti*, her chin pressed down against her neck to hold up the front *pallu* of her sari. "What is all this commotion you are making? So much shouting through the house!"

"Mamma, we have been sent an angel! Do you remember a boy who Pappa helped, paid for his education? Would have been a long time ago." Silloo was so excited that her words tumbled over each other. Mamma sat down, confused, a little less annoyed, and thought for a while. Silloo impatiently rubbed her hands together.

"A boy who Pappa helped?" Mamma said to herself. "*Areh*, hah, hah. Yes, yes. *Apreh doodwalla's* son. Pappa had some strong connection with that *doodwalla*. He would disappear for hours on many mornings, just walking and talking to the fellow. I would scold him when he came back, so agitated by what he was doing." She paused, wagging her finger, reflecting on that time. "Pappa always said that that man was meant for bigger things than just delivering milk. It bothered him that such a smart man hadn't had a chance at an education, and he said that if he could, he wouldn't let that happen to his son. After Pappa died, I sent money every month, as he wished for me to do, until the mother came to me to tell me the son had finished up at the police academy. I was not so keen on the arrangement, but I promised Pappa." She smiled at the memory of her husband. "*Dikri*, why are you asking me about the *doodwalla?*"

Silloo could not contain her excitement. The universe had indeed brought her an angel.

"Mamma, the *doodwalla's* son came to see me today. He has been assigned to our case. He is arranging a meeting with the boys!" She was crying now. "He knows the boys are innocent and that all of what is happening to us is wrong. He wants to help us!"

"*Areh*, the *doodwalla's* son was here?" Silloo nodded. "*Areh Bapre.*" Mamma held her hand over her mouth. "*Areh Khodajee.*" She wiped the tears from her face and closed her eyes. Picturing her husband, she thanked him in her mind's eye.

Silloo felt lighter that day, as though a huge weight had been lifted. She would soon see Dara—which made her very happy.

December 31, 1971

Ahmed Kazim returned to her apartment later that afternoon. There was little left for the men to take—furniture, clothes, a few essentials. Everything else was gone. The apartment was bare, emptied of the amenities of their previous life. Left on the walls were only the outlines of pictures that used to be there. Kazim had arrived with two of his lackeys. They stood awkwardly, trying to look intimidating. Silloo was no longer fazed by them and had begun to let her guard down. Kazim entered the apartment as if it were his own home, dropping himself onto the sofa and stretching his arm across the back cushion. His machine gun dangled from his neck like a medal.

"Why don't you come and sit here with me. I'm such a nice man, why don't you let me show you how nice I am. I can make you happy."

"You're disgusting—get off my sofa. You just wait! My husband will destroy you when he gets his hands on you."

Kazim's face contorted, flushed with humiliation and anger. He stood and marched toward her.

"Get those children here now!" he shouted at one of his goons.

"You leave my children alone. I swear, if you touch them—"

"Shut. Your. Mouth. Woman! Shut up!"

The children, crying, were ushered into the room, followed

by a protesting Fatima and Mamma. Ahmed Kazim's men shoved the children into a lineup against the wall. They screamed and wailed. Silloo tried to run to them, but one of the men grabbed her and pulled her back. Everything moved in slow motion. Silloo watched in horror as her worst nightmare began to unfold. Ahmed Kazim's yelling over all the crying was deafening. He shouted at them to be quiet, then walked up to Rustom, only seven. Her son's eyes were shut tight as he cried uncontrollably. Kazim pushed the barrel of the gun into Rustom's temple.

"Open your eyes, boy," Kazim bellowed.

Silloo held her breath, frozen, desperate not to scream or cry or move, her body stuck, her pulse racing.

Rustom slowly opened his eyes, standing perfectly still. Tears streamed down his face. He stared into the bleakness of the room, into his mother's eyes, his cheeks soaked, his bottom lip trembling.

"I can pull this trigger now, ah, what do you think? I could just take care of you right now. Do you understand me?" Kazim made the sound of a gun going off in the boy's ear. "Your mother needs to start showing me some respect. I'm the only reason you all are alive. Maybe she will understand this now." He looked at Silloo and pushed the barrel of the gun even harder into the side of her son's head. Silloo struggled with the man holding her. Ana cried louder. Mamma buried her head into Fatima's shoulder.

"Make her shut up!" Kazim bellowed.

"Ana *jan*, can you play a game with Mummy?" Silloo's voice trembled as she tried to calm her daughter. "Let's close our eyes and pretend we are playing hide-and-seek on the beach. Come on, close your eyes and be very quiet so you stay hidden." Ana closed her eyes, crying softly. Paralyzed, Silloo could barely breathe. Was this the end?

Suddenly, Ahmed's voice broke the band of tension in the room. In the chaos, no one had heard him enter. He stood stoic in the doorway. "So you will kill a child? Is that how you make yourself feel powerful?" he said, his shoulders now slightly hunched, his back arched. He looked like a lion ready to pounce.

"What do you know? All you do is serve your pathetic master, like a dog. I'm a real man. I'm taking control of my life and taking my country back from all these bastards," Kazim spat.

"Really? You are a man, are you? You're holding a gun to a child's head. Are you a Muslim? Do you think Allah will bring a man who kills innocent children to heaven? *Ittaqillah*, you should fear Allah and consider your actions long and hard. Look at yourself," Ahmed said with disgust. "I proudly serve a family who has taken care of me and my family—that is honor. What do you have? You're a thief, a liar, and now you will be a murderer, of a child no less. Allah sees everything. Remember that."

Kazim glared at Ahmed and pulled the gun away from Rustom's head. "I tell you this: I will decide their fate. I am the master here now. God doesn't care for this dirt." He spat at Silloo's feet and stormed out of the apartment, followed by his goons.

Silloo rushed to her children and collapsed to the ground.

Fear and angst pulsated through her veins. She was fixed to her spot. Looking up at Ahmed, she managed to utter, "Thank you."

She knew she needed a new plan, a plan to protect her children. This had made things crystal clear for her.

❧ ❧ ❧

Later that evening, Silloo stood on her balcony, looking out at the blue harbor. A cool breeze caressed her face and ran its wide fingers through her long, billowing hair. She wanted so desperately to feel hopeful, to be excited about what lay ahead, to have something to look forward to. Instead, she was overcome by desperation and the overwhelming fear of what might happen to them.

It was New Year's Eve. *How odd*, she thought. In years past, she would have been primping and preening at this time, preparing for a night out with friends, dancing into the early hours of the morning. This year was so very different. She was responsible for everyone's lives. Her children, Mamma, Dara and the rest of the men. Their fate lay in her hands. She was worried and quite unsure if any of them would even have another New Year's Eve ever again. She desperately searched her heart for gratitude but settled on being grateful to leave this year behind, terrified of what the new year might hold for her, unsure of how much worse this situation could get.

"*Sayidati*," Fatima called from the window. "Telephone. It's Lieutenant Fuad Hizam."

Silloo moved inside and picked up the receiver. "Lieutenant, hello."

"I have good news, *Sayidati*. I've received permission for you and your mother-in-law to visit your husband and brother-in-law tomorrow."

"Really?"

"Yes, please come to the station at eleven tomorrow morning. I'll meet you there and take you up to where they're being detained."

"Thank you, Lieutenant."

"It's my pleasure, madam. Em, are you okay? Your voice sounds...well, different."

"I have men walking in and out of my apartment all day, every day, taking whatever they want. Taking my belongings." Her voice broke. "Today, Ahmed Kazim held a gun to my son's head and threatened to kill my children." The lieutenant gasped audibly. "He makes lewd comments all the time. I fear for my life and for my children's lives. I'm very grateful for your story and your desire to help me and my family, but no one is helping fast enough. I'm not sure what it is exactly that you're expecting to hear in my voice. This is the best that I can do."

"*Sayidati*, I'm truly sorry that you had to endure that. I-I'm not sure what else to say. Like I told you before, I have no control over these men. They come in the president's name."

"I'm not sure that there is anything you can say, Lieutenant. I will see you tomorrow. Thank you for arranging a meeting for us."

That night, Silloo brought all three children into her bed. She lay alongside Rustom, stroking his hair. Aram and Ana were both asleep. Rustom stared at the ceiling.

"Mummy, why do those men keep coming here? Why did that man want to shoot me?"

Silloo wrapped her arms around her young son, shuddering at the image of the gun to his head. "They are fighting for their country, this country, and they are angry," she said. "Very angry."

"But we didn't do anything to them. Mummy, I'm scared. I want Daddy to come home now."

"I know, my love, so do I. We must be patient and take care of each other. We know that we are good people, and we have to believe that there are good people that will help us out of this. Now, try to sleep, my sweet boy. I am right here by your side."

Rustom closed his eyes and nuzzled into his mother. She held him tight, tears silently streaking her cheeks and wetting the pillow beneath her. They had been very lucky today, lucky that they were still breathing, still alive, but luck was not going to be enough. She needed to keep her children safe, and in her heart, she knew that there was only one way to do that. Tomorrow, she would call Mr. Mardden and ask him to come over to discuss her plan.

January 1, 1972

The fluttering in her stomach persisted, and her body tingled. Silloo's anticipation was palpable. She had not slept the night before, and her eyes stung with exhaustion. The police station was quiet when she and Mamma arrived. Lieutenant Hizam was waiting for them, giving them both a warm welcome before taking them straight to the office where the men were being held. As the door to the office opened, she was smacked by a wave of warm, stale air. She immediately started to perspire as she fell into Dara's embrace. Before he could say anything, she hushed him.

"Please, just hold me quietly for a minute."

Mamma grabbed Jamshed and pulled him into her bony shoulder, her tiny body swallowed up by his.

"Enjoy your visit. You will have about thirty minutes," Lieutenant Hizam said, smiling, before stepping out of the room.

"Dara, I wasn't sure if I would ever see you again." The tears flowed down Silloo's face as her husband held her tight.

"I know, my love. I know."

They talked quickly, filling each other in on what had been happening in their separate worlds. Silloo and Mamma told Dara and Jamshed of the looting, thievery, and threats. Silloo was careful to leave out Kazim's attack the previous day and his advances. She didn't want to enrage her husband.

Jamshed told them how Kazim's men had come to the

police station several times asking for money in exchange for their release. They had started at five hundred thousand pounds sterling, but Dara and Jamshed insisted that they didn't have that kind of money, and subsequently each week the amount was reduced by fifty thousand. Kazim's men had already seized all their assets; there was nothing left to give them. It infuriated Dara and Jamshed that these thugs had ransacked their homes, taking their personal belongings. Silloo wondered how they would react if they knew the whole truth.

"Dara, I have been in touch with the British and Indian embassies. John Goodwin came to see me, but he is going back to England and there will be a new person assigned to our case. I have spoken to Mr. Das Gupta at the Indian embassy multiple times as well. He has been to see Freny but has not been able to see us yet. I am also trying to get in touch with the Ministry of Interior here to see if we can get someone to help. The problem is that Kazim and his men are representatives of the president's office, and unless we can put pressure on the president's office itself, I am not sure we can get them to back down."

"Hmm, well, my love, it is really good that you have managed to get in touch with the embassies. We must keep that pressure up and have them contact the president's office. You will also need to call Zarir in Dubai. He can arrange for money to be sent to the Indian embassy. Mr. Das Gupta has agreed to receive it and get it to you safely for anything that you need. Have you talked to my sister at all?"

"No, I have not tried. I will call Maki today." Silloo smiled feebly, happy to be near her husband, yet feeling the distance.

Mamma cupped Jamshed's face with her hands and started to cry.

"Mamma, everything will be okay. Look, we are fine," Jamshed said as both men embraced their mother. Silloo watched. She had no way of knowing if that was true. In that moment, their reality hit her like a freight train.

The lieutenant opened the door gently and informed them that their time together had come to an end and that he had a typewriter that would be delivered to her apartment later that day. Their meeting was over before it had a chance to begin. The women walked home in silence. Just to be outside, walking, gave them some relief. The reunion had quelled some of Silloo's anxiety, but it had also magnified the emptiness she felt inside.

January 11, 1972

Sitting in the armchair, her elbows on the armrests, a cup of tea balanced between her fingertips, Silloo watched the steam rise and dance gracefully as it met the cool air of the room. She envied its freedom as it ducked and rolled and unfolded. Taking a deep breath, she exhaled, disturbing the performance in front of her. As the vapors dissolved into thin air, she reveled in her control, in awe of the steam's ability to vanish before her eyes.

Chapter 9

A loud knock on the door made her jump from her chair, spilling the tea all over her lap. The heat scorched her skin through the soft cotton fabric of her skirt. She opened the door to Ahmed Kazim, who barged in with a black book held aloft. She shuddered, realizing that she was alone in the apartment. Fatima had just taken the kids down to play outside, Mamma was in her own apartment, and Ahmed was checking in on his family. In retrospect, she shouldn't have let Fatima go until Ahmed was back. She stood by the front door and decided to leave it open and stay as close to it as she could. Kazim had entered the apartment and was now staring at her, waiting for a response. She had no idea what he had said or asked, so she looked back at him blankly.

"What did you say?"

"I said, what does your husband know of the situation here?" He leaned, forward winking at her. His voice softened, and the sound made her skin crawl. "Because no one has to know anything, you know? I mean, I won't tell anyone." He leered at Silloo as he moved in closer to her. The strong stench of cigarettes and sweat preceded him. Chills ran down her spine as her body stiffened. His voice dropped and slowed even more. "Would it make you happy if I resigned? You know, he's never going to be released. I can take good care of you. Make you happy." He wrapped a lock of her hair around his finger and pushed it behind her ear.

"You are disgusting. I don't care about you, and I would rather die than be anywhere near you."

Kazim's face reddened with fury. He moved in swiftly, grabbed both her arms, and pressed his face into hers. She managed to turn away just as his wet, open mouth landed on her cheek. He pushed his mouth hard onto her face, his saliva soaking her cheek. She struggled to get away from him, but he was heavy and strong. She gave up, her body going limp. Confused, he backed away. Adrenaline pulsed through her, and she took the opportunity to run into the hallway.

"Get out!" she screamed.

Kazim glared at her. "You will regret this," he said, chasing her into the hallway. "Come back here now!"

She managed to duck and run past him and back into the apartment, slamming and locking the door. The door shuddered with the rage of his fists.

"You will be sorry!" he bellowed.

She sank to the floor in a flood of tears, wishing she were steam, able to vanish into thin air.

10

*"In the depths of your hope and desires lies your silent knowledge
of the beyond; and like seeds dreaming beneath the snow your
heart dreams of spring. Trust the dreams, for in them
is hidden the gate to eternity."*
—Khalil Gibran

January 11, 1972

Later that evening, the two younger children played on
the living room floor with pots and pans and wooden spoons.
They were surprisingly calm—innocent and blissfully unaware
of the turmoil and strife that surrounded them. Silloo watched
as they played, in awe of their resilience and ability to accept
their situation and move forward. She wondered how long that
would last. Her children were her universe. Even in these dark
hours, the darkest of her life, their presence brought light.

The latest encounter with Kazim had shaken her to her core.
Once more, she was forced to rethink things. She needed a plan
not only to keep her children safe but to keep herself safe. It had
been too easy to casually accept the hand that had been dealt to
them. She was tired, but she knew better now than to blindly
trust that all would be okay. She no longer trusted that God would
protect them. Her conversation with Rustom continued to play in

her mind. Her children's safety was in her hands—and hers alone. She clenched her jaw.

The removal of every belonging from her home that had ever meant anything to her, the absence of her husband, and the uncertainty of her children's safety now only emboldened her. She wouldn't be broken. This, her universe, this beauty that sat before her, would be her fuel, her strength, her power. She had helped create and then carried these three children. Their light would be the force that empowered her. It had come from her, and she would bask in its beauty and strength, and it would be what pushed her forward. She was grateful for Lieutenant Hizam, but she understood that he could not protect her or her children.

The serenity of sleep was a forgotten notion for Silloo. She would drift into a haze only to be startled at every sound, convinced that someone was in her home or watching her, unsure if it was a figment of her imagination or a living, breathing threat. Sleeping with the lights on helped only a little. Her mind played games with her, triggering her angst and reveling in her despair. So, at midnight, when she heard what sounded like a stampede outside her apartment, loud voices and heavy footsteps, she bolted out of bed, ran to the door, and looked through the peephole. There in the stairwell stood a mob of people, policemen and plain-clothed men, but then there among them was Uncle Burjor! Silloo threw open the door to see Dara, Jamshed, Uncle Burjor, and Darius surrounded by a group of police officers walking up the stairs.

"Dara!"

Her husband stopped in his tracks and took her in with his warm, loving eyes.

"We're being moved to Jamshed's apartment. I'll be right upstairs."

He looked triumphant, and in that frozen exchange, it was almost as if nothing had happened. The police officers ushered the men upstairs, and Silloo watched, incomparably grateful for this small gift. For the first time in weeks, she slept.

January 12, 1972

The relief of that night was short-lived. She thought that with Dara upstairs she would be able to see him, speak to him, maybe even hug him. How she missed and longed for her husband! But the police posted a guard outside Jamshed's apartment; no visitors were permitted. Only Ahmed was allowed to go in for a few minutes to drop off food and collect laundry. Silloo made several calls requesting a visit, but her requests fell on deaf ears.

Later that morning, Silloo opened the door to the young lieutenant, standing tall, stately, and apologetic.

"I wasn't sure if you were told the news, but your husband and the other men have been moved here to your building. The space was needed at the police station, and since there are no proven charges against them, I was granted permission to move them to your brother-in-law's apartment. They *are* under house arrest. I know it's not what you were hoping for, but it's a small step."

"Thank you, Lieutenant. I did hear them last night as they went upstairs, and I got to see Dara briefly. Thank you so much."

"Please, don't thank me yet. This will take time and will likely get worse before it gets better, if I'm being honest. I will not be able to call you too much. I need to lay low and focus on your case. I can't have anyone questioning my integrity. It will compromise everything. I hope you understand."

"Yes, of course. Thank you."

"Did you get the typewriter?"

"Yes, thank you, I did. I have started typing up my journals. There are a couple of keys missing but otherwise it is fine."

"I am glad to hear it. I should go now, please take care." The man bowed his head, donned his beret, and left.

"*Sayidati*," Fatima whispered as she slipped out of the kitchen. "Come, come."

Silloo followed Fatima into one of the back bedrooms. The window was open, and a bucket tied to a rope sat on the floor in front of the window.

"Fatima, what is this?" Silloo asked.

Fatima pointed to the ceiling, then grabbed a note from inside the bucket. "*Sayidati*," she said, handing her the note. "For you, from up. *Sayid*." She pointed to the ceiling again.

Silloo unfolded it, revealing her husband's distinctive, slanted longhand.

Chapter 10

My Dearest Silloo,

*I can't believe that we are separated by just one floor.
When I saw you last night in the doorway, I wanted to hold
you and tell you everything would be okay. To think how
many times we've been in that hallway, walking in and
out of our home, coming and going freely—to this. Seeing
what they did to Jamshed's apartment makes me so angry. I
can't imagine what you have gone through. I'm so sorry that
you've had to handle this all on your own.*

*The phone lines here in Jamshed's apartment have been
cut, but I was thinking that you could send up one of our
intercoms in the bucket. Do you still have them? You will
have to unscrew it from the wall. It will allow us to talk.
Wait until it's dark. When you tug on the rope, I'll know
you're ready. I have it tied to a chair.*

Well, love, until I hear your voice.

Love, Dara

She read the letter again and again, running her fingers
over the indentations of his writing. Waiting impatiently for
darkness to blanket the city so she could hear his voice, she
refolded the note along its creases and placed it in her pocket,
feeling him just a little bit closer.

As soon as the last slivers of amber and burnt orange
disappeared from the sky, Silloo took the screwdriver and
unscrewed the intercom from the bedroom wall. She found
an extension cord, plugged one end into the intercom, placed

everything in the bucket, then tugged on the string and waited. Nothing. She tugged again and watched the bucket slowly lift up and away to the floor above. She hurried to her bedroom and waited a few minutes before lifting the receiver and hitting three on the keypad.

"Silloo." His voice blanketed her whole body.

"Dara." She inhaled the peace and calm that hearing his voice gave her. She smiled, holding the receiver to her ear and playing with the cord.

"Love, how are you?" He paused briefly between each word, speaking slowly and deliberately. Her eyes filled with tears. She wanted to tell him everything—how broken she felt, how scared she was, how she found it hard to breathe, how she never slept, how alone she was.

"I'm okay. The kids are okay too, and Mamma is managing." She told him about the visit from Lieutenant Hizam, and he reiterated Kazim's constant demand for money.

"Silloo, I'm not sure how long they'll keep us here. They want to take us to the People's Court for a hearing."

"A hearing?"

"Yes, they're charging us with smuggling. They have no evidence—it's all rubbish." Dara spat his words out like discarded pumpkin-seed shells.

"Smuggling? We need to get you a lawyer. I can call the embassies tomorrow." She grabbed paper and a pencil to start a list.

"You should definitely call the British and Indian embassies. They need to know what is happening so they can push the appropriate people in the government. We can't let any of this go quietly. We need people to know what is happening. You know what I mean?" Dara said. "We were allowed phone calls from the police station but have no access from here. Oh, and we aren't allowed a lawyer. They have said that one of us can speak for the group. Probably best if it's Jamshed."

"How can they not allow you to have a lawyer? That's crazy!"

"I know, I know, but what can we do? We're stuck."

"Oh Dara..." She paused. "I thought I might be able to see you now that you're upstairs, but they won't let us up. Lieutenant Hizam said he would try to get us permission, and I'll just keep calling everywhere until someone says yes."

"They'll probably make you ask a hundred times before granting permission, those bastards. What has Hizam said, has he stopped Kazim and his guys from coming around every day?"

"No, he has no authority over them. They are backed by the president's office."

"This is why it is so critical to keep the embassies involved and interested in this case."

They talked some more about the children. It had now been two months since Dara had held them. He wanted to know everything: what new words Ana was saying, what Rustom and Aram were getting themselves into. She told him about their daily shenanigans, as simple as they were. An hour passed, and then two, and Silloo drifted off into a hazy sleep. Realizing this, Dara lay listening to her rest. At four in the morning, when she woke, they decided they should put the intercoms away for the night. Dara sent the intercom back down in the bucket. Silloo changed out the wire, hid the long one under her mattress, and screwed the intercom back into the wall. *Until tomorrow night,* she thought.

✧ ✧ ✧

Every day for a week, Silloo sent Fatima and Ahmed to the shop, where Kazim and his men had set up base, to request permission for her to see Dara and the men. Every request was denied. Finally, Fatima and Ahmed were told that they were banished from the shop, and if they came back, they would be beaten. In desperation, Silloo sent a note to the commissioner of police, who said that he would arrange a meeting. But nothing came from that either. So, Silloo, dressed in one of her finest saris, decided to head to the police station herself. When the guard outside her building tried to stop her, she told him that she was going to the police station and he was welcome to come with her. He left her alone.

"*Sayidati*, what is it that you need? Why are you here?" Inspector Suleiman asked when he saw her stride in. He was not a tall man, but still managed to somehow look down on her, and even though he had known her and her family for many years, she was weary of him. Was her sense of him legitimate or imagined? She no longer felt she could trust anyone.

"What is it that I need?" She was tired of being polite. "I need to see my husband, who is being held for no good reason.

Chapter 10

Why is it that you people won't help us? We have been law-abiding residents in this country for over a hundred years. You of all people know that. Where is your empathy and common decency? I want to see my husband, and the fact that I must ask permission is ridiculous!"

"*Sayidati*, the police have no jurisdiction over the *lugna*. Those men have permission from the president's office. It's out of my control. They believe that they have a case against your husband."

"They have nothing. Nothing!"

"You know, *Sayidati*, perhaps it is time for you women and children to leave Aden. Get away from here."

His attempt at empathy failed miserably. "Time to leave, you say." Silloo paused, looking at him thoughtfully. "Let me explain something to you, Inspector. I will not leave without my husband."

"There is nothing that you can do by staying here. This is no place for a woman."

"Oh, but you see, there is something I can do, as long as I'm here—and I'm very much here. I'm a voice for my husband. I'm not going anywhere. This woman is going to stay close to her husband. Do you understand? I want a visit arranged, and I will sit here until it is granted."

The inspector took a deep, exasperated breath, walked into his office, and closed the door. Silloo found a seat and folded her trembling hands in her lap, trying to steady them. She wasn't exactly sure what she was waiting for, but she couldn't turn back. She sat in the waiting room, listening to the clicks of a typewriter in the next room. An hour passed slowly before the inspector finally emerged from his office.

"Mr. Saleh, one of the men from the president's office, is on his way here. The *lugna* is refusing permission for you to see your husband as they are in the middle of an investigation."

"Inspector, with all due respect, who are those men? You're an inspector, an official. Who is it that has the authority to grant me permission? Is it them, or is it you?" Silloo wasn't sure where her courage was coming from, but she pressed on. She had nothing to lose.

The inspector was taken by surprise and looked embarrassed. "Well, we'll see what happens when Mr. Saleh gets here," he said.

Saleh was with the *lugna*, the *intifada*, one of the president's men, an enforcer of this new reality—another Kazim. He walked into the police station wearing dusty sandals, a white collared shirt stained with sweat, and gray trousers. He was balding but wore a thick mustache, which looked odd on his fleshy face. He had been a driver for the shop since the custodianship, brought in to spy on her husband and his brothers. She shook her head when she saw him.

"*Sayidati*," he said cheerfully as if he hadn't expected to see her there. She nodded at him.

"Saleh, *Sayidati* is waiting for permission to see her husband," the inspector interjected.

"Ah, *Sayidati*, yes, I see, but it's not possible for me to say yes or no, you understand." He laughed.

Chapter 10

"So why don't you tell me who does have that power and authority. Who is *actually* in charge?" Her words hit them both like daggers.

"I have plenty of authority, *Sayidati*!" Saleh retorted.

"Really? Where? Where is all this authority of yours? It doesn't seem like you have any. I want to know who the person with real authority is. That's who I need to talk to." She folded her arms in front of her and leaned back, hoping that neither man could see how much she was shaking.

Saleh shuffled into the inspector's office, and Silloo overheard him on the phone yelling at someone in Arabic. He slammed the phone down, then repeated the process. More yelling on the phone followed by more slamming of the receiver. She straightened herself in her seat, wondering if they would call her on her bluff. These were simple men who wanted to feel important. If she knew anything, it was that knowledge was her weapon.

Saleh finally emerged from the office, looking triumphant. "*Sayidati*, you can see your husband tomorrow. I want you to know that *I* am the one who authorized this, eh? You see." He puffed out his chest and strutted around the room. He reminded her of an ostrich—a small, round ostrich, if that were possible.

"Are you absolutely sure about that? Because I have heard this now a few times. What guarantee do I have that your authority means anything?" Silloo was getting very adept at this game, and he was playing right into her hands.

"My authority means everything, *Sayidati*. I will come to your home at 1:00 p.m. and take you to your husband myself. Eh! There, you see!" He threw his arm into the air and swept it across the room to show what he had authority over.

Success! Silloo got up to leave.

"Oh, and *Sayidati*," he called out.

She turned to look at Saleh.

"This will be the last time that you see him before he is moved," he said, smirking.

It felt as though someone had slowly poured a carafe of ice water down her back. "Moved? Where is he being moved to?"

"They will be moved to Mansoura."

"Mansoura? What have they done that they need to go to jail?" She could feel the bile rising in her throat but held her composure. Ever since the men had been detained, she had managed each situation as it presented itself. The house arrest, Kazim, the looting. She realized at this moment that she had never really considered where this all could go, how bad it could continue to get, or how truly dangerous a predicament they were in. She trembled.

"There will be a hearing at the People's Court. We will see who is innocent then, eh? See you tomorrow."

And yet again, as quickly as she had felt triumph, the tables were flipped.

Chapter 10

January 26, 1972

Silloo stood under the stone archway of the *Atash Padsha*, the wide-open wrought-iron gates welcoming her into the *agiary*. The cloverleaf-shaped reflecting pool glimmered between the gates and the entrance to the sacred building. She was early. She took the extra time to revel in the tranquility of the gardens. A mix of carefully picked trees and herbs grew in wild abundance all around the temple. A sanctuary away from the extreme weather of Aden surrounded by lush greens, tall, meandering trees, and an array of colorful wildflowers. The air was cooler than usual but still warm; it moved and danced with calm anticipation. A wind chime somewhere close sounded a soothing melody of harmonic pitches. She looked up at the building and noticed for the first time its stately facade, understated in size but not structure. It was reminiscent of a miniature Parthenon, flanked by six pillars that supported a geometric frieze before giving way to the intricate detail of the pediment. Within the pediment was an image, carved and painted, of mountains and a sinking sun, its rays reaching up and out. Underneath were the words *In Memoriam*, and hanging between the central pillars was the *Asho Farohar*, the guardian angel.

Silloo closed her eyes and tried to settle her mind, focusing on the wind chimes and surrendering to the gentle breeze.

"Silloo *Bai*, how are you?"

She opened her eyes. "Mr. Mardden, hello. I'm better—now that I'm here."

He smiled at her, a genuine smile. She peered over her shoulder, just to check that none of the *lugna* men had followed her.

"*Chal,* come inside the *agiary*. We have much to discuss," Mr. Mardden said softly, tipping his head from side to side and offering her his hand.

Inside, a small woman was sitting on a bench with her head covered. Silloo recognized her immediately. She waited for Mr. Mardden to close the *agiary* doors, and then the woman, Jeroo, rose and greeted her with a long, tight hug before the three of them made their way into the sacred room where the fire burned.

Mr. Mardden had sent word to the ever shrinking circle of Parsees still in Aden, in search of someone whom they knew and trusted who was leaving the city soon—someone willing to take Silloo's three children out of Yemen. Jeroo had come forward. No one knew of this plan; it had to be kept secret. If the *lugna* found out, they could sabotage the whole thing.

"Mr. Mardden, isn't it disrespectful to have this discussion in here?" Silloo asked.

"On the contrary, madam, this is where *Ahura Mazda* can hear you and feel your presence best. It's not at all disrespectful. We are discussing the safety of your children, after all."

His gentle demeanor soothed her. She realized how much she had missed being in the presence of someone she trusted.

Chapter 10

She had become so accustomed to adversity that it now seemed surreal to feel safe.

Mr. Mardden pulled three folding chairs from outside the room and offered the ladies a seat before taking his own.

"Silloo," Jeroo said, "I want you to know that the whole Parsi community is behind you and we want to help. *I* want to help. I can get the children out of Aden and take them with me to Bombay." She paused, allowing her statement to settle in.

Jeroo was an old family acquaintance, small and petite with olive-colored skin and long, straight, silky black hair that swayed gracefully as she moved. Silloo was overwhelmed by her compassion. She could feel all her emotions and fears bubbling up to the surface, looking for release, but she suppressed them—she was here for her children. Her fragility suddenly felt so obvious. She wanted to sob and wondered what would happen if she did. Would Jeroo step toward her and wrap her arms around her? What would that kind of comfort feel like? Would she crumble in her arms, finally the one being consoled instead of having to console?

She had thought that this meeting was meant to initiate a plan to get the children out, but Mr. Mardden had already started to put a plan into action. This would and could happen—and soon.

"Silloo, we need to get plane tickets for the children. I am booked on the Air India flight on March 2nd," Jeroo told her.

"March 2nd, that's so soon. I need to get passports for the children. I will have to call the British embassy and see if they can expedite them." She sat up straight and tilted her head to each side, stretching out the tension in her neck and shoulders. "How much are the tickets? I don't have much money. I have some hidden in the house, so I can pay for the tickets with that maybe?"

"You don't have to worry about paying for the tickets, and honestly, if you come up with money to pay for them, it will look suspicious to those thugs," Jeroo replied. "Mr. Mardden has been in touch with the Parsi community inside and outside of Aden. The *agiary* will take care of the payment through donations."

"But I can't accept that. It's too much."

"Poppycock! Of course you can!" Jeroo's voice flew up several octaves. "How many years has Bhicajee Cowasjee been in Aden? How many people has *your* family helped over the years? Parsi and non-Parsi!" She cut the air with her hand as she spoke, fierce and resolute, reminding Silloo of her boys when they practiced karate. "This is how we'll do it. We need to move fast and make all the arrangements."

Silloo's immense feeling of gratitude pushed her over the edge. Two tears trickled down her cheek. She knew in her heart that there was no other way: her children had to go. It was no longer safe for them to be in Aden with her. And it was not safe for Dara to remain in Aden without her. She abhorred the idea of being parted from her children, but the plan was practical, sensible. She folded one hand into the other and, staring down at them, nodded her head in agreement.

Her stepmother would meet Jeroo and the kids in Bombay. Mum would take care of them until Silloo could join them. *If* Silloo could get there. There was a possibility that she would never get to hold their tiny hands in hers again or hear their sweet voices call her name. She was well aware of the tremendous risk involved in her decision, but she also knew that if she left Aden with her children, she would never see her husband again, that her departure would seal his fate and the fate of the others. This would be their best hope for survival. Her family, their lives, would all be determined by the choices she made in this moment.

✤ ✤ ✤

The ichor of centuries of battles has seeped through Yemeni soil—the blood of warriors, soldiers, innocent women and children—from generation to generation. Religious myth holds that Aden is where Cain killed his brother, Abel, out of jealousy. Some believe that the soil of Aden was cursed by this heinous crime, the first murder, and that the city would forever be a slave to this fratricide.

Aden is rooted in its deep connection to religion and culture, but the new Communist-inspired regime was anti-religion at its core. As it spread to the masses of mainly illiterate, uneducated, impoverished Yemenis like Kazim, the founding fathers of this new regime avoided the topic of religion. They glazed over the real principles of Communism—liberation, organization of labor, equality—and instead drew attention to the end of a century-long occupation. Focusing on their fight for independence allowed the political leaders in Aden to convince uneducated men all over the country that fighting the foreigners was their right and the only way to take back their country. It was curious how these Yemenis, typically so entrenched in their faith, had so quickly abandoned it.

Silloo's visit to the *agiary* had given her a lot to think about. Back at home, she had to move fast to get the children passports and arrange for her stepmother to fly from London to Bombay to pick them up. The plan seemed unbelievable and crazy, but she knew she had to try. She would not risk having to see them lined up again with a gun to their heads. She imagined their small, innocent bodies, their big brown eyes, and her heart hurt. She pushed her emotion aside and moved forward, sitting at her dining table, busying herself with the details.

Mamma stood in the doorway in a navy-blue chiffon sari embroidered with silver thread. She looked tired, empty, and defeated. She looked the way Silloo felt.

"Mamma, come, come sit."

"*Dikri*, what did you do at the *agiary*?"

Silloo hesitated. She didn't want to scare Mamma or worry her even more. But if the children were going to leave, she didn't want it to come as a surprise. She wanted Mamma to have this time with them too. As Silloo searched for the right words, Mamma reached her hand out and took Silloo's in hers.

Chapter 10

"Silloo *Mai*." It was the first time that she had ever called Silloo by her name and not *Dikri*, Gujarati for "daughter." "*You* are the reason that the boys are still alive. *You* are the reason we are still alive. *You* are the one fighting for all of our lives, and—" Mamma's eyes filled with tears as she clasped her daughter-in-law's hand even tighter. "Thank you for your strength. I would never have been able to do this without you."

Silloo reached over and kissed her mother-in-law on the cheek. Nothing else needed to be said.

Later that night, she spoke to Dara for the last time on the intercom. Their supervised visit in the apartment had been brief, and even though it was far from what they had hoped, it was comforting to be together. She was grateful to have had the warmth of his arms wrapped around her and as they sat hand in hand, at a loss for words, listening to Mamma as she continuously asked what would happen next and if they would ever be released from Mansoura. Silloo focused on the feeling of her fingers intertwined with her husband's. Dreading whatever it was that was to come next. Mansoura was a dangerous place and this new turn of events did not leave her feeling confident.

And so, with the characteristic swiftness of the past few months, their lives would change, yet again, the very next day.

Part Three

"Tenderness and kindness are not signs of weakness and despair,
but manifestations of strength and resolution."
—Kahlil Gibran

11

"Out of suffering have emerged the strongest souls;
the most massive characters are seared with scars."
—Kahlil Gibran

January 27, 1972

The four men stood in the doorway of the prison cell. It was a huge room with barred windows along one wall and heavy double-steel doors along the other. The doors opened to an enormous courtyard where they could see prisoners in forest-green jumpsuits congregated: walking, talking, smoking, and chewing *khat*. The room was flooded with light, and the beams of the gabled, corrugated-steel ceiling were dotted with ceiling fans that wobbled with precarious haste. Each of the men carried a bundle of bedding and clothing with them. There were no beds in the cell; the prisoners slept on the floor on whatever bedding they were lucky enough to bring.

"Put your things in this corner. This is where you'll sleep." The prison guard spoke to all of them in Arabic and pointed to the far-right corner. "You can wear your own clothes—you are political detainees, so you don't have to wear the prison uniform or do any labor. The other prisoners in this cell work in the kitchen, so they won't be here during the day. You are not allowed to talk to them when they come back in the evening.

You can walk outside if you need exercise. No talking to any of the other prisoners. You understand?" the guard asked. He was neither friendly nor unfriendly, just matter-of-fact. They all nodded, a little stunned by the reality that lay before them.

"Dara, do you see those men across the courtyard?" Jamshed whispered to his brother. "Look carefully. Recognize them?"

Dara scanned their faces. They were all men whom they knew, good men, successful Yemeni businessmen, lawyers, and government workers.

Jamshed leaned in. "They must have denounced the new regime. They are now considered traitors of the Communist government, British sympathizers." He shook his head. "What will become of us?"

Dara wasn't sure what to say. He shared his brother's sense of uncertainty. They had tried hard not to think of how bad this could get, but each time things got worse, it became increasingly difficult to keep their thoughts positive. Despair was beginning to seep its way into them.

"You think it will actually be only four days that they keep us here?" Jamshed wasn't really asking.

"They're trying to scare us. To pay them all this money they think we have," Dara responded.

"I just don't know how this will end, Dara. Will I see Nazneen and my children ever again? This isn't how I imagined my life ending."

"I know, but we can't lose faith—that's what you always tell me, isn't it? My turn to remind you, big brother."

Chapter 11

"Yes, yes. True. Thank you. You are right, or I should say I am right." He gave Dara a melancholic smile. "My letter should reach Maki soon. I asked her to talk to cousin Shapur. I'm sure he will be able to help us."

Jamshed looked at his brother, younger by ten years, and couldn't help but feel pride in who he was. They were very different men. Dara, in Jamshed's mind, was less cautious, too wild for his liking. However, it was Dara's fearlessness that had helped them through this time. Helped them stay focused. It had even saved Jamshed's life in the early days of the unrest and was the reason that they started paying the regime for protection. Jamshed's kidnapping had shaken them both, but it was in that moment of need that he had asked his kidnappers to contact Dara for the ransom. Dara had disappeared for three days, returning home with his brother. Neither of them ever felt the need to share the details of what happened; only the two of them knew the truth.

"I just know that Shapur will help. He is our only hope, and I do have faith. We must always fall back on that. Thank you for reminding me," Jamshed said.

Mansoura Prison was built in the early 1960s and designed like most government buildings during British rule—in a traditional colonial style. It was a sand-colored fort, large and stately, reminiscent of old grand palaces. Imposing steel gates were flanked by smaller passing ones. Dara remembered reading about the design in the newspaper when it was completed. It had been built so that the large cells surrounded a wide, expansive courtyard. Each cell held about fifty men or more comfortably. The four corners of the building were reserved for the most violent offenders, female prisoners, and, last but not least, torture.

The cell for the latter group, as Dara recalled from the article, was located to the right as you entered the prison and was succinctly referred to as the "torture chamber." When the British designed and constructed the prison, they consulted interrogation experts to create the most intimidating environment. Four interrogation rooms flanked a small hallway that led to the solitary confinement cells. The interrogation rooms had small windows and were soundproof, with low ceilings, concrete floors, and blinding lights. The paper had reported that even the interrogators felt uneasy when they entered those rooms, specially built to induce feelings of claustrophobia and anxiety.

Dara sat on the floor on his bedding, leaning up against the cool wall. He scanned the cell and tried with all his being to keep his mind from slipping into a dark place. He really hoped that Shapur would come through for them.

February 3, 1972

"Silloo, it's Maki here, calling from Bombay." Dara's sister spoke loudly into the receiver to be sure she could be heard. "What's happening on your end? I just received Jamshed's letter, *Areh Khodah*."

Chapter 11

"I am so glad you called, Maki. I have been trying to reach you. There is much to tell you, but most important is that they took the men to Mansoura Prison a few days ago."

"What? Oh no, what is going on? What is this? Now they are just taking innocent men and throwing them into prison—why?" Maki spoke with a strong British Indian accent, enunciating certain syllables while elongating others.

"It's been very difficult."

"Now don't you worry, Silloo. Jamshed has asked me to talk to Shapur. I will go to him tonight. I hope he'll know the right people to put some pressure on the government in Aden. I'll do everything I can. That, I promise."

Silloo could hear her own fear mirrored in Maki's voice, which cracked as she spoke. Maki could not bear the thought of her two brothers stuck in a prison.

"How is my mummy? How is her health? Is she eating properly? Oh, I wish I could be there with you. Thank you for taking care of her."

"Mamma is managing. This isn't easy for her, not easy for any of us, but she's managing. Her health, God willing, is good, and we are fine, really. We need you to do everything you can from there to help get the boys out of that place."

"*Areh Khodah.*" Maki smacked her tongue on her top teeth and took a deep breath.

"Maki, have you talked to my mum?" Silloo asked.

"No, no, I haven't. Is your mummy here or in London?"

"Mummy is in Bombay. She just arrived two days ago.

Could you make sure to speak to her soon? There is something else, but I don't want say too much on the phone."

"All right, I'll call her tonight, but after I come back from Shapur's place. I am going to go now. This cannot wait. Be careful *mai*, please."

"Yes, I will. Bye, Maki, and thank you."

❖ ❖ ❖

Maki looked at her watch. It was 8:30 p.m.—not exactly the best time to drop in on someone, but this couldn't wait. Maki wasn't really one to drop in on anyone, ever. She was a strong woman, and proud, *very* proud, but this situation softened her. These were her little brothers. Maki had been a teenager when Dara was born. She had held him, fed and changed him, and loved him like he was her own child. As much as she despised having to ask anyone for anything, this was different. This was a matter of life and death. She had felt the desperation in Jamshed's letter that had arrived earlier that day.

She took off her housecoat and gently pulled on a light cardigan. She was a small, remarkably beautiful woman, with fair skin and a chiseled nose, delicate lips, and prominent brown eyes. Her hair was cut at her shoulders and fell in layered waves, framing her face. Reaching into her drawer, she took out a pale-blue silk scarf, carefully wrapping it around her head, tying it into a neat knot under her chin.

Chapter 11

As she exited her building, her driver was waiting for her and held the heavy white door of the car open as she gracefully climbed in. The drive from Lands End to Nariman Point was especially pretty at night. Marine Drive, also known as the Queen's Necklace, was lit up by pearl-like lights lining the coastal drive. Shapur and his wife, Zarine, lived in a newly renovated high-rise in the elite business center of the city. Maki sat in the back of the white Ambassador, her driver safely at the helm. Her line of sight drifted over and out into the dark expanse of the Arabian Sea, knowing it was there but unable to see anything but darkness. She felt an ocean of emotion within herself. Straightening her back in the leather seat, she pressed her palms over her skirt, flattening it out, collecting herself.

The ornate entrance of the building was intimate but impressive with its marble tile floor and slim, uniformed security guard. He called Shapur's apartment to inform him of her arrival and then escorted her to the elevator. Kanta, the young, portly houseboy, led her to the drawing room, and Shapur rushed to meet her shortly after. Shapur was a tall man, balding, with warm eyes. He wore his burgundy dressing gown and searched the table for his glasses.

"Maki Bhen, to what do I owe the pleasure? Please forgive my robe, but I wasn't expecting any company."

"Shapur, I'm so sorry to intrude at this hour, but I've come to share a very sad story with you." Tears welled in her eyes.

"Oh no, please, Maki, have a seat. It is only 9:00 p.m. Still early for us night owls." He gestured to the couch. "Kanta, bring some tea, please." Shapur sat down next to her, deducing instantly the seriousness of the situation by her presence at this hour alone. "Now tell me, please, what has happened?"

"The boys, my brothers, have been rounded up in Aden and taken to prison. Mamma, Freny, and Silloo are under house arrest with the children."

"Oh my word!" Shapur gasped.

Maki pulled out the letter she had received from Jamshed. Holding it in her hands, she began to tell her cousin the whole story as she knew it. He had been aware of some trouble in Aden but had no idea how dire the situation was. He listened intently while she spoke.

Shapur's mother was Mamma's younger sister, Maki's aunt. She had three children, two boys and a girl, and had married into a priest's family. In the Zoroastrian faith, priests must be born into priest families, and once born into the family, a boy can choose to go through the intricate training to become a priest. Shapur had chosen to become a priest, and in addition to his religious obligations, he had traveled and pursued a solid education. After becoming a chartered accountant in London, he returned to India to work for one of the oldest accounting firms, AF Ferguson. His career progressed, and eventually he was offered a prestigious executive position at Wyman Gordon in India, one of the leading suppliers of aerospace and military materials. Shapur's job had made him powerful connections in the government—really powerful connections. Maki hoped that he might be willing to call on those connections to help her brothers out.

Chapter 11

"Maki, I will do my best to help. I have some ideas, but I need just a little time to process all that you have told me. Do you mind if I just write a few details down?"

"No, no, of course." They talked some more before Maki rose from her seat. "Thank you, Shapur. Thank you so much."

"No thanks yet. I promise, I will do whatever I can."

She smiled at him, and as her eyes welled with tears, their hands clasped each other's.

✧ ✧ ✧

After Maki left, Shapur retreated into his home office and began making notes, checking his calendar, and sketching out a plan of action. He picked up the phone and dialed a Delhi number.

"Agarwall residence, good evening."

"Hello, good evening. Mr. Vijay, please."

"Who may I say is calling?"

"Shapur Rao, from Bombay."

"One moment please."

Shapur could hear the sound of slippers hitting a hard tile floor as he waited for Vijay to come to the phone.

12

"A man's true wealth is the good he does in the world."
—Kahlil Gibran

February 5, 1972

What makes good people good? What makes someone choose to risk their own safety or well-being and help another human being? It's a question that has fueled discussions since the days of the great philosophers. Socrates believed that true happiness is derived from virtue and character. Living well consists of not only being in a certain situation of happiness and security, but doing things that actualize those virtues. Certain people are more inclined to actualize those virtues, while others are not. Shapur was inherently equipped with that fortitude. He did not spend a moment thinking about whether or not he would or could do something to help someone. He acted without question; his only focus was on how.

Two days after they had spoken on the phone, Shapur walked into Vijay Kumar Agarwall's office in New Delhi. Vijay was well connected with the Delhi political factions, even in the highest ranks of the Indian government. Vijay, like Shapur, was more than willing to help.

"Shapur, dear old friend, so good to see you!" Vijay emerged from behind the rosewood desk and clasped Shapur's hands in his own. He smiled graciously and bobbed his head from side to side ever so delicately, as if it were attached to a spring, in warm welcome.

"Vijay, so good to see you. Thank you for taking time for this."

Vijay was in his mid-thirties, with a smile that spanned his whole face. He stood at about five feet tall with a receding hairline that exposed his shiny latte-colored head. "Come, come, sit. Tea is on the way. Now tell me more about this situation your family is in."

Shapur shared all the details as the clerk poured them cups of hot, milky chai and Vijay jotted down notes. Vijay's desk was long and intricate, a beautiful, rich reddish-brown rosewood with light streaks of gold embedded in it and carvings of flowers and leaves all along its sides.

"The new government in Aden, it is quite nationalistic, isn't it? Communist, I believe, and in the most conservative of ways, from what I have heard." Vijay paused. "I want to ask my dear friend Krishna Menon for his help."

"V. K. Krishna Menon?" Shapur asked, surprised. Krishna Menon was an Indian icon.

Vijay laughed, showing all his teeth, bobbing his head again from side to side and raising his eyebrows in agreement. "He has strong connections at the United Nations and a long-standing relationship with Indira Gandhi. If we want to put pressure on this government to release your relatives, then we have to get the highest-ranking people here to put pressure on the highest-ranking people there, you see. Krishna Menon is our best hope."

Shapur knew all about Krishna Menon, mostly that he was a brilliant man—mighty and eloquent. He was adored by his supporters for his unabashed passion for the fight for India's independence in the face of Western imperialism. In contrast, his Western critics viewed him more as a menace. From pictures, Shapur recalled that he was a tall man, with wavy graying hair combed back into tufts at the back of his head. Shapur wondered how old Menon must be now. Surely in his mid-seventies at the very least.

"Many people think that he himself is a Communist, you know, but he's actually more moderate, more of a simple socialist." Vijay smiled, his head bobbing with even more gusto. "He has a strong sense of justice. Did you know that he wrote the preamble to our constitution?"

"No, I didn't know that."

"Oh, yes, 'independent sovereign republic' were his own words and his only! He's a man who believes in taking care of things properly. I think that must come from all those years he lived in the UK." Vijay's permanent smile grew even wider.

"Vijay, I'm curious. Why do you think he would be willing to help us?"

Vijay threw his head back in laughter. His leather chair shrieked along with him as it dipped back and bounced forward, almost propelling him across the table. "For the same reason that you and I are here, my friend." He almost catapulted out of his chair. "He is a good man and believes in justice. Right, I just told you that." His smile stretched even further now. "And Krishna can't stand to see good men treated badly. Also, he will do absolutely anything for the best *mithai* in Delhi! Absolutely anything!" He laughed heartily, bouncing up and down in his seat, his white teeth sparkling. "Just give me a few days—he's not easy to locate, you know. He's quite busy, but I think I know where to find him."

February 10, 1972

Shapur and Vijay walked through the high arch of the Secretariat Building in New Delhi on their way to meet the prime minister of India. The structure consisted of two blocks parallel to each other that flanked the president's residence. Each block had four floors and close to a thousand rooms. The buildings were made of red and cream sandstone from Rajasthan. Small domes topped each building, and each wing ended with a colonnaded balcony. The main building housed a much larger dome with arched balconies. A long reflecting pool anchored the complex. The architecture was a mix of Mughal and Rajasthani styles, symmetrical and elaborately decorative. Needless to say, it was impressive in all its splendor.

Indira Gandhi's office was in the north block at the end of a long, wide hallway. Attached to her grand office was an impeccably decorated waiting room adorned with tufted leather chairs, heavy draperies, an oversized Persian rug, and a grandfather clock—its decor a stark reminder of the deep-rooted British occupation left behind not so long ago. The two men stood in silence while they waited, admiring the rosewood and tapestries.

A small man wearing a white *kurta* with a black waistcoat, white pants, and a Gandhi cap opened a door and invited the men into the main office. The walls of the room were covered in dark wood panels with large decorative moldings that ran along the tops of the walls, giving way to arched ceilings. The prime minister's desk was made up of two pieces forming an "L" shape. The main desk was covered with several neat piles of paper, a large calendar, and vase of bright-yellow daffodils. Two telephones and a notebook rested on the other end of the desk.

"Good morning, gentlemen. To what do I owe this pleasure?" Prime Minister Gandhi walked over to a sitting area in her office by the window. She was wearing a bright-yellow sari with an emerald and silver border, which matched the daffodils on her desk perfectly. She stood with her back straight, her hands at her waist elegantly placed one on top of the other. She smiled and gracefully tipped her head in greeting.

"Madam Prime Minister, thank you for taking the time to see us." Vijay and Shapur stood side by side and bowed in a respectful *namaste*. Smiling, Prime Minister Gandhi gestured to the oversized armchairs in front of her. The men took their seats, unbuttoning their suit jackets and settling into the luxurious leather chairs. The prime minister sat in front of them in a cream and gold upholstered chair. Even as she sat, her back remained straight, her shoulders pulled back. A swirl of gray hair swept up from the left side of her temple to the top of her head.

Vijay began explaining the situation, and Shapur jumped in to fill in details as she listened intently. The clerk served tea in a fine china set on a silver tray. When they finished their report, they sat in silence as she sipped her tea and stared past them through the window. Focusing through the blur of the *jali* peering at the *chatri*, she slowly followed the contours of the dome as her eyes gently fell on the slender beauty of the grand north wing dominion columns that proudly flagged the Secretariat Building.

"Well, this all sounds quite atrocious, and you say that one of the wives is under house arrest with three young children?" Her voice was calm; she spoke thoughtfully, her head dipping with certain words as if in agreement with herself. Every so often, she would look past them, searching for words in the expanse of the room. As she found them, she would nod, look at the men, and smile gently. Her every move and statement was deliberate, intentional.

"You know, gentlemen, I was taught from a young age to have a deep compassion for people who need help and support. It was my mother's calling as an activist, and as you know, my father was much the same. There is something about this story that I find quite compelling." She stopped to scratch the tip of her sculpted nose. "Perhaps it is the fact that you are Parsi like my late husband," she said, smiling at Shapur, pausing as she thought of her beloved Pheroze. Even though his faithfulness had not always been with her, hers had been with him, and she had loved him wholly and completely since the day she'd met him.

"Human dignity and decency are important values that we must all uphold. It's important to share not only our joys but also our sorrows, don't you think?" Prime Minister Gandhi said, pacing herself once more, and the men nodded along, unsure if they were expected to answer her question. "Mr. Rao, I commend you for taking this up for your family."

Shapur smiled, bowing his head in gratitude. He shifted his gaze to Vijay momentarily before speaking with some hesitation. "Madam Prime Minister, my friend here, Vijay, and I would be delinquent to not inform you of his close relationship with Krishna Menon."

Krishna Menon had advised that Vijay talk to Indira Gandhi on his own at first because of their long history. It was well known that she and her late husband, Pheroze, had shared a close relationship with Menon until 1962, at which time they felt that he was steering her father, Jawaharlal Nehru, in the wrong direction. Pheroze and Indira encouraged Menon's resignation as the minister of defense. Ultimately, his relationship with her father, her husband, and her had made it hard for her to cut him off completely, and so, although their relationship was somewhat strained, they managed to put their differences aside and maintain decorum. Menon was eager to help Shapur and Vijay but understood that the pressure that Prime Minister Gandhi could exert on the government of Aden could work in parallel to whatever he could do. All in all, it would be a tricky balance.

At the mention of Menon, she tipped her head to one side and smiled encouragingly.

"We have been in contact with Mr. Menon and have also met and talked to him." He nervously twisted his fingers with his other hand.

"And why did you decide to do that, Mr. Rao?"

"Well, as you are aware, I am sure, the president of Yemen is a staunch Communist. Krishna is respected among the Communist world leaders and has direct access to them, frankly, through the United Nations. He met Salmin Rubaya Ali, the current president of Yemen, in the UN Security Council."

"Well, that is quite a connection," she said, seemingly genuine. "As you know, I know Krishna Menon very well. He's an old family friend and was very dear to my father. I would like to talk to Krishna about this matter and understand what angle he is pursuing. It's unacceptable to me that Indian nationals are being detained in a prison on no grounds of criminal activity. That's completely unjust. Mr. Rao, please leave your contact details with my assistant, and let's follow up in a few weeks after I have had some time to talk to Krishna Menon and the Indian embassy. And I assume the British embassy is involved as well?"

"Yes, they have been working in conjunction with the Indian embassy."

"Good, good. That is important. It has been a long time since British India ruled over Aden, but still these citizens belong to both India and the United Kingdom. We must be united in our efforts."

"Thank you so much, Madam Prime Minister."

"I will see what I can do. Now, gentlemen, I must get back to work."

The men stood, offering another deep *namaste* before leaving.

✺ ✺ ✺

Indira Gandhi leaned back in her chair, looped her finger through the handle of her teacup, and gazed out the window, focusing again on the columns. Her mind drifted back to Pheroze, their roller coaster of a relationship seemingly doomed by her success, or perhaps luck, in her father's political shadow. It had been almost twelve years since her husband had passed away, and her heart still ached for him.

She took a deep breath and called for her clerk. "Please ask Mr. Chavan to come to my office and also get Krishna Menon on the phone."

13

"Be a lamp, or a lifeboat, or a ladder. Help someone's soul heal.
Walk out of your house like a shepherd."

—Rumi

February 14, 1972

Dara kept his eyes shut, trying to drift back into a hazy sleep, hoping perhaps that what lay on the other side of consciousness was familiar and safe, that the past few months had just been a bad dream. The lumps from his bedding pushed up into his hip. His ears settled in on the ceiling fan droning incessantly above him. Slowly opening his eyes, he focused on the fan blades. They spun slowly and off-center, looking as though they may unhinge at any moment. A glaring metaphor for his life.

The men had been at Mansoura for almost three weeks and had settled into something of a routine. They were now allowed visitors and the women wasted no time in getting there. They would come together in an entourage. Darius's wife, Hufrish, would bring their young daughter, only a year old. The guards would allow her to hand the baby to Darius, so they began placing notes with updates in her nappy. Darius would slip the note out and into his pocket while bouncing her on his arm. Guards supervised each meeting, but never noticed the exchange. Embassy officials were not allowed to visit the men at the prison, but they kept in touch with Silloo, so the notes were the men's only access to what was happening outside of Mansoura.

As Dara pulled himself up onto his elbows, his vision blurred slightly. He settled his eyes on the wall of windows and took a deep breath, exhaling slowly. The cell was filled with a cacophony of sounds, from the constant, steady pace of the fan to the grumbling, grating symphony of snores that emanated from every direction. Hauling himself up off the bedding, he made his way to the bathroom, suddenly feeling queasy and unsteady on his feet. His vision blurred again, followed by lightheadedness and an overwhelming need to vomit. He moved quickly for the toilet as the burning throw-up clawed at his insides in search of a rapid escape. Collapsing on his hands and knees, his whole body retched, releasing the fiery monster within him. He gasped for breath, gagging between bouts of projectile vomit, expelling vile bits of food and fluids into the urine-stained toilet. With barely anything left in his stomach, his body relentlessly convulsed, desperate to oust the foreign parasite brewing within it. His throat and chest ablaze, the rancid stench of his purge made his body heave continuously. His face paled and his eyes teared as beads of sweat formed on his clammy forehead, a cold chill coming over his body. He closed his eyes as his head spun, slowly drifting into unconsciousness.

He could hear his name being called, seemingly from far

away, then the voice got closer and closer. Finally, he opened his eyes to see Jamshed hovering over him.

"Dara, Dara, *sum thayum?* What happened?" It took Dara a few minutes to register what was going on, but just as he opened his mouth to speak, his stomach tightened again. It was as though someone had slid a knife into his gut and was twisting it slowly. He pulled his knees up to his chest, clutched his stomach, and groaned in pain. His mouth and chin were crusted in vomit. He lay on the floor of the prison bathroom, writhing in his bodily fluids. Jamshed shouted for a guard.

⬥ ⬥ ⬥

When the prison doctor realized that there was little he could do for Dara at Mansoura, he had him transferred. The Queen Elizabeth Hospital in Khormaksar was a state-of-the-art medical center with extensive facilities. The foundation had been laid by the Queen during her visit to Aden in 1954. It had been built in the quintessential colonial architecture of the British Raj—archways, wooden screens, overhead fans—and accommodated close to five hundred patients at a time, with wards for both medical and surgical care along with a private wing. The hospital also boasted a modern nurses' training school. The wards were flanked by oversized verandas painted a brilliant white, and the rooms were small but filled with sunlight.

Dara was admitted for food poisoning and severe dehydration. His stomach cramps continued for several days, and a dull throbbing in his head persisted. He grew so weak that it became impossible for him to even stand. On Dara's third day at Queen Elizabeth, Silloo was allowed a visit.

A slim nurse showed Silloo to his room. She found him sleeping. He looked pale, his cheeks sunken and his body gaunt. The shell of her husband was lying in the steel-framed hospital bed, and it shook her to see him this way. She sat and watched him for a long while as he slept. In a strange way, she was grateful to be with him. It felt safe. Her husband in the room, bright lights and people all around them. She sat comfortably in silence until the doctor and a flurry of nurses came to check his vitals, stirring him from slumber.

Silloo smiled with surprise and delight when she saw the doctor was Nizar Hussain, a dear old friend of theirs.

"Dara, Silloo, nice to see you both after so long! Although I wish it were under different circumstances. These are difficult times for our country, and I'm sorry for what you and your family have been going through." He looked embarrassed, as though he were responsible for the hand they had been dealt. "My friend, you're lucky they brought you here."

Dara smiled feebly. He opened his mouth to speak, but Nizar interrupted him.

"Now, now, you're very weak. Don't try to talk yet. I'll tell you what I can. You seem to have caught a bad infection, really bad. When you arrived, you were seriously dehydrated, so we'll continue to give you fluids for the next few days to build up your strength, and then we can slowly, slowly introduce some food. Do you know what you ate that was different from everyone else?"

Dara shook his head. He had only eaten what he'd been allowed to eat at Mansoura.

"What has happened to you is quite serious, and I can't be certain that it was caused by bad food alone. It is a little suspicious that nobody else was sick there. Be careful when you go back to Mansoura, Dara." With a pained look on his face, he continued, "I'm happy that I saw your name and quickly took you as my patient. I'll make sure that you get better, my friend."

"Nizar, thank you. This is a blessing," Silloo said.

"I know things haven't been easy for you. There are many Yemenis who know you and have gone to the NF and spoken on your behalf, myself included. Please don't lose hope. For now, we'll get him better! You have as much time as you'd like, Silloo. The guard outside the door just needs to see you keep some distance from Dara."

Alone again, Dara reached through the railing of the hospital bed for Silloo's hand. She peered over her shoulder at the guard, who thankfully wasn't paying attention. She moved closer and took her husband's hand between both of hers.

"Dara, I have something I want to tell you." She looked down at the floor. "I have decided that it would be best to send the children to Bombay. Mum is flying from London and will meet them there. I think it's safer for them to go."

He nodded. He wished he could tell her how worried he was about how this would all end. His eyelids felt heavy, and before he could say or think anything else he drifted off into a restless slumber.

March 1, 1972

Carrying Ana on her hip, holding Aram's hand in hers, and with Rustom by her side, Silloo walked into the hospital. The boys were dressed in matching shorts and shirts, and little Ana wore a white lace dress with a complementary clip in her hair—clothes that had been sent to them from friends in town through Valerie. Silloo had mentioned to Valerie in one of their visits that the children were growing out of their clothes. There was no money to buy clothing, and it would have been suspicious if she pulled any money from its hiding place. Valerie got to work and within a few days, she had clothes for all three children.

As soon as they saw their father, they squealed with delight and ran to him. Dara had made a strong recovery and was sitting upright in a chair. For the first time in months, he scooped his three children up into his lap as they laughed and shrieked. The guard came rushing into the room, but the moment he witnessed gave him pause. In an act of mercy, he left the room without a word, closing the door to give the family some privacy.

"Daddy, tomorrow I am taking Aram and Ana on an airplane," Rustom announced to his father. "I have to take care of them so Mummy can stay here and take care of you."

"Rustom, you are a very good big brother, my son. I know you will take very good care of your brother and sister." Dara fought back the lump in his throat.

"I don't want to go on an airplane," Aram said. He folded his arms in front of his chest and pouted.

Little Ana had no idea what was going on. She clung to her father, just happy to be in his arms. Dara pulled Aram onto his lap along with Ana, tickling him until he howled for him to stop between bouts of high-pitched laughter. The visit was short but filled the painful void of their absence over the past several months. Dara kissed and squeezed his children goodbye, trying hard to ignore the unspoken reality—the truth that there was no knowing how long it would be before he saw them again, or if this might be the last time he would ever get to hold them. Silloo gathered the children up, and after multiple goodbyes, they turned to leave.

"Silloo," he called out to her. She was stunningly beautiful, even when she was consumed with so much despair. "They are taking me back to Mansoura tomorrow. Nizar kept me here as long as he could. He has given orders that I am to be allowed to receive food from home."

Silloo looked at him and nodded. He didn't think it was possible for her to look any more defeated, but he knew his words had crushed her. As she walked out of the hospital room with their children in tow, he felt numb. Tomorrow she would have to put them on a plane and say goodbye to them. There was a chance that he would never hold them again, smell the sweet scent of their skin, or feel their arms wrapped around his neck. All he could do was pray for a miracle.

March 2, 1972

Three suitcases lined the wall by the front door. There was a heaviness in the apartment, a sadness that Silloo could not shake. She found herself hugging and holding each of her children constantly, desperate to savor each second with them.

Mr. Mardden arrived right on time to drive them to the airport. The plan was to meet Jeroo there. Fatima smothered the children with hugs and kisses, unable to hide her tears while Ahmed loaded the car with their luggage. Mamma did the same, as they passed the children from one to the other like parcels. Mr. Mardden, with subtle finesse, eventually coaxed the children into saying their final goodbyes and ushered them into the car.

Fatima grabbed hold of Silloo's hand. "*Sayidati*, Ahmed and I will be here waiting for you."

The children, blissfully unaware of their future, waved madly out the window, waving goodbye to the only home they had ever known. Silloo watched them in all their innocence, wondering if they would ever return. Ana sat on her mother's lap, playing with her silver bangles, and the boys sat on either side of them. Silloo chatted with them about how much fun they would have with their grandma and Auntie Nazneen in Bombay and how exciting it would be on the airplane. She ignored the tremble in her hands, the heaviness in her heart, and the pit in her stomach. She wanted this moment with her children to last forever.

Jeroo was waiting by the door to the terminal with her bags, her long black hair glistening in the sun. She knelt down and looked the kids in the eyes as she greeted them and introduced herself. She handed each of them little gift-wrapped packages and promised them a lot of fun on their adventure together. Then she stood and embraced Silloo. "I'll take good care of them, Silloo. They'll be safe," she whispered. Silloo nodded and smiled feebly, unable to speak.

The airport was quiet, so they were able to check in and drop off their bags quickly. They walked together as far as they could, reaching the doors to the tarmac, where a bus waited to transport passengers to their planes. Silloo could see the Air India 737 from behind the glass window. A security guard stood at the door, checking boarding passes. It was the moment she had been dreading.

She wondered if this was a mistake, if she should just call it all off—take her children and go home. Aram hung on her hand, and Ana's arms tightened around her neck, sensing their impending separation. She thought back to the day that Kazim had held the gun to their heads in her apartment. Keeping that image in mind, she took a deep breath, let go of Aram's hand, hugged Ana, and handed her to Jeroo. She swept up Aram and squeezed him tight, fighting back the lump in her throat.

"I love you, my sweetheart." Silloo put him down and wrapped her arms around Rustom. "Will you write to me from Bombay?"

Rustom nodded and hugged his mother's waist.

"Why don't you hold Aram's hand, darling? I love you."

"I love you too, Mummy."

Silloo looked at Jeroo and nodded her head. "Thank you."

"Don't worry, my friend. I will take good care of your babies."

Ana was crying, her arms outstretched toward her mother. Rustom and Aram walked together, and the four of them filed through the doors. The security guard watched as Silloo stood, one arm wrapped around her own waist, the other covering her open mouth as the group boarded the bus and it began to drive away.

The guard called out to someone in Arabic. She looked at him, her heart pounding in her chest. She turned away, trying to appear nonchalant as the guard walked out and stopped the bus. She now watched in horror. What was happening? Had Kazim caught on and stopped them from leaving? Her heart *thumped, thumped, thumped* in her chest. The children and Jeroo got off the bus and stood on the tarmac. Jeroo looked nervous too. The guard came back through the doors and marched toward her.

"They are your children?"

"Yes. Yes, they are," she said, her voice shaking.

"It's okay, Mamma, you can go with them on the bus to the plane. I come with you. You say bye there. It's okay, come." He smiled gently, nodding his head and leading her to her children.

Silloo took a deep breath. "Thank you, thank you so much." She ran out to the tarmac, scooping her children into her arms.

$$\diamondsuit \diamondsuit \diamondsuit$$

Dara sat in his hospital room, ready and waiting to be returned to Mansoura. He had not seen Silloo since she had sent the kids to India; he hoped all had gone off without any issue. He hated being in the dark. Having to wait for word that his family was safe. Not being able to keep them safe. Alone with his thoughts, he worried. She was aloof the day she had visited with the children, not her usual self. He was so lost in his thoughts that he did not notice Nizar come into the room.

"Dara, Dara, are you okay?"

"Ah, yes, Nizar, sorry, I was just thinking about my children and Silloo." He smiled feebly.

Nizar flinched; he could only imagine what his friend was experiencing. "I am sorry, Dara. I just wanted to let you know that I signed all your release papers." Nizar pushed his glasses up the bridge of his nose. "They are bringing the ambulance around to take you back to Mansoura. I have given strict instructions for you to receive home-cooked food only."

"How did you manage that?"

"Oh, it was easy. The police are not happy that they have to hold you men with no formal charges. There is a lot of sensitivity around this case, and when I suggested that you might have been poisoned, well, they got worried. Anyway, they agreed to home-cooked food for you. I hope it makes this a little easier to deal with."

"Thank you, Nizar."

"Be careful, Dara."

✧ ✧ ✧

The days passed even more slowly without the children. The apartment echoed with its emptiness. Silloo spent all her time making phone calls. One embassy to the next, and every Yemeni office that would take her calls. She was determined to use every minute she had to find a way to get the men released. They had started sending the men messages in the food that they prepared and took to Mansoura. Silloo and Mamma busied themselves with day-to-day details, desperately trying to ignore the void left by the children's absence.

March 27, 1972

Mamma sat at the dining table with a strip of paper an inch wide and six inches long. She wrote meticulously in Gujarati.

Chapter 13

Though her handwriting was sometimes hard to decipher, Silloo knew that Dara and Jamshed would be able to read her notes. Silloo dictated.

"Heard back from Maki. Shapur is working on a plan."

"Areh *Dikri*, there is not enough space for all those words."

"Oh, sorry, Mamma. Okay, just say Shapur is working on a plan. Then when you are finished, give it to me."

"What will you do with it now?" Mamma asked quizzically.

"Look, I am going to roll it up like this." Silloo took the small piece of paper and rolled it around a toothpick so it was a tiny tube. She poked a hole into one of the kebabs that she had made earlier and placed into a tiffin box on the table. "Here I will stick it into the kebab like this," she said, as she used the toothpick to push the paper into the kebab.

"*Dikri*, how will they know which one has the message?" Mamma sat confused.

"It is always the kebab in the middle of the bottom tiffin, Mamma." Silloo arranged the tiffin box meticulously, placing the most important kebab at the very bottom of the third tin.

While Silloo busied herself in the other room with Fatima, Mamma scrolled an *Ashem vohu* on another small piece of paper and taped it to the bottom of the tiffin in hopes that prayer would bring her boys some protection.

⟡ ⟡ ⟡

The guard took the two tiffin boxes from Ahmed and walked down the long corridor to the men's cell. He was new at Mansoura and wasn't friendly like some of the other guards. Short and round, his stomach cascaded over his cinched black belt, and the buttons on his shirt fought to keep the two sides together.

The brothers walked over to take the boxes from him, but the guard just stood there, glaring with narrowed eyes.

"This is your food," he said, pointing at the tiffin.

"Yes, it is," Jamshed said.

"What is this?" The guard had dropped one of the tiffins and was pointing to something taped to the bottom of the tiffin box. Dara looked in horror as he recognized his mother's handwriting.

"I don't know what that is. Maybe if you let me look at it, I can tell you," Jamshed said calmly.

"You think I'm *ahmar*, a donkey. You think I'm stupid?

Dara began to sweat. "We don't think you're stupid."

"What is this? Explain!"

Jamshed looked closely at the handwritten note, and when he read it, he was relieved. "It's a blessing from our mother. A prayer that we stay healthy and safe. That is all. Nothing to fret about."

"You're a liar."

"I'm not a liar," said Jamshed, stung by the accusation. "You can ask anyone who reads Gujarati, and they'll tell you the same."

Chapter 13

"You'll come with me, and we'll see what kind of blessing this is."

"No, this is not my brother's fault," Dara jumped in. "The food comes for me because I was sick. The note is for me, not for him. If you want to take someone, you take me." He looked at Jamshed, urging him to follow along.

"You think you're the strong one, ah? Okay, let's see how strong you are." He yelled over to a couple of guards. One grabbed the tiffin boxes, and the other took hold of Dara. Jamshed tried to protest, but the guard raised his baton, making it clear that he needed to back off.

14

*"Endurance is one of the most difficult disciplines,
but it is to the one who endures that the final victory comes."*
—Buddha

March 27, 1972

Dara's heart pounded as the guards roughly escorted him to the front of Mansoura Prison. He quickly realized where they were leading him: toward the torture chamber and interrogation rooms. The three guards shoved him into a small room with a waist-level barred window that was about two feet tall by two feet wide. They chained him to the window and left him there.

Multiple ignored requests to use the bathroom led Dara to relieve himself through the bars and out of the window. The chain was too short for Dara to sit on the floor, so he stood leaning against the wall while he waited for them to return to interrogate him. His legs grew weak and his arms locked up, pulling on a muscle in his neck.

Hours passed before the three men filed back into the dismal room. The new guard seemed thrilled to be there, full of an inflated sense of power.

"What was the message? Are you going to tell us, or do we need to beat it out of you?"

"There was no message. It was a blessing, a prayer from my mother."

"Liar! Tell me what it said."

"I told you already. Why don't you go and ask someone who speaks Gujarati, and they'll tell you exactly what it says. I have nothing to hide."

"Mohammed, *'ahdir alsawt*. Bring the whip."

The second guard left the room and returned with a bamboo cane. The new guard took it and *thwacked* it menacingly against his hand. "I don't think you understand me—I want to know what was written on the paper. You tell me, or I'll beat you."

Dara stiffened, bracing himself for the inevitable. "I have nothing to tell you. I have already told you everything. My mother wrote a prayer."

"You're lying."

The sound of the whip cutting through the warm air instantly brought with it a sharp, hot pain that radiated through Dara's back. He arched his torso, yelling out in anguish. Then came the next strike, and another, and then another. His back was on fire, the stinging heat reaching down deep into his body, burning all the way through him. He sank to the floor, his wrists still chained to the barred window, his mind a blur. A dull throbbing encompassed his whole body.

"You want to tell me what was written on the paper now?" the guard shouted as he stood over Dara, looking down on him. Dara could barely hear him over the ringing in his ears.

"I already told you what I know."

Ahmed returned to the apartment with the tiffins still full of food and a message from Mansoura that the women weren't allowed to send food anymore.

"*Sayidati*, they wouldn't tell me why, just no more food."

"Who told you that, Ahmed? And what else did they say?"

"The guard was a new one. I haven't seen him there before. He shouted at me to leave."

Silloo began making some phone calls, starting with the British ambassador, followed by the Indian ambassador and Dr. Hussain. She hoped that one of them could help her understand what had changed. She retreated to the balcony while she waited to hear something, from anyone, so anxious that all she could do was pace.

"*Sayidati*, there's a phone call for you from Dr. Hussain," Fatima announced. Silloo rushed to the living room.

"Silloo, I called Mansoura like you asked. It took me some time to find out what was happening, but I finally got some information," Nizar said. "It seems a prison guard found a note under one of the containers that the food was delivered in."

"What? Oh no." She rubbed her forehead with her hand.

"Dara is being held in solitary confinement. He insists that the note is a prayer from his mother, but they don't believe him. They won't allow food for now, but I'll see what I can do. In the meantime, I think you need to notify the British and Indian ambassadors of Dara's situation."

"Yes, I have already called them, Nizar. Thank you."

"I'm sorry that I don't have something better to tell you."

"No need to apologize. It's not your fault." Silloo hung up and went to the kitchen to check the tiffins. Sure enough there it was, bright as day. Mamma had written a prayer in Gujarati on the bottom. *Oh, Mamma,* she thought. She walked back out onto the balcony to look at the ocean, barely making out the ripples of the waves as they coaxed each other into the bay. She missed her children, her husband, her life. Here on the balcony in her solitude, she allowed a steady stream of tears to flow down her cheeks in silence.

March 30, 1972

For three long days, Dara endured violent beatings, heavy whippings, and verbal abuse. He was growing weak, becoming more emaciated than ever; he had been allowed only a few pieces of bread and some rice in his time in isolation. He had learned to recognize the sound of the guard approaching the room, the all-too-familiar shuffle of his boots under the weight of his heavy body.

On the fourth day, the torture escalated. The guard, unsatisfied with his lack of progress, came in with a rifle. Dara looked up at him in a daze, thinking that perhaps this time the guard might finish him off once and for all—almost wishing that he would.

They went through the same round of questioning, again. *What was written on the paper?* Dara pleading, *It was just a prayer, a blessing.* But the guard's rage was brimming over. He released Dara from his chains, turned as if to walk away, but then in a split second spun to strike. Dara caught a glimpse of his thick knuckles before they crashed against his face. Pain vibrated through his head and knocked him off his feet. The next strike, this time with the butt of the rifle, landed on his lower back. Hard, sharp, and solid. He arched his body, screaming in torment, as one blow led to the next and then the next and the next. The guard continued to pummel the rifle butt into Dara's lower back as hard as he could. The door flew open. Dara heard yelling as he curled into a fetal position. Blood gushed from his nose and mouth. His body felt broken.

✛ ✛ ✛

When Dara opened his eyes, he was still lying on the cool tile, drenched in his own blood and sweat. His back pain had abated slightly, so long as he didn't move.

"Are you all right?" a voice asked from behind. Dara looked over and saw the outline of a small man sitting on a burlap sack. He had bedding folded next to him.

"Who are you?" Dara asked, dragging himself up to sit against the wall. He inhaled sharply from the pain. His face was bloody and bruised, and his eyes were so swollen it was hard to keep them open. He clutched his ribs and leaned his head against the wall, his lungs hungry for air.

Chapter 14

"Faisal. Faisal Al Khoury. They put me here with you because there is no more space in the prison," the man said as he hugged his knees.

"Nice to meet you, Faisal. I am Dara. Dara Barucha."

"Are you okay, Dara Barucha? Looks like they beat you quite badly." Faisal leaned forward, and he finally came into focus. He was slim and wore a crocheted prayer cap. He shifted his body and now sat cross-legged on his burlap mat with a concerned look in his eyes.

"I will be fine, thank you. Just a little banged up." Dara attempted to smile but his face would not permit it. "Where are you from, Faisal?"

"Mukayras," he said proudly. "I am from Mukayras."

"What did you do to deserve being thrown in here with me? Must have been quite bad."

Faisal smiled at Dara and looked down at his feet. "I refused to do something for the new government, and they didn't approve. What did *you* do that they did this to you? I want to make sure I do not do the same."

"I told the truth," Dara answered. "They just don't believe me."

"Oh. I'm sorry for the behavior of my countrymen. I am ashamed of my government, but you know, we aren't all like this."

"Thank you, Faisal, but you don't need to apologize. I was born in Aden. This is my home. I understand what you're saying; my heart bleeds for this country. This is my country too."

"It seems we are quite similar."

"Yes, so it does. What exactly did you refuse to do? If you don't mind me asking."

Faisal grimaced and clasped his hands together. "I'm a teacher. I teach math and science at the Al Ghazaly School in Mukayras. I have taught for fifteen years. I love my students. Some of them have even moved on to study in Aden College," he said proudly. "One student of mine, he received a scholarship to study in the United Kingdom! In any case, the new government, they asked us to do things that are wrong, things that I just couldn't do. I'm a very proud Muslim, Dara Barucha. I refused to spy on my students' families. I, also, will only tell the truth. If that gets me killed, then so be it."

"Spy on your students' families? How and why did they want you to do that?"

"Mukayras is a mountainous area, and the schools are small, but we are very proud of the education that we are able to provide to our students. The government came into our schools and wanted us to find out from our students what their parents are saying at home. We are expected to ask the children, every day—*every day*—what their parents are saying and if they support the government or not." Tears fell down Faisal's face. "Then they will arrest the parents if they've said anything against the government. This isn't right. This isn't what the Prophet Mohammed taught us. I refused, flatly refused, and so now I'm here, but I have my honor and dignity. Allah will protect me." Faisal sat slightly taller as he wiped his eyes with the back of his hand.

Chapter 14

"I'm so sorry, Faisal. That is terrible. This is a very difficult time for many of us, but the truth will prevail. I have to believe it. If we don't believe that we will come out of this, what is left?"

"*Insha'Allah.*"

The men sat silently after that.

For the next four days, the two men got to know each other, sharing stories and experiences. The aggressive guard never returned, and miraculously, Dara was left alone and not asked about the message again.

After a week in semi-isolation, he was returned to the communal cell. He limped back and was reunited with the others in an emotional moment. Jamshed had worried himself sick about his younger brother. Dara, a proud man, didn't speak of what had happened to him in that room, but at night he would lie on his bedding and his back would pulsate and throb. He lay in silent agony, wondering if this nightmare would ever end, and if it did, how they would ever move forward. He never saw Faisal again but his cellmate remained etched in his mind.

❖ ❖ ❖

The British ambassador, Arthur Kellas, paced the floor of his office, his hands clasped behind his back—it was how he cleared his mind. He was a tall man with a receding graying hairline and thick, dark eyebrows. His nose was long and pointed, hanging over his wide mustache and bending down toward his chin, his harsh features muted by his kind and gentle nature. An Oxford man who had already devoted thirty-plus years to the British diplomatic service, his career had placed him throughout the Middle East: from Tehran to Cairo, Baghdad to Tel Aviv, and Nepal to Aden.

His ambassador role in Aden was an important one, and the case of the Barucha brothers and their employees' detainment was a priority for him. He was not an overly emotional man, but he felt for them, and as subjects of the British Empire he was undoubtedly responsible for them. Moreover, Arthur and Dara had become friends, he was yet another friend who had been taken out on the boat. Both Arthur and the Indian ambassador had worked tirelessly to have the men released, but to no avail. He was determined to get the minister of foreign affairs to agree to some resolution on their impending phone call, and this time he had a trump card in his back pocket.

"Ambassador Kellas, how are you?" Muhammed Salih Aulaqi's thick Yemeni accent reached through the phone receiver.

"Mr. Aulaqi, I am well, sir, and you?" Although Arthur didn't speak a word of Arabic, his many years in the Middle East had taught him how to pull his consonants from his throat when pronouncing Arabic names and words.

"*Alhamdullah*, we are very busy, as you know, taking back our country." Arthur ignored the dig. The reality was that Muhammed Salih Aulaqi repulsed him. A former trade union leader and moderate, the Yemeni foreign minister was young, inexperienced, and undereducated.

Chapter 14

And the further truth was that he and his party were struggling: the National Front's recruits, like Ahmed Kazim, hailed mainly from the tribal regions of Yemen and from poverty-stricken corners of the city. Most of them had little to no education, and yet they were being promoted to high-ranking positions in companies that had been nationalized by this new government. These low-skilled men were suddenly executives.

It was difficult for legitimate Yemeni businessmen, who were now considered elite Adenis, to be shoved out of their livelihoods by, and forced to cower to, these thugs. Educated Yemenis watched their own countrymen turn on them and view them as the enemy. The tribal men didn't really understand what Communism meant: they were young, fueled by decades of imperialism and desperate to have their country back. They only wanted to enjoy their country the way the British and other expatriates had enjoyed it, with no idea of how to do so. One could hardly fault them; at times, however, their methods were barbaric and savage.

The president, Salmin Rubaya Ali, had placed these men in positions of power, but many of them were just too angry. Angry at being occupied for so long, angry at having to be the server in their own country, angry with anyone who had, in their opinion, contributed to their long-term persecution.

Their anger extended to their own people, the upper class, the educated realm of Adenite society. They were, in the minds of these new National Front recruits, the ultimate traitors: British sympathizers. There was just too much anger. Authority placed in the hands of the simple man made the anger morph into something extremely dangerous. The men came into businesses on the authority of the president's office, with little to no supervision, they heckled, they stole, and they threatened. Salmin and his administration's lack of awareness disgusted Arthur, and he was convinced that it would only be a matter of time before it all came crashing down on them.

"Mr. Aulaqi, I want to discuss the case of the Barucha brothers." Arthur dove in. "These men are being held on no grounds; they have neither committed any crime nor been accused of any criminal activity. This is a matter of utmost importance for our government, and I want you to know that it is receiving some very high visibility back in the UK." Arthur waited for the response.

"Mr. Ambassador, I'm not familiar with this case, but I promise that I will report your concerns to my government. I hope that such a minor matter will not affect our relations."

"I assure you, Mr. Aulaqi, neither I nor my government considers the unlawful incarceration of our subjects as a minor matter." This was not how Arthur had wanted this conversation to go. Aulaqi laughed a hearty, deep smoker's laugh.

"I will speak with our officials and get some information on this case. Now, more importantly, I want to discuss if your government has decided on a sum of money to be set aside for the financing of Yemeni scholarships in Great Britain?" Arthur's neck immediately stiffened as he took in an audible breath, pausing to contain himself.

"That is indeed the case," he stated.

"But, Mr. Ambassador, what is the amount that has been allocated? We would like to finalize this open issue with our British friends." Arthur could hear Aulaqi's smirk over the phone.

"Mr. Aulaqi, originally, we had allocated twenty-five thousand pounds, but following certain recent events and budget restrictions in the Indian subcontinent, the amount had to be reduced to fifteen thousand pounds. We have sent over all the paperwork for this offer but have had no response. Frankly, the ball is firmly in the South Yemeni court. We are awaiting the names of your scholarship nominees."

"What about courses that our nationals can take? What level of education will the scholarships include?" Aulaqi pressed on, and Arthur shook his head.

"Mr. Aulaqi, we can discuss the details once we have the nominees. I assume that each nominee will have a unique situation."

"Ah, yes, *walahi,* this is tr—"

"Mr. Aulaqi. The Barucha brothers?" Arthur interrupted him.

"Mr. Ambassador, I will have to get back to you on that matter."

15

"Don't grieve. Anything you lose comes round in another form."
—Rumi

April 4, 1972

Silloo wrapped the *pallu* of her sari around her head
as Mr. Mardden pulled the car to the front of the Court of
Justice. Gracefully, she climbed the sandstone steps into the
courthouse. It was a large building with a distinct red-tiled
roof. Arched windows and terraces surrounded the structure.
She stood inside the main terrace, escaping the intrepid heat
and glaring sun while waiting for Mr. Mardden. They walked
into the courthouse, Mr. Mardden trailing a few steps behind.

"I am here to see Officer Sharaq," Silloo announced to the
clerk behind the reception desk. He nodded and gestured for
her to take a seat in one of the white plastic chairs lined up
against a wall. The clerk ogled her while she waited, coughing
and clearing his throat, stopping to spit into a small trash can
every so often. She stood in the corner of the waiting room—
blocking his line of sight as much as possible—Mr. Mardden by
her side, standing guard.

"Hello!" the clerk yelled with irritation and pointed to a
door down the hall, signaling for her to go into the officer's

office. She gathered herself, gestured to Mr. Mardden to wait for her, and then walked down the long corridor. About halfway along, she saw the officer sitting in an office behind a large desk.

"Officer Sharaq," she said, nodding her head in greeting.

"Please, please, have a seat." He twirled a toothpick between his teeth.

"I would rather stand," she replied. "I am here to find out what is happening with my husband's case."

He smirked. "And who is this husband of yours?"

"Dara Barucha. He and his brother, uncle, and one of his employees have been held since November with no formal charges against them. I want to know when they will be released."

Officer Sharaq sat back in his chair. She was intriguing, alone with her husband incarcerated, yet she was bold for a woman. And very attractive in a demure way. No woman had ever spoken to him in this tone. He felt a stirring within him.

"Ah, yes, okay. Yes, they will be called to appear in the Madinat A'shahab on April 8th." He smiled. "They will be tried in the criminal court."

"Well, I would like to know about a bail consideration."

"You can fill out a bail application and bring it on trial day to present to the judge."

"Okay, that is what I will do then. Where do I get this application from?"

"Mustafa at the reception desk can give you one. Or… "

She glared at him.

"You could close the door, come here, and I will take care of everything for you."

"Excuse me?"

He approached her, taking the end of her *pallu* in one hand and shutting the door swiftly with the other. "Why don't you tell me how badly you want the bail consideration and I can see what I can do about it." He pushed her up against the door, moving in close. His mouth hovered over hers.

Silloo shoved him off her, taking back her *pallu* and staring at him in disgust. "I will get the application from Mustafa. I have nothing that I want to tell you." She turned to leave, her body trembling.

Silloo dreaded the thought of having to deal with the beast at the reception desk. She was constantly forced to interact with these despicable, uneducated, uncouth men who feasted on her with their eyes and mocked her resilience. To them, she was nothing but an object, only good for one thing, and they made it very clear that they were imagining that one thing with every look they gave her. They were amused by her tenacity, but their misogynistic minds were not capable of more. She found them deplorable, arrogant, and they collectively made her stomach turn. She approached the reception desk and asked the clerk, Mustafa, for the bail form. He threw it at her and then walked away.

Chapter 15

April 8, 1972

The four men were led into the courtroom handcuffed and in single file. The judge, Mohammed Nasser, sat behind an elevated wooden desk, a court reporter to his right and a clerk to his left. The accused were led to a podium with a microphone, where they stood forlorn and exhausted.

Dara looked over at Silloo, Mamma, and Hufrish. He smiled. It seemed like an eternity since they had been able to meet. The court had forbidden visits, and now any visitation had to be requested and approved through the Ministry of Interior.

The judge hit his gavel. "Are you directors Dara D. Barucha and Jamshed D. Barucha and employees Burjor S. Barucha and Darius Master of Bhicajee Cowasjee Limited?"

"Yes, Your Honor," Jamshed spoke for the group.

"You are being charged with smuggling money and goods out of Aden under Criminal Law 11, sections 16 and 24. How do you plead?"

"Not guilty, Your Honor."

"Please reappear for your appeal on April 15 at nine o'clock in the morning. Return them to Mansoura," Judge Nasser said, never lifting his head from his papers.

"Excuse me, Your Honor," Silloo interjected.

Judge Nasser peered at her over his glasses. "What is it?"

"I am the wife of Dara Barucha. I have with me a bail application for my husband and the other men."

"Bail application? Let me see." The clerk handed him the documents. As he scanned them, he glanced up at the women every few seconds, his double chin preventing his head from looking down any farther. "You want bail for them, okay. Bail is set at £80,000."

Silloo's jaw dropped. £80,000? Was he crazy?

"Please, Your Honor, can you reconsider the amount? We don't have that kind of money."

"Come back on April 11th for reconsideration." He slammed the gavel again and called the next case.

"*Dikri.*" Mamma tugged on Silloo's arm. "What is happening? Where will we get that kind of money?"

"I don't know, Mamma, I don't know. We have to try to make some calls and get as much as we can before April 11th. Come, we have work to do."

❖ ❖ ❖

Silloo sat at her dining table with her telephone, a pad, pen, and her telephone address book. She began with family and close friends, calling each one, explaining the situation and requesting their help. One of her first phone calls was to Valerie.

"Silloo! *Comment est tout?* How are you? What 'appened at the 'earing?"

"Oh, Valerie. Well, they did set bail."

"That is good news, no?"

"They set it at £80,000." They sat in silence for a long moment.

"Okay, it is okay, *mon ami*. We just need to make some calls and see 'oo can 'elp. Shall I come and 'elp you make calls? I can also talk to Pierre and see what he suggests."

"Thank you, I can make the phone calls. You know how much I appreciate you for offering to help me, but this is something I need to do on my own. I can't ask you to do this for me."

"Oh, *mon ami*, I will come later this evening. We can see how far you get and make a plan for tomorrow. 'Ow does that sound?"

"You know I would love to see you tonight. That sounds wonderful."

April 11, 1972

Judge Nasser was at his elevated desk, alone in the courtroom, when the women arrived. He ignored them as they took their seats. Silloo, with Valerie by her side, reviewed the bail application as other people filed in. She had met with and called everyone she knew in the past few days, begging for help with the bail money—from the British and Indian embassies to the French and Russian embassies, and to every friend and acquaintance they had known during happier times in Aden. Valerie had contacted everyone she and Pierre knew at every embassy in Aden. Sharing her friend's diabolical story had the ambassadorial crowd up in arms and ready to help.

Silloo was humbled by the kindness she had received, the empathy that was extended to her. As she sat on the wooden bench, the buzz of the courtroom gave her a sense of calm. *How odd*, she thought, *that I feel safe in this courtroom, surrounded by strangers, many of whom want to see my husband rot in jail. Yet here, no one can hurt me.*

The judge called the court into session, drawing Silloo's attention back into the room.

"Bail reconsideration hearing. Do you have the application?"

"Yes, Your Honor. Here it is."

"I will reconsider your request and set bail at £40,000, but it is only for the uncle and the employee. Your husband and his brother will remain in custody."

"With all due respect, Your Honor, there was never a distinction made between the men. The application was for all four."

"Well, now it is not." He smacked his gavel with contempt, stood, and left the courtroom.

Chapter 15

April 15, 1972

Dara stood with the other men, each of them dressed in white trousers and white shirts that hung loosely on their bodies, waiting for the judge to enter from his chambers. The table where they stood faced a group of seats where Silloo, Mamma, and Hufrish sat. Silloo smiled softly at him. How he longed for her, for normalcy, for their life to be what it had been. There were so many things that he now wished they had done differently.

As the guard removed the men's handcuffs, a small group of people shuffled into the courtroom. Dara began to recognize some faces: the ambassadors of India, the United Kingdom, the USSR, and, of course, Pierre and Valerie. They all looked over to the men and nodded their heads in greeting and support.

"Jamshed, look who just came in."

Jamshed glanced up from studying his papers—he was their spokesperson, their lawyer, or as close to one as they were going to get.

"*Areh.*" He looked over in disbelief. Then whispered, "Why do you think they're all here?"

"I don't know, but I am not complaining. This is a good thing." Dara patted his brother on the shoulder.

"Yes. It would be nice to have something good happen for a change."

The court was called into session, and everyone took their seats except Dara and the men. The bailiff read the court summary charging the four men with smuggling. All four men took their seats while the prosecutor rose. A tall, gaunt man, his waist, almost indiscernible, gave him the appearance of a flat board. He walked around to the front of his table to address Judge Nasser. The judge held his hand up to the prosecutor and then pointed to Jamshed, signaling him to come over as well.

"Your Honor," the prosecutor said. "I am representing the government of the People's Democratic Republic of Yemen. The PDRY is charging these four men of Bhicajee Cowasjee with smuggling money and goods from 1967 to 1971. The prosecution will call Mohammed Al Haq as our first witness."

"Yes, yes. And you, Jamshed Barucha, will be representing all the men. You both will be able to ask the witness questions, and since you are also representing yourself, Mr. Barucha, you will be allowed to cross-examine as we go."

Jamshed nodded at the judge and then returned to his spot behind the desk. Mohammed Al Haq took his place next to the judge.

Dara shook his head, barely able to look at Al Haq, an employee who went rogue and was now the managing director at his family's business.

"Mr. Al Haq, what is your position at Bhicajee Cowasjee Limited?"

"I am the managing director." He glanced over at Jamshed and Dara, sneering. They both looked away.

"And as managing director, do you have access to all the financials of the company?"

"Yes, I do."

"Mr. Al Haq, as managing director and with the access that you have to the financials, can you say, yes or no, that the brothers were smuggling money and goods outside of Aden?"

"Yes, I can."

Dara shook his head. "Son of a bitch," he said, just quiet enough that only Jamshed could hear. The prosecutor stood down, and Jamshed took his turn questioning Mohammed Al Haq.

"Mr. Al Haq, what proof do you have of this allegation?"

Mohammed Al Haq hesitated, shuffling his worn leather dress shoes on the gritty tiled floor. "I will provide it."

"Can you provide it now?"

"I did not bring the evidence with me. I will produce it."

Jamshed shook his head. The judge called for the next question. The prosecutor ran his hand over his balding head before his turn at recross.

"Bhicajee Cowasjee has branches in Dubai and Djibouti, is that correct, Mr. Al Haq?"

"Yes, but they are hiding them from us."

"That is not true," Jamshed interrupted. "Bhicajee Cowasjee does not have branches anywhere outside of Aden and certainly not in Djibouti! We recently engaged in opportunities in Dubai, but they are unrelated to Bhicajee Cowasjee. The businesses have no connection to each other."

Al Haq slithered in his seat. The prosecutor glared at him, his nostrils flaring. The judge yawned before taking a heavy inhale of his cigarette.

"Bhicajee's has invested in cotton mills in the United Kingdom, and they have shares in multiple accounts that relate to mills in London and Cairo—correct, Mr. Al Haq?" the prosecutor asked.

"Eh, yes," he said, cracking his knuckles and shifting in his seat.

"And you have accounts to show this?"

Al Haq's eyes flitted around the room. "Um... yes, I saw them. In some paperwork."

Jamshed jumped out of his seat, startling Dara. His nostrils flared and his cheeks flushed red. "Your Honor, this is another false allegation. I would like to see some proof of these so-called accounts connected to cotton mills in London. It will be the first time that I will have seen anything like it. Mr. Al Haq, how long have you worked at Bhicajee Cowasjee?"

"I have been there for six years."

"For six years?"

"Yes."

"And what was your position when you were hired?"

"Umm, I was, I was a cashier."

"Mr. Al Haq, isn't it true that you were a part-time salesman in the provisions department and have only been a cashier since the custodianship of 1971? So that means, if my math is correct, that is only one year as a cashier. And currently you are the acting managing director of the firm, yes?"

Al Haq's face turned red, with beads of sweat forming on his forehead. He was a simple man, and it was clear that

Jamshed was rattling him. It was Jamshed's time to strike. But before he could say anything more, the prosecutor interrupted.

"Your Honor, Bhicajee Cowasjee was a discredit to the government of Yemen and was running at a loss. That is why the workers like Mr. Al Haq had to take it over."

"Excuse me, sir," Jamshed interjected, staring at Al Haq. "Can you show us the numbers of how the shop is doing currently compared to how it was operating before the takeover?"

Al Haq's eyes grew wide. Was he supposed to answer this question? He looked at the prosecutor for help. Judge Nasser sucked long and hard on his cigarette; the butt emerged from his mouth soaked in saliva. "Answer the question," he said.

"No, I cannot."

"Why not? If we were running at a loss and were a discredit to the government, surely you must have proof of that. Can you show the court the proof?"

"I-I will have to look at the papers."

"Do you have the papers here today? Or is this also something you will have to go look for?"

"I-I, do not know. I have the papers. I have to look."

The stench of stale cigarettes permeated the courtroom. The judge coughed a long, thick smoker's cough and lit a new cigarette. The room was quiet except for the constant shuffling around of the viewers.

"You call yourself businessmen. Bhicajee's was nothing but a soda factory," Al Haq said with disdain.

"You are absolutely correct," Jamshed said proudly. "My

grandfather started Bhicajee's as a soda factory a hundred years ago. He, my father, my brothers, and I built our business and expanded it from the soda factory to a business serving the entire Adeni community. We are proud of our origin and our success and how we have contributed to the community and economy of Aden."

Beads of sweat dripped down Al Haq's forehead. The prosecutor continued with his disjointed and unclear line of questioning, and it was becoming easier and easier for Jamshed, eloquent and prepared, to knock them off their feet. Dara watched his brother as he exuded a confidence he had never witnessed before.

"Prosecutor, what is the purpose of these questions? Do you have something specific that you want to ask the brothers?" the judge asked.

"Yes, I do." He looked at Jamshed. A shuffle of heads following the prosecutor's gaze could be heard across the room. With Jamshed acting as the brothers' council, the questioning and testimonies moved along somewhat awkwardly. "Did you and your brothers use members of the Indian community and embassy to smuggle property and money out of Aden?"

"No, we did not."

"Yes, you did!" the prosecutor shouted.

"Where is the proof? Must be with all the other proof that you all have forgotten to bring with you today," Jamshed quipped.

"I will show the evidence," Mohammed Al Haq said.

Chapter 15

"Please do!" Jamshed replied curtly.

"The bank gave you and your brothers a time limit to honor an overdraft, but you and your brothers did not comply with the time limit, and that is why it was absolutely necessary for the takeover of the business," said Al Haq. He was completely rattled, sweat now pouring down his face. His hands fidgeted.

Dara watched as the prosecutor's face distorted. He looked concerned, worried. Perhaps this was not going as they had planned. Dara smiled.

"Mr. Al Haq, I think you are confusing the timeline," Jamshed said. "You see, there was no overdraft before the takeover. The bank didn't authorize one because there was no need for one. After the takeover, you and your men ran our company so far into the ground that *you* requested the overdraft, and that is when the timeline for paying back the overdraft was given. Are you aware of that? That the overdraft was an issue when our company was under custodianship? The overdraft amounted to £40,000, and I took it upon myself to honor this debt to the bank after the company was returned to us. We had worked out a payment schedule with the bank that was just going into effect when we were detained."

Mohammed Al Haq looked down at the floor. He was struggling to keep the facts and timelines straight in his mind. He was unraveling.

"Furthermore, Mr. Al Haq, the chairman of the custodianship committee investigated this matter in 1971 and found that our books were clean, which is why they handed the company back to us. There was no proof of any smuggling then, and there is no evidence now because it never happened."

"You made a private arrangement with the chairman at the prime minister's office," Al Haq said in desperation.

"How is that possible? The chairman is a representative of your government," Jamshed retorted.

Judge Nasser was beginning to get annoyed. "Mr. Prosecutor, control your witness. Do you have anything that you can prove? Or a real question you can ask?"

"Yes, Your Honor." The prosecutor tried to pull himself together and gave Al Haq the eye. "Mr. Al Haq, please tell the court about how these men hid what was happening in the accounts."

Mohammed Al Haq rearranged himself in his seat before speaking. "They had their own man manage the accounts, and then they lied about them."

Jamshed jumped out of his seat again. "That is simply not true!" he yelled. "We hired a reputable chartered accountant who works for an accounting firm approved by the government and the bank."

Jamshed had the prosecutor and Al Haq cornered. The judge looked even more irritated.

"Mr. Prosecutor, do you have any other witnesses?"

"No, Your Honor."

"Then we will adjourn until May 6, at which time I want to see the evidence for all these allegations."

"Yes, Your Honor."

Chapter 15

"Take these men back to Mansoura."

The men were escorted out of the courtroom through a back door. Darius and Uncle Burjor were all smiles, patting Jamshed and Dara on their backs.

The three ambassadors rose from their seats and walked over to the judge. Silloo could not hear what they were saying but remained seated until they were finished. Ambassador Das Gupta from the Indian embassy came over and greeted her and the others in a deep *namaste*.

"Mrs. Barucha, I, along with the honorable British ambassador and ambassador from the USSR, have made statements to the court regarding the innocence of your husband, his brother, uncle, and employee." His head bobbed solemnly from side to side. "I'm hopeful that the judge will take our opinions into consideration."

Silloo returned his *namaste* with one of her own. Valerie came from behind and slipped her arm into Silloo's. "Come, *mon ami,* you need to eat something, or soon you will disappear."

✤ ✤ ✤

On the van ride to Mansoura, Uncle Burjor and Darius were in great spirits, recounting Jamshed's victorious blows in the courtroom, but Dara and Jamshed sat quietly.

"*Areh*, Dara, Jamshed, why are you both so quiet? That was a good show, *yar*." Darius jabbed at them.

Dara smiled. "My friend, my brother did an excellent job

cross-examining that rat, but he knows as much as I do that there is no guarantee."

"What do you mean?"

"Even if we prove our innocence in court, it doesn't mean that they will release us or exonerate us of any of these charges."

"It's too early to get optimistic," Jamshed said.

Darius closed his eyes and leaned his head back. "We've been in this situation since November. It has been one hundred and twenty-two days since I've been with my family, and all for what, because I was in your office at the wrong time? This is crazy, I want to go home. I want to get out of this hell."

"Do not despair, Darius. We will continue to conduct ourselves with dignity and respect. Our Creator has not forsaken us, and I'm sure that He will, in His own time and in His own way, lead us through."

They continued the ride in silence, each lost in his own thoughts, fears, and doubts, but hopeful that Jamshed's victory in court would be the start of something good.

16

"What hurts you, blesses you. Darkness is your candle."

—Rumi

April 16, 1972

"Ah, Vijay, my friend, right on time, how are you?" Krishna Menon leaned back in his chair, elbow on the armrest, his forefinger cradling his chin.

"*Ah va*, Krishna, I'm just fine," Vijay responded between chuckles. "What is the news?" He bobbed his head, flashing his ever-present smile.

"I wanted to tell you that I spoke to Salmin, you know, the president of PDRY." Krishna hung on to the last letter and let it drag out. "He is claiming that he's not familiar with this case, but he promised me that he would look into it." He paused, eyes squinted.

"Well, Krishna, my friend, I received a call from Mr. Chavan today. He has been in contact with Mr. Das Gupta, you know him?"

"Ah yes, of course, the Indian ambassador in Aden, isn't it?"

"Yes, yes, that is absolutely correct. It seems that he is very close to this case and meets with one of the wives quite frequently. He has informed us that just yesterday the men were called to the People's Court on criminal charges. You will find it quite interesting that they weren't allowed to have a lawyer—they were made to represent themselves."

Krishna frowned and pursed his lips. "Oh my, and how did that go? Did he say?"

"Well, actually, Mr. Gupta was very pleased with the outcome. The opposition called one witness—a man who the government had inserted into their business. You know, one of the guys who are causing all the nonsense, you follow?"

"Yes, yes, please continue."

"Well, it seems that the older brother—his name is Jamshed—missed his true calling as a lawyer!" Vijay laughed a deep hearty laugh. His belly shook as he rubbed his bald head. "He was very swift with his questioning and made those government guys very nervous. The judge has pushed the trial to another hearing date next month and has asked them to come up with some *real* evidence."

"That is very promising, and actually this is probably a good time to put more pressure on Salmin. I had made it clear to him that both the British and Indian governments are watching how he is handling this case and that they have all eyes on him. I'm sure he didn't like that at all."

"Do you think he really cares about this, my friend?" Vijay asked.

"I think he's young and wants to be seen as a success. I *do* think that he cares, but not for the same reasons that we would. I also think that if pushed far enough, he'll throw his own guys into jail before claiming he knew anything about this." He paused, thoughtfully. "Vijay, what is it that the government wants from them exactly?"

"You see, almost one year before this, the government took the company under custodianship."

"Custodianship? Meaning what exactly?"

"Meaning that the government brought in custodians— these young guys with no education—to watch over the business."

"Ahh, their way of getting ready for nationalization?"

"Yes, yes, but these guys who took it over were merely the coolies and drivers and such at the company, who were then promoted to positions like managing director overnight. It was ludicrous. They didn't have even one clue about how to run a company." Vijay explained the events that followed, leading to the brothers being accused of smuggling.

"Are they guilty of smuggling?"

"No, but they did fill a *dhow* and send the goods to Dubai for a new shop that they opened there."

"Well, that sounds a little suspicious."

"*Areh*, no, no, but from everything that Mr. Gupta sent us, it was all legal. No funny business at all, and we have the paperwork to prove that the business in Aden sold the goods to the business in Dubai. All legitimately conducted business."

"Hmm, so what are they holding them on then? What do they want from these men?"

"They are of the belief that the family has a lot of assets

outside of Yemen, and they want the money. So, they keep asking for large sums to release them, but then they change the number very readily. Also, Mr. Gupta told Mr. Chavan that they looted their homes. They took personal belongings, claiming they belonged to the company, which now belongs to the government. Even photos. *Areh*, what do they need somebody's family photos for?" Vijay's smile disappeared momentarily.

"They have no proof of any wrongdoing then?"

"Correct. They keep trying to find something, but it seems there is nothing to find. There is also the argument that the government is holding the family responsible for the overdraft."

"Wait, wait, the overdraft that these other guys piled up from mismanaging the business?"

"Yes, yes. This family seems to be very well respected. The community is really struggling with how to help them. I think they also understand that this could be any one of them. This family was the only big business left, and the government targeted them in the hopes of extracting money. What do you think this government will do, Krishna? You understand the way these men think, no?"

"I wouldn't say that I understand how they think, but I do understand what drives them. They are proud and passionate about their country. They want to show the world that they can survive without the British or any other outsider. They don't want to be embarrassed, and they won't be coerced into doing anything. If we want to get them to do something, it will have to seem that it is their own idea—you understand what I'm saying?

I will speak with Salmin again, and I know just what to say to him. We need to do this quickly, before the court reconvenes."

The president's office was located in Al Ittihad, a new compound constructed between Khormaksar and Sheikh Othman. It was built in the late 1960s in commemoration of the British exit from Aden. Five two-story white stone buildings sat against a backdrop of mountains on one side and an ocean view on the other. The compound, surrounded by a white wall and imposing metal gate, housed each of the government's ministries. The buildings were contemporary for the time. Each one had narrow arches reaching up to the second floor and windows set inside the arches on the first floor, while the second-floor windows housed *mashrabiyas* of wooden latticework and lined with stained glass.

Mohammed Al Haq waited nervously for his meeting with Salmin. Being summoned to this office was either very good or very bad, and he had no idea why he was here or which way this meeting might go. Mohammed was dressed in Western clothes, gray trousers with a collared, short-sleeved white shirt. He scratched at his three-day old stubble, and sweat stains marked the armpits of his shirt. A scrawny clerk ushered Mohammed into Salmin's wing of the building, where his rosewood-walled office overlooked the ocean. Two Yemen Arab Republic flags flanked the window behind the desk. Salmin was on the phone. Mohammed sat waiting.

"Mohammed Al Haq?" Salmin asked, slamming the receiver down on its cradle.

"*Aiwa, Ya-rais.*" Mohammed jumped to his feet and saluted the president.

"Your name is coming to me a lot these days, *ya-rafiq.* Sit, sit."

"I work very hard to make you proud. How can I serve you and my country?" Mohammed was sweating profusely, and Salmin enjoyed how uncomfortable he made his young comrade.

"Mohammed, tell me about the family of Bhicajee Cowasjee."

Mohammed relaxed slightly. This should not be hard, he thought. The president was going to agree with everything that they had done. After all, the orders had come from his office. "Bhicajee Cowasjee? *Aiwa, Ya-rais,* I can tell you anything you want to know. I am the managing director there now." Pride dripped from his mouth like a salivating lion.

"*Yallah,*" he said, giving him the green light.

"Eh, we started the nationalization process of their shop as we were ordered to do. They had one of the largest operations in Aden, *yaani.* We've been trying very hard to get them to pay up the money that they're hiding out of the country, but it hasn't been so easy. They are stubborn. We are still trying to prove that they're hiding money outside of Yemen and that they were smuggling goods out of Aden and to Dubai."

"*Wallahi?* Hiding, you say, and smuggling? You know this for sure?"

"*Ya-rais*, eh, they are a big company with goods coming from Britain and America—very expensive goods—there *has* to be so much money, but they're hiding it! I'm sure, yes, because our orders from your office said so."

"*Yakhi*," Salmin leaned in. "Mohammed, tell me, did you hear this from me?"

"Eh, no, *Ya-rais*, no, but—"

"*La, la, la*, no, no, no. No more of this 'coming from the president's office.'"

"But, *Ya-rais*—"

"No!" He raised his voice. "Have you put women and children here in Aden from this family under house arrest?"

"*Ya-rais*, yes, we were authorized to. There is money, we will find it. We just have to scare them enough that they admit it."

"Did you put women and children under house arrest? In *my* name? *Wallahi!*" Salmin shouted, spit flying out of his mouth with each word.

"Yes. *Ya-rais*. Yes." His eyes were now downcast.

Salmin rose and strode toward Mohammed. "*Yakhi*, do you know what my job is?"

Mohammed held his hands in a tight grip, nodding his head.

"Do you understand that it is my job to save this great country of mine?" He held out his hands as if he were holding a globe within his palms. "My job is to show the entire world that the people of Aden are strong and that we can run a successful government without Britain, that we can provide education and a better economy than when the *Inglise* were here. You understand what my job is, hmm?" Salmin raised the back of his hand and slapped Mohammed hard with the force of his entire body. Mohammed fell off his chair. "You are a humiliation. A disgrace to this country!" Salmin shouted.

He leaned in toward Mohammed and grabbed his shirt collar. "I spoke to the judge who presided over this case yesterday. He told me that you were a fool, that you couldn't answer one question, that the small little Hindi man made you look like a snake. There were high-profile men there— the French, Russian, British and East German ambassadors, in addition to the Indian, British and Russian officials—all watching you make an idiot of yourself. This case has too much publicity, and I can't just get rid of them now. You did this!" He snarled in Mohammed's face. "Without any evidence that they were smuggling, and with all the people of the world watching, what will we do with this case? Huh? What will we do? You weren't told to do this by the president's office, you understand? You have one job before the next hearing: you go and make evidence of these things you say these men did because if you don't bring anything, you'll be the one going to Mansoura, and I'll make sure that you never come out! *Faham?* Now get out." He let go of Mohammed's shirt, pushing him onto the floor.

Mohammed scrabbled to his feet and swiftly left Salmin's office.

17

"To be able to look back on one's life in satisfaction, is to live twice."
—Khalil Gibran

The waves crept up to the shore, inching their way around her as the tide rolled in. The sun, hidden behind one lone cloud in the sky, moved lethargically. The air hung heavy and still in the afternoon heat. Silloo dug her hands into the hot sand, finding her way to cooler spots under the top layer, grabbing fistfuls of light, golden grains. She watched as the sand trickled down from her hands in a steady stream. The frothy waves were warm and pleasant on her bare skin; it was as if they were coaxing her into the ocean. She leaned back on her elbows and closed her eyes, searching for a memory she could escape into. Smiling as the images of her honeymoon in the African plains flickered in her mind.

They had always loved an adventure, she and her husband. They wouldn't hesitate to spend a weekend camping in the desert or on one of the surrounding Adeni islands. Socotra Island was their favorite, with its unique flora and fauna. So when it came time to plan their honeymoon, they both agreed that an African safari was the obvious choice.

They were married in a traditional Parsi wedding at the Merwan Baag in Aden, greeting over a thousand guests, standing for hours on a stage lined with white and red carnations and built in the shape of a boat because of Dara's love for the ocean. Silloo wore a hand-embroidered white chiffon sari and Dara was dressed in his traditional Parsi *dugli* and *pagri*. They were a handsome couple.

Silloo thought back to the moment when she was finally able to sit down and eat, after shaking hundreds of hands and kissing a thousand cheeks. She sat in front of a large banana leaf, and the server, his white uniform stained with *daal* and prawn *patio*, shoveled food onto the leaf before graciously flashing her a toothless smile and an offer of congratulations. She turned to Dara, who had watched the whole scene and instinctively smiled along with her. The first moment they shared together as a married couple was so simple and light and inconsequential, filled with gratitude and so vividly embedded in her mind's eye.

After seven grueling hours on their feet, they went home to their apartment. They had set it up and furnished it prior to the wedding but arrived together for the first time to stay on their wedding night. Dara poured his bride a Martini Rosso and a Johnnie Walker for himself, and they kicked off their shoes and danced to Miriam Makeba. Three weeks later, after working and living life as a married couple, they finally set off for Nairobi.

Silloo and Dara arrived at the newly renovated Nairobi airport. It was unlike anything they had seen before. The building was mostly windows, and light flooded every corner of the inside. It was spectacular. Silloo and Dara had stopped to take pictures with Dara's new 8mm camera. He took a movie of Silloo in her blue dress pointing to the sign that read "Aden 1124 M."

The lonely cloud moved on, and Silloo could feel the sun penetrating her skin, enveloping her in heat. She slid all the way down onto her back and closed her eyes, slipping into the warmth of her memories.

On their way to the hotel, they drove through the streets of Nairobi, packed with people, roadside cafés and restaurants, even a hippopotamus or two crossing the roads. All the intersections had traffic police standing on platforms with small fences around them, somehow maintaining order. They looked as if they were conducting an orchestra.

Dara wasted little time finding a tour company and arranging the next three weeks of their trip. Within hours of arriving in Kenya, they met Kiinju, and a bond quickly formed with their trusted guide. They gave him free rein to plan the whole trip, asking him only to take them to the best places. Kiinju decided on five game reserves: Ngorongoro, Tsavo, Amboseli, Aberdare, and Kruger National Park. Each park was just as spectacular as the others. They saw cheetahs running across the plains, lions basking in the sun, giraffes, hippos, rhinos, and so many other animals that they lost track. They enjoyed mountain views, ocean vistas, and spectacular sights like Victoria Falls. It was on this trip that Dara had shot an arrow into an Amstel can; it had been one of their most treasured souvenirs from their honeymoon. They camped for a few days in each reserve campground, then returned to Nairobi for a couple of nights to hit the restaurants and dance at the hip, modern nightclubs.

The trip was exhilarating, from waking up to learn that they had slept next to a hippo all night, only separated by the canvas of their tent, to sitting up into the early hours of the morning on the veranda of the Treetops Hotel to watch the elephants come to the water hole—a spectacular sight, worth the many hours of waiting. They watched in awe as a family of elephants was led to the water hole by larger males. While the females and babies drank water and washed, the males kept guard, pacing. Each male took his turn to drink and wash, then returned to his shift.

On safari, during the days, Dara was so enthralled with his new camera that on more than one occasion he had to run to the already moving jeep while elephants began to encircle them or annoyed hippos closed in. Kiinju had to keep telling him that when he said it was time to go, it was *really* time to go. Dara would laugh, stick out his tongue, and then roll it up to his top lip, assuring Kiinju that he could outrun a cheetah if he needed to. They would all laugh, reveling in the mystique and excitement of this beautiful country.

Digging her hands deeper into the warm sand, Silloo basked in the joy of those happy days, savoring once more the blissful life she had lived with Dara in the early days of their marriage. She shifted her body on the sand, now wet beneath her, cooling her down.

Kiinju had taken them to meet a Maasai tribe. Accustomed to tourists, the Maasai put on a performance for them. They danced traditional warrior dances, pulling Silloo in to join the women. Dara, his eye behind the lens, recorded every moment of her as she moved in sync with the colorfully dressed tribeswomen. Later he told her how he was in awe of how elegant she looked even when whirling her arms and legs around in the middle of the African plains. She smiled just thinking about it.

On their final days in Africa, on the return from Kruger National Park, Kiinju stopped in his village to introduce them to his new wife. A sweet young girl with a solid education, Amara was the new head teacher at the village elementary school. Dara and Silloo spent the afternoon with her and Kiinju, drinking tea in their home and then walking through the small town where they lived.

Silloo sat up and looked out over the ocean. The dark wooden posts of the shark nets protruded out of the water. The shadowed gullies of the mountains contrasted with the blue-green hues that shimmered on the surface. She cherished her ability to remember their trip in such detail, especially now that all those pictures and hours of movies Dara had meticulously taken were gone.

She wondered if anyone was watching those movies and then hoped that they had just destroyed them. Witnessing the men take them had been violation enough; the thought of someone watching them was so much worse. She wrapped her arms around her knees and cried openly. She was completely alone. She missed her children, her husband, her life. Would this ever end? Would she ever see her children again? Would she ever be able to smile with complete abandon as she had in Nairobi? Or would this time, should it eventually end, follow her wherever she went, forever casting its dark shadow, reminding her that she would never really be safe, ever again, anywhere?

18

"Nothing is more noble, nothing more venerable, than loyalty."
—Cicero

Ahmed, dressed in his traditional *thoob* headdress and *khanjar* around his waist, hurried through the narrow cobblestone streets of the fishing village in Little Aden, on his way to meet Hassan, who had asked to see him today. To get to Little Aden, one had to pass through the area of Al Itthihad, the new headquarters of the NF. He looked out over the sandy shore of the bay to the rocks of Aden proper. The ocean was a spectacular shade of light blue and almost blended into the pale blue of the sky. The only sound was that of his sandals hitting the bottoms of his dry, cracked heels and crunching on the sandy road beneath him.

The café was tucked away in the lower level of a white stone building. The thick chocolate aroma of coffee mixed with hints of cardamom wafted in the air while the low intonations of Fairuz sang through a transistor radio set up in the corner. Local men filled the small room, drinking coffee, chewing *khat,* and smoking *shisha.* Layers of smoke danced toward the ceiling and shimmered in the thin bands of light cascading through the narrow windows.

"*Rafiq, qahwa, law samaht.*" Ahmed held one finger up to the server, ordering his coffee, and made his way over to the table.

"*Hala, hala.*" He placed his hand on Hassan's shoulder. Hassan rose from his chair, and the men greeted each other with the traditional three alternating kisses on each cheek.

"Ahmed, *Akhi*. How is *Sayidati*? Any news on *Sayid*?"

"*Sayidati* is *al'hamdullah*, okay. She's very worried all the time, misses the children, the house is quiet, you know?"

"*Ya-haram*, and *Sayid*?"

"*Ya-aib shom*, it's really a shame. *Sayid*, he is still in Mansoura." Ahmed leaned in and whispered, "I'm not sure what will happen to them if *Sayidati's* people don't get them out soon."

"Ahmed, Mohammed Al Haq came to see me at the beach club, while I was working at the dock. *Ya'ahmar*, the donkey, he wanted me to tell stories about *Sayid*. You know, make up lies."

"No! Really? What did you tell him?"

"He wanted me to confess to him. I told him that the only thing I would confess was the truth. *Sayid* is a man of honor, a loyal man, and as good as any Yemeni. *Wallahi*, I swear on the Qu'ran, in front of Allah, *Allah Azim*."

The server put a cup of coffee in front of Ahmed, and Hassan gestured for another.

"And then?" Ahmed asked.

"And then he shouted and kicked the boat that I was working on, *wallah*, then he left." Hassan took a long, indulgent sip of his coffee. His eyes filled with tears, and he wiped at them with the end of his headdress. "*Akhi, Sayid* is a good man. You know he wanted me to go and work for him at his *dukkan*.

I told him so many times that I was just a simple man, only meant to work outside with the sun and the sand. But, *wallahi*, he wouldn't give up," he said, smiling and shaking his head. "He kept asking me, and I kept saying no. I'm a man of the sea. I understand it, and it understands me. We are like brothers—we know each other's boundaries. When *Sayid* knew I would not leave, he went to the manager at Gold Mohor and told them that I was too good for them; if they did not promote me, he would take me to work for him." His eyes teared again.

"How do you know this?"

"Ah, the boy who works in the kitchen in the club, he heard it all and ran to tell me. The manager did it, and I became head of security for the club. *Yaani*, it is an important job." Hassan brought the tips of his fingers together and waved them in the air. "*Sayid*, he never told me that he did that. He just kept asking me to go work for him, acting like he didn't know."

"*Aiwa, Sayid*, he only wants to help *everyone* he meets."

"*Ya*-Ahmed. What he did helped my family, and me. What he did for me is something you do for family. *Fahim? Wallahi*, he is a good man, a good man."

"*Wallahi*." They sat silently for a few minutes.

"Ahmed, my cousin, he is young, but he knows *Sayid*, and in fact, my uncle and *Sayid's* father knew each other also. My cousin Fuad, he is very clever, not simple like me. He went to college, speaks English. He works for the police now, in the Criminal Investigations Department. I talked to him a while ago about *Sayid* and *Sayidati*. He knew the case and was trying to help. He came to me yesterday and told me to tell you to give a message to *Sayidati*."

"*Akeed*, certainly."

"Tell her that he is working very hard inside of the CID, talking to the prosecutor and judge, and he cannot come see *Sayidati* or call her for a long time because they are watching him very close and he does not want to jeopardize the case. *Fahim?*"

"Yes, yes, I understand."

"Tell *Sayidati* that my cousin will go to Mansoura this week to see *Sayid*. Okay? *Insha'allah*. You know that Sufi, what's his name? Ah, Rumi, the Irani one?"

"*Aiwa.*"

"I'm a devout Muslim. I don't believe in the mystics with all their dreamy discussions, but my son, he likes to read a lot, and he brought this, *iqtabas*, eh, you know, quote to me, one from Rumi. He said, 'When the world pushes you to your knees, you're in the perfect position to pray.' I don't like mystics, but this one, this quote, I like it."

"Yes, this is true. For all of us. Faith is everything."

The men asked for a backgammon board and played a few games together, exchanging fond stories of *Sayid* and *Sayidati* before gathering themselves and making their way to the mosque for evening prayers.

Chapter 18

April 20, 1972

Lieutenant Fuad Hizam was saluted as he entered Mansoura. Most of the guards had worked at the prison for many years, and they all knew the relatively young chief of investigation from the Criminal Investigations Department: a Yemeni prodigy, a boy who had come from nothing and garnered himself an education, a lieutenant in the Aden Police Force, and now a high-ranking chief at the CID. He was well respected, often envied, but always admired. The prison superintendent met him at the main door, and they found a quiet meeting room to talk.

"Lieutenant Hizam, it's always a pleasure to see you. Can I offer you tea?"

"No, no, *shukran*. Thank you. I'm actually here to talk to the brothers, the Barucha brothers."

"Aye, *Allahi*." The superintendent turned and closed the door, walking back toward the lieutenant and speaking in a hushed tone. "Do you have any idea what will happen to them?"

"I'm responsible for the investigation, you know. And I need to ask them some questions."

"Fuad, I know you well. I'm holding four men in this prison who have no charges against them. How long am I supposed to do this? *Akhi*, do you have any idea how long this will continue?" He was genuinely concerned.

"That is up to the court and the president." Fuad trusted no one, not even people whom he should have been able to trust. If anyone learned that his education, which had led to his ultimate success, had been provided by the father of these brothers, he would get pulled off this case and then they would likely rot in Mansoura, if they weren't executed first. He couldn't risk it. He was fully committed to helping them.

"Can't you tell me anything?"

"Right now, no, I can't, and I have a lot to do in the next few weeks before the hearing. I need to speak to them, so can you bring them, please?"

The superintendent, outranked by Fuad, understood that the conversation was over and that the request was not optional. He left the room to get the men.

Dara and Jamshed were shown into the meeting room. The brothers were cautious, though they had met with the lieutenant before at the police station, and he seemed like a good man.

"It is a pleasure to meet you both again," Hizam said. "Mr. Dara, I have met your wife several times now, and she has kept me up to date on some of the details. It seems the president's office has been very particular about who can visit you."

"It's good to meet you again, Lieutenant. My wife did tell me the interesting story that you shared with her—your father knew our father, is that correct? You didn't mention that the last time we met."

"Yes, yes, it is. My father, God rest his soul, spoke very highly of your family." He smiled at the memory of his father. "Please have a seat. As you may know, I'm in charge of your investigation, and I've spent a significant time at Bhicajee

Cowasjee looking over the books, and I need to ask you some questions."

"Absolutely, but that would be my brother's department."

"Ah yes, Mr. Jamshed. I was interested to see how well your company was doing, and I couldn't understand why you would need this big overdraft. Can you explain what happened and why you needed it?"

"Yes, of course. You see, the bank draft was not our doing. Those chaps in charge of the custodianship, they ran the shop into the ground. You know that they came overnight and seized the premises?"

"Yes, that's right. But the dates in the ledger at Bhicajee Cowasjee show that the overdraft was taken before the custodianship." Hizam lingered on the last word.

"That is simply not true. Can I see what you are referring to?"

The inspector handed over the accounting ledgers from the store, and Jamshed scrutinized them. Dara watched the lieutenant, trying to gauge him. He seemed genuine but Dara wasn't sure if this was all just another ploy to try to put him and Jamshed away once and for all.

"What is this? This is not right," Jamshed said quizzically. "Lieutenant, you need to go to the bank and talk to the bank manager. He will show you the original statements. These are not real." He stared up at the lieutenant. "I believe that they falsified documents. Our financials were quite robust before the custodianship, before those thugs tried to ruin my father's business. They did not understand how to extend credit or what a letter of credit even was, for that matter. They kept borrowing from the bank until the bank put an end to it. That was when the prime minister's office called us to come back and asked us to take control of the company again. I just do not understand why they would do this."

"Hmm, I will go and see the bank manager, that would explain a lot of this," Hizam said.

"He will have copies of everything, I am sure," Jamshed said confidently.

"Well, then I will get them from the bank itself. Are you okay with me using what you're telling me today as an official statement?" the lieutenant asked.

"Yes, absolutely."

"Thank you. How about the details of assets and liabilities of the company? If the overdraft was, in fact, after custodianship, what did the financials look like before? As far as you know."

Jamshed broke down all the numbers as he knew them, perfectly ingrained in his mind. He detailed how the company was operating prior to custodianship and what the numbers were after. Dara watched him in amazement as he recited every number without hesitation, pulling them from his memory as though reading from a piece of paper.

"Lieutenant Hizam, under the present circumstances, I don't see any reason why we should be burdened with this additional liability, of which we've had no control. They keep asking us to pay for an overdraft that we didn't request, for a company that they have taken control over. They have stripped us of everything that our father and his father worked so hard to build. They have demeaned and diminished our very existence, terrorizing and vandalizing our lives. What more do they want from us? This is preposterous!"

"I understand this has been a very difficult time for you and your family. This meeting has been very helpful. I could not understand what it was that I was missing, but now it all seems a lot clearer. I promise you that I will pull together all the facts and present them at the next hearing. I'll also bring this to the attention of the minister of interior. I'm not sure who truly knows what has been happening at this level. We are a country that has had its most vital organs torn from it. We are bleeding and in pain, but we don't always know the true cause of the injury. We are trying to heal, but it takes time. Allow me to show you that this country is still inherently good and just. I'll do everything I can to help you."

Dara took the lieutenant's hand and pulled him close, embracing him with his other arm.

"Thank you, *Akhi*. My brother."

Hizam straightened himself and smiled.

"See you on May 6th."

19

"And forget not that the Earth delights to feel your bare feet
and the winds long to play with your hair."
—Khalil Gibran

May 6, 1972

The air was sticky and humid, but Silloo still chose to sit
out on her balcony and drink her morning cup of tea. What
had once been a daily ritual was now only possible with a lot
of luck. Fresh herbs had become scarce in the city, and as much
as Silloo tried to grow her own, she couldn't focus enough to
make it happen.

She sat on a white plastic outdoor chair and inhaled the sweet
aromas of mint and lemongrass. Beyond the dancing forms of
steam above her cup lay the ocean. The port was quiet, no cruise
liners or big tankers, no sounds of ship horns. She found herself
suddenly missing that sound and the sight of the ships. She had
never realized, until now, what they represented: hope, progress,
prosperity. The call of a ship horn would mean that the streets
would soon flood with visitors, the city restaurants and shops
would come alive, and the buzz of happiness would fill the air.
It was hope that she was holding on to.

Today was the day. Today they would reveal their future

and whether it would be one of freedom. If not, and the men were found guilty, they could face sentences from ten years in prison to execution. Silloo closed her eyes tight, desperately attempting to shed the thought. It had been six long months of this uncertainty and two agonizing months of being a mother without her children. She wasn't sure how she would move forward if Dara wasn't released today. She tried to keep her focus on watching the waves bounce and bob on the ocean, and on the mountains, solid and unwavering. The call to prayer sounded and she let the tension in her shoulders drop. She tried desperately to feel hopeful.

The shrill ring of the phone interrupted her, and she quickly went to get it.

"Hello?"

"Mrs. Barucha, good morning. Arthur Kellas here." The British ambassador's voice was immediately calming.

"Mr. Ambassador, good morning."

"It's a big day today, how are you feeling?"

"I was just thinking about that. Not sure what to think about it really."

"Well, Mrs. Barucha, I would be remiss if I did not point out all possibilities to you, hence my call."

"Arthur, thank you, but I think that I am aware of what is at stake today."

"Silloo, do you understand the scenarios, though? Do you understand that if found guilty"—he paused briefly—"they will either be sentenced to ten years at the very least in Mansoura, or they…well, they will receive the death penalty." They sat in silence for a long moment.

"Yes, I do understand that, but I cannot think about that right now. I need to focus on the other possibility. The possibility that they will be released, that all my prayers will be answered, that my children will get their father back, and I will get my husband. That someday I will be able to reassemble my family somewhere, as far away from Aden as possible, and forget this nightmare. So, Mr. Ambassador, with the utmost respect, I think I will focus on that possibility for now, at least until I have no other choice."

"I understand. I will be at the hearing today and will be available afterwards should you need me."

"Thank you, I appreciate your support. I will see you there." Silloo returned to her balcony and in a daze watched the waves bouncing and bobbing on the ocean. She numbly gazed, feeling no emotion, just emptiness.

Two and a half hours later, Silloo and Mr. Mardden pulled up to the courthouse. She was dressed in a purple sari with white embroidered flowers, Dara's favorite sari of hers. Her long hair was twisted up into a bun. Mr. Das Gupta waved emphatically from the entryway when he spotted them. He ran toward the car, barely waiting for it to stop before opening Silloo's door.

"Mr. Gupta, are you okay? What is happening?"

"Oh my, oh my, Mrs. Barucha, I have great news."

"Oh my goodness, Mr. Gupta. Please don't get run over or you won't be able to share your good news!" She hurried to get out of the car. Mr. Maarden saluted as he drove off to park the car.

Mr. Gupta broke into a fit of laughter. "Yes, yes, of course."

She stood in front of Mr. Gupta about four inches taller, her black purse hanging off her arm. "Now, Mr. Gupta, what is this very exciting news that has you running in front of cars?" She couldn't remember the last time she had seen someone bursting with such enthusiasm. What a heartwarming sight it was.

"Mrs. Barucha," he said quietly. "I think we have the bail money!"

"What? How?"

"The Indian community here in Aden came together, and they are offering the combination of their properties to the government. The value is being determined as we speak."

Silloo was stunned. "But why would they do that? Has anyone talked to the judge yet? Why would they offer their properties?"

Mr. Gupta smiled. "Madam, the properties will most likely need to be handed over at some point anyway. And, yes, my associate is inside negotiating with Judge Nasser now. I'm hoping we will know if it's acceptable before they call us into the court."

Silloo was overcome with a wave of emotion, she could feel hope coursing through her veins, her insides on fire. Outwardly she mustered a smile for Mr. Gupta.

"One other thing," he continued, "the ambassadors of Britain, East Germany, and France have put pressure on the government to make sure that the bail must include all four men. They have agreed just this morning!" His smile grew longer. "Come, come, let us go inside. I want to make sure that we don't miss anything, hmm?" He placed his hand on her elbow as he guided her up the stairs. She was grateful, for she suddenly felt as if her knees might give way.

Inside, the stench of stale cigarettes followed them through the hallways and into the courtroom. Light poured in from the windows, and Silloo could see the clear blue sky and the tips of the mountaintops from where she sat between Mamma and Valerie. Arthur Kellas walked in with the Russian and French ambassadors, who all walked over and greeted Silloo.

"Mrs. Barucha," said Ambassador Kellas, "how are you feeling?"

"I am still focusing on the possibilities, Ambassador." Silloo smiled. As she waited, she continued to fiddle with her sari. She imagined leaving the courthouse with Dara that day. Could that really happen? Could this be it—could their nightmare be over? She took several deep breaths, waiting for what seemed like an eternity before the judge entered. Dara and Jamshed were led in after. The public prosecutor came in from the back of the room, followed by Lieutenant Fuad Hizam. She looked at him and greeted him with a nod of her head, which he reciprocated in kind. A hush settled over the room, and the court was called into session. The prosecutor read a summary of the charges and called Lieutenant Hizam to the stand.

Chapter 19

"Lieutenant Hizam, can you please state for the court your role regarding this investigation."

"Yes, my name is Lieutenant Fuad Hizam. I am the chief of investigation for the Criminal Investigations Department here in Aden. I am the lead investigator of this case."

Silloo smiled. The young lieutenant had changed the course for them.

"Lieutenant, can you tell the court what you've done as part of your investigation?"

"Yes, I've spent a lot of time at the office of Bhicajee Cowasjee, and I went through all the financial statements and asset and liability statements. I also interviewed staff members, the brothers themselves, and other key community members."

"Lieutenant, is there or is there not a discrepancy in the statements? Yes or no, please."

"Ahh, well…?"

"Yes or no, please."

"Yes, there is."

"So, Bhicajee Cowasjee has a large outstanding amount of money in the form of a bank overdraft that is owed. Yes or no?"

"Yes."

"Thank you, no more questions." The prosecutor turned away triumphantly.

Jamshed walked around the table toward the lieutenant. "Lieutenant Hizam, from the records that you investigated, were you able to determine the timing of this overdraft?"

"Yes."

"And could you tell the court when the overdraft was, in fact, implemented?"

"Yes, it was in October of 1970."

"Lieutenant, can you tell the court who was running Bhicajee Cowasjee at that time?"

"Yes, it was under custodianship, so officially it was under control of the prime minister's office." He stared blankly at the prosecutor.

The prosecutor jumped to his feet. "Objection, Your Honor! It is only his word against that of the prime minister's office. The ledgers at Bhicajee Cowasjee show that the timing of the overdraft was before custodianship—it is the reason they were put under custodianship!"

The judge glared at the prosecutor and turned to the lieutenant. "I hope you have some proof of this accusation."

"Your Honor," the lieutenant said, "I verified this information with the bank manager at Chartered Bank, and what the prosecutor is saying is just not true."

The prosecutor laughed. "This is just what you say. Where is the proof?"

"Lieutenant, please don't waste the court's time. Can you prove this?" Judge Nasser asked.

"Well, yes, of course I can. I asked Mr. Humphreys of Chartered Bank to come today and bring the official bank statements of Bhicajee Cowasjee that show the dates of each transaction that led to the overdraft."

The prosecutor's smile disappeared. "You did what?"

Chapter 19

"I asked him to come today and present the statements of the overdraft to the court. The only way to actually prove the timing is with the actual bank statements, which were removed from Bhicajee Cowasjee. The ledgers were adjusted, and the originals were also removed from the office, so I went to the bank manager and requested the original statements. The bank manager is just there." The lieutenant pointed to the back of the room.

Chatter filled the air as all heads turned and looked around the room, finding the lean English man with an imperial mustache, Mr. Humphreys. He was dressed in a three-piece suit, his pocket-watch chain perfectly positioned in his vest and a folder tucked neatly under his arm. Too tall for the chair he sat in, he leaned to one side of it, his long legs crossed.

"Mr. Humphreys, do you have papers that you want to submit to the court?" the judge asked.

Mr. Humphreys rose from his seat. He was even taller than he had looked sitting down. He loomed over everyone from his perch at six foot five and slowly meandered his way to the front of the courtroom.

"Your Honor, I would be delighted to submit my papers to the court."

After looking over the documents for several minutes, the judge called the prosecutor up. They engaged in a hushed, heated discussion, which eventually ended with Judge Nasser waving an agitated hand for him to go back to his corner of the court. Dara and Jamshed watched in anticipation. There was no way of knowing what might happen, which way this would go. The reality was that the judge could interpret the evidence in any way he chose. That he had the facts in front of him really didn't mean anything. It was all the other factors, like the motivation of the president's office in particular, that could and would weigh in and ultimately push him to make a decision—in their favor or not.

Mr. Humphreys stood placidly with his hands clasped behind his back. His navy pinstriped suit stood out against the dullness of the courtroom.

The judge turned to the tense crowd. "I will accept this evidence for the case. I might have some more questions for you, Mr. Humphreys. Take a seat next to Lieutenant Hizam." The judge turned to the court clerk. "Please make a note that this evidence provided by the bank manager, Mr. Humphreys, clears the issue of the bank draft. Let the record show it was incurred by the men representing the prime minister's office. Mr. Prosecutor, please continue."

The prosecutor was rattled. He was representing the president's office, which should have made this very clear-cut, but it was far from easy, and his case was falling apart. There had been too many men involved in this case, too many inexperienced men.

"Lieutenant, this evidence and witness whom you called may address the issue of the bank draft, but there is a much more serious charge for smuggling. That is the bigger charge and the one that we, the president's office, are more concerned with." He attempted to change his focus.

"There is no evidence that any smuggling occurred," Lieutenant Hizam interrupted.

"That man over there," the prosecutor said, pointing to Dara, "took a *dhow* and filled it with goods from the shop here and smuggled it into Dubai. Can you prove that he did not do that?" he yelled in the lieutenant's face.

"Yes, I can. He did rent a *dhow*, and he did fill it with goods from his store."

"You see? What did I tell you?"

"*But* he filed a petition to move the merchandise from Aden to Dubai with the Ministry of Interior. I have a copy here."

Lieutenant Hizam handed a sheet of paper to the judge, who rubbed his forehead while looking it over.

"Mr. Humphreys, did you see any of these transactions on the business account?" the judge asked.

"Your Honor, I have included in the folder that I gave to you the remittance of payment through the bank in Dubai when the goods were received. If you look under the bank statements, you will see it there. Every item shipped was received and accounted for, and all appropriate fees were paid. There is nothing missing. On the request of the lieutenant, I went back and cross-referenced every line item to be sure that I wasn't missing anything."

"And did you find anything at all suspicious?" the judge asked.

"No, sir, nothing at all." Mr. Humphreys sat back in his seat, his pale skin tinted red at his cheeks and tip of his nose.

"Who are you?" the prosecutor snarled at the lieutenant. "They must have you in their pocket!"

The judge's eyes narrowed. "Mr. Prosecutor, may I remind you that you are in my courtroom. Please ask a legitimate question or sit down," he ordered.

Lieutenant Hizam spoke up. "Your Honor, I would like to answer the prosecutor's question. You see, sir, *I am* Lieutenant Fuad Hizam. My father delivered milk for a living. I was very lucky that my father, even though an illiterate man, realized that if I was to have a real future, more than delivering milk, I would need an education. He worked hard to give me that gift, and after successfully completing my secondary education at the finest international schools in Aden, I was accepted into the police academy here in this city. I worked hard and worked my way through the police department to become a lieutenant. I was recently promoted to chief of investigation at CID. I take my job very seriously, sir, and I will conduct my investigations with the sole intention of uncovering the truth. I will condemn a guilty man, but I *will not* punish an innocent one. *That* is who I am."

"You're a liar. You made these documents," the prosecutor snarled.

"Why would I make documents? How could I manufacture bank statements? If they're guilty and you have proof, then why don't you just execute them? Execute them now!" Hizam shouted.

Silloo gasped. Why would he say that? Dara and Jamshed stared at the lieutenant. What was he doing?

"There is absolutely no proof anywhere that anything they did was illegal or wrong. I have looked at everything. They followed every process. There is no wrongdoing, yet you have held them for six months, desperately looking for proof of wrongdoing that doesn't exist. If you're determined to just get rid of them, then do it—get rid of them—but stop trying to make them guilty of something."

"That's enough!" The judge, large and unwieldy, smacked his gavel. "We will break for fifteen minutes." He stood up and motioned the prosecutor into his chambers.

Silloo stood, though her legs felt wobbly. She rushed to talk to Dara and Jamshed.

"Dara, what will happen? Why did he say those things? Why would he put such crazy ideas into the prosecutor's head?"

Dara threw his hands in the air. "I really don't know, my love. We just have to wait and see what the judge comes back with. If it's my time, then it's my time." He looked at her defeatedly.

"What? Dara, don't be so stupid!" Silloo's heart was pounding in her chest. She wanted to scream, and her husband's complacency in this moment made her angry. A hundred different thoughts ran through her head, but the most haunting was the prospect of her husband being shot and leaving her as a widow with three young children in tow.

"Mrs. Barucha." Silloo turned toward the voice. Arthur Kellas and Valerie were by her side. "Let's get some water and then take our seats again. Come, please. Mrs. Barucha, come with me." Ambassador Kellas took Silloo by the arm as she stared blankly at her husband. "He is as shocked as you are, madam." He leaned in and spoke softly. "This was never going to be easy. We need to trust the young lieutenant. He is a terribly good chap. I do believe that this is all part of his plan. Let's trust him, hmm? What was it that you said earlier today? Ah, yes, that you were going to focus on the positive possibilities until that was no longer an option."

"Focus on the possibilities." Silloo took a deep breath and composed herself. "Yes… okay."

Judge Nasser returned to the courtroom without the prosecutor and clambered into his seat. The buzz in the room settled to pin-drop silence. Valerie took Silloo's trembling hand in hers. The judge looked over some papers and made some notes. After what seemed like an eternity, he asked the four men to rise.

"Mr. Jamshed Barucha, Mr. Dara Barucha, Mr. Burjor Barucha, Mr. Darius Master, on behalf of the government of Aden, and in accordance with the Adeni judicial system, I hereby address the charge of smuggling under Criminal Law 11, sections 16 and 24."

Silloo felt heat rise to her cheeks as tears filled her eyes. She clasped Valerie's hand tighter. Dara and Jamshed stood side by side. The end was in sight. The moment had arrived.

Silloo looked at the four men. The culmination of stress and fear of the past six months sent chills through her body. She settled her eyes on her husband. Dara had his hands clasped behind his back. Would she ever hold those hands again? Feel their warmth on her? The pain was overwhelming. She shifted her gaze to Jamshed and pictured Nazneen and their three beautiful children. This was the moment that would determine if he would ever hold them again. A chill pulsated through her body. To Dara's left were Darius and Uncle Burjor. They had been in the wrong place at the wrong time. She watched as her husband looked over at them and she knew instantly what he was thinking and what he wanted most in that moment: their freedom. She knew that he felt responsible for their misfortune. And it was just like Dara, in his bleakest moment, to be thinking of anyone other than himself.

The judge continued, "In accordance with the investigation conducted by the Criminal Investigations Department, the Aden Police Department, and on written instructions from the president's office, this case is being withdrawn from the People's Court as a criminal case and will be transferred to the Ministry of Interior, who will then transfer this case to civil court, where they will address any issues of the business and financials of the business. I hereby dismiss the charge of smuggling under Criminal Law 11, sections 16 and 24."

A roar went up through the courtroom. Silloo burst into tears. Dara and Jamshed turned to each other in disbelief and embraced.

The judge hit his gavel on the sound block. "Order, order. In addition, the Indian community has appointed a spokesperson, whom I met with this morning. They are willing to put up bail for the release of all four men, now set at £50,000. The bail transfer will happen tomorrow morning, *Insha'allah*, and then the men will be released from Mansoura." The judge hit his gavel one more time and then rose, immediately disappearing into his chambers.

Silloo ran to her husband and locked him in a quick embrace before they were pulled apart, again. He would spend one last night in Mansoura, and then they would finally be together.

20

"Do not judge us, you who boast your purity.
No one will indict you for the faults of others.
What is it to you whether I am virtuous or a sinner?
Busy yourself with yourself!"
—Hafez

May 7, 1972

Krishna Menon picked up the telephone receiver. "President Rubaya Ali, nice to hear your voice. How are you?"

"Mr. Menon, *al'hamdullah*, I'm good. And you?"

"Everything is going well, as we say. I hope you're calling with good news?"

"Mr. Menon, you know I'm very grateful to your country. India's active support of my country's independence, well…it means a lot to me."

"Of course, Salmin. No one can understand the shackles of colonialism more than an Indian…except perhaps a Yemeni. But please, call me Krishna."

"Yes, certainly. Well, I want to inform you personally that the case you asked me to look into has now been dismissed. There was no evidence of wrongdoing by those men, and I have found that men working *in my name* have done things *in my name* that I don't agree with. They have been dealt with appropriately, I assure you. We are a young country—my brothers, fathers, and grandfathers, none of us have lived in a Yemen that is truly ours. We are learning, but I care very deeply about my country. Ultimately, I want this government to be fair and to provide equal opportunities for everyone, not just the more fortunate."

"Some can argue that that is all anyone wants. Except the more fortunate, of course." Krishna smiled to himself.

"Mr. Menon, Krishna, I want to reiterate to you that the men who acted in my name, they are not going unpunished. I'm embarrassed that this happened this way, and I won't tolerate it. I'm grateful that you came to me. I do want to be taken seriously on the world stage. Men like you are good to help men like me. I want to do the right things, and I will, but I have a whole population that I need to educate. And that takes time."

"Indeed. One step at a time, my friend. They are lucky to have you as their leader." Krishna meant what he said. He knew that Salmin's intentions were earnest and all that he really wanted was what was best for his country. His job was not an easy one.

"*Mashallah*, thank you. You understand that I also need to be taken seriously here. The case has been dismissed, and I had it moved to civil court. They will drag it out and then dismiss it there also, but that might take a little time. It has to be that way. You know I have to be very conscious of the perception."

"Yes, of course I understand. Thank you for addressing this situation. It gives me a lot of confidence that you will find your way to the path of your choice and your country will find its way."

"Of course, of course. Thank you. I will speak with you again soon."

Krishna Menon put the receiver down and immediately called out to his assistant, "Get Shapur Rao on the line, please."

Shapur picked up the phone to hear Krishna's shrill laugh. "Shapur, Krishna Menon here. How are you?"

"Mr. Menon, I'm well, thank you. How about you?"

"Ah, I'm doing very well indeed! Now you and our friend Vijay need to bring me some of the best old Delhi *mithai*, please. The Barucha brothers were released, my friend!" He laughed loudly.

"Krishna, that is just the best news!" Shapur roared. "Thank you so much. I won't only have Vijay bring you *mithai*, but I'll send you the best Alphonso mangoes from Bombay!"

May 8, 1972

Light filtered in through the curtains of the balcony windows, speckling the walls and furniture with warm yellow kisses. Dust particles jammed into the streaks of light. Silloo lay on her side, her arms curled under her head, watching her husband's chest rise with each inhale and fall with each exhale, accompanied by a symphony of snores. The past few days had felt like a dream, and she caught herself on more than one occasion pinching her arm just to be sure that Dara was really with her.

Dara began to stir. The light in the room enveloped him in a sunny cocoon. He turned to his wife, who was lying beside him, smiling. He leaned over and took her in his arms. They made love slowly and deliberately, as if time were standing still. Afterwards they lay together in silence for hours, holding each other, each one lost in their own thoughts. In that moment, they held on to the promise of a future—something that they now realized they had taken for granted and had come so close to losing.

"Dara." Silloo finally broke the silence.

"Yes, my love."

"I just wanted to hear your voice. I still can't believe that you are here with me."

"I know, me either." He looked down at her and smiled. "Honestly, I didn't believe that it was really going to happen until I was in the embassy car on the way here."

"That was so nice of Ambassador Kellas to arrange a car for you all."

"It really was."

"What happens now? Did they say when Jamshed will get his apartment back?"

"No, he might not get it back. There is no logic to any of this and I feel that between the president's office and the *lugna* men there is no real direction. I think, for now, it's fine for Jamshed. Mamma will love having him with her, I am sure."

"Oh yes, I am sure she will. Hufrish said that she is going to book tickets and that they are going back to Bombay as soon as possible. I don't blame her."

"I think Uncle Burjor will do the same. There is nothing stopping them from leaving, so they should go as soon as possible," Dara said.

Silloo lay quietly by her husband's side. "When do you think you will be able to leave?" she asked, wishing she hadn't.

"I don't know. They are taking the case to civil court. Who knows how long that will go on for. I can't leave until they give me my passport back."

"So, what happens now? Where will we go? What will we do?"

"Well, I think you should leave as soon as possible and go to the children. Ana is much too young to be away from you this long. This whole nightmare has been terrible for them."

"Yes, I agree, but what about you? What if those men come after you?"

"That won't happen. All the *lugna* men—Ahmed Kazim, Mohammed Al Haq, Ali Nagi, and all their cronies—have been rounded up and sent off to Mansoura. They will probably never see the outside world again."

"And after I leave, when will *I* see you again? Where will we all go?"

"I don't know yet. Silloo, I still need to close things up here. Zarir has set up the business in Dubai. I suppose we can go there."

"No, Dara. I'm not sure staying in this part of the world is the right thing." A lump formed in her throat and tears sprang to her eyes. Silloo's emotions surprised even her. "What if the same thing happens in Dubai? What is the difference between Aden and Dubai?"

"There is a big difference, and almost everyone who has left here has gone there. I can't just leave my family business, Silloo. This is my father's legacy."

"What about our life?"

"What about my brother? We struggled through this together. How can I abandon him?" His voice cracked as he clutched his lower back with his hand and rubbed it. All he wanted to do was make Silloo happy, but he could not walk out on Jamshed.

"And what about me? Did I not struggle through this also? What if they had killed you? And me? We have three children. We have been given a second chance, a second chance at our family. A second chance at a life. I want to go far away from here and try desperately to forget all of this."

Dara rolled onto his stomach and looked into her eyes, pushing her hair behind her ear. "My love, I did not choose this. What is it that you want me to do?"

"I think we should go and live in London, close to my mum. She says that there are many houses for sale in her area. We could invest in real estate. We could try something new."

"Silloo, I don't know anything about real estate, let alone in London. My life has always been here, working for my family business. This is what I know, what I love. This is not over yet. We still have work to do here. Let me talk to my brothers. I can't...I can't just abandon them. I need some time to think through all of this. I never imagined my life anywhere other than Aden. I don't know what is next, I really don't."

Tired and unsettled, Silloo unwrapped herself from her husband and left the room to make some tea. Dara lay in bed and closed his eyes. His back cramped in a deep, agonizing spasm, which had not stopped since news of their release. He let out a gasp of pain when she left.

Silloo returned with two cups of tea, handed one to him, and perched herself on the side of the bed.

"I think I should leave as soon as possible then. I do need to go to the children. I miss them and really don't want to be away from them a minute longer than I have to. Then I can go to London with Mum. The boys need to be in school, and Mummy is going to enroll them. She said there is one across the street from her house. We don't need to decide our future right now, but I want you to think about where we would be safest. This nightmare has torn our family apart. It could have been irreparable. I don't know how we all survived." She quieted. "We have been very lucky."

"I know. I promise you I'll think about it, and yes, you should leave in the next few days. You've stayed long enough, Silloo. And the reason we came out of this alive isn't because of luck, my *jan*, it's because of *you*. You kept the pressure on here in Aden, you never gave up."

She smiled at him, grateful for this acknowledgment. He slid over to her, setting his cup and then hers on the bedside table, and then pulled her to his chest. "It's all going to be okay."

May 16, 1972

Dara poured himself a scotch and sat on the sofa in their bare living room. Valerie had brought over a box of some of the things that Silloo had handed to her over the balcony: three albums and the Amstel can with the arrow that he had shot into it on their honeymoon, among a few other smaller items, all personal belongings that in one quick moment his wife had deemed important enough to save. All that was left of a very full life. It angered him that anyone could take their possessions away, strip them of their precious memories, of their idyllic life.

Reaching into the box, he pulled out a photo album with a white plastic-coil binding. The cover was a deep, rich blue, thick and padded, it was solid. Dara flipped it open, eager to see which of their memories had been spared. He smiled at the first picture in the album. It was a photo of him and Silloo, her parents, and her brother in Iran. Settling into the sofa, he brought his ankle up to the knee of his other leg and rested the album on his bent knee. His mind flooded with memories of the trip. The colonel had decided that he wanted to do a once-in-a-lifetime road trip, from Bombay to London.

Chapter 20

Dara smiled. His father-in-law was forever an adventurer. "*Millecinquecento,*" he said out loud in his best Italian accent.

"What are you doing, *jan?*" Silloo came into the living room, her long hair wet from her shower.

"I found the album of the trip we did with your parents, the road trip to London," he said, beaming.

"Oh really? Was that in the box from Valerie?"

"Yes. Come and look at it with me."

"I don't even remember what I gave her to take. I am so glad we have that still." She slid in next to her husband on the sofa and slipped her arm through his. "Oh wow, look at these. What a great trip it was. How did Daddy even outfit that Fiat with those tents?"

"He used luggage racks and had canvas tents made that would roll up to the bar. Remember how those tents all connected to each other so that it was all sealed up around the car? Then we had the spokes that went into the ground to secure it."

"Ah, yes, that's right. It was genius. My daddy was such a clever man."

"Yes, he was."

"Where did we stop first, the place where we saw that beautiful flower that only blooms once a year at night?" she asked.

"The Queen of the Night. It was in Nashik. That was our first stop on our way to Delhi."

"It was beautiful. Those petals were two different shapes, do you remember? They opened like a hand holding a goblet." She cupped her hands, mimicking the shape of the flower.

"It was spectacular."

"Then we went to Delhi, Agra, and Jaipur, right?"

"That's right, and from there we drove up through Kashmir to Gilgit. Trying to avoid the dacoits, or looters, as we say in English," he recounted.

Silloo rested her head on Dara's shoulder as he turned the page. "Let me think, from there we drove to Lahore, then Karachi and Rawalpindi. Then before we went to Quetta, there was that shop owner who told us to buy a trailer, remember, because the roads in Quetta were so bad, he said our car would be too heavy. It was good advice; we would not have made it through those hills of Baluchistan without it."

"Where was this picture of Mummy and me taken?" She pointed to a picture on the page.

"This was in Iran."

"Ah, yes, when we first drove into Iran. What was that town called, eh…Zahedan. That was it!" she said proudly. "That was where we picked up that teenage boy and drove him to his village."

"*Becharu*, poor boy, remember we dropped him off, and then when we reached Kerman, we heard there had been an earthquake and the village was destroyed."

"*Becharu*." Silloo's cheeks turned pink and tears welled in her eyes. Dara loved how her heart felt everything. He kissed her forehead, and she snuggled in even closer.

"From Kerman we drove to Shiraz and then Isfahan. There was that American couple we met there, at the *agiary*. Remember them? They were learning Persian and studying the Zoroastrian religion. Do you remember their names?"

"Mary and Bill!" she recalled.

"That's right!"

"Can you believe that we drove through Pakistan and Iran camping on the side of the road in a car?" She laughed. "Remember when Mummy's suitcase was stolen from the top of the car while we were sleeping?"

"We are lucky that that was all that happened!"

"I know, really," she said, shaking her head.

"And what about that bridge that almost collapsed. Thank God your dad decided to stop and make sure it was safe."

"What was wrong with it again?" she asked.

"The planks had moved and were not on the track. We were able to fix it, but he made us all walk over the bridge while he drove over it. But if we had not stopped—"

"We would have gone *pishh* down into the ravine." She motioned with her hand. He smiled. "From Tehran to Tabriz, and then Turkey, right?" she continued.

"Yes, all along the Black Sea to Ankara and then Istanbul."

"Oh, the Bosporus! It was so beautiful. And Hagia Sophia and the bazaar with all the spices."

"It was something really special." Dara said thoughtfully.

"How long did it take us? The whole trip?" Silloo asked.

"Let's see, we left in July, and we reached London sometime in the middle of October. So three months."

"I feel like the trip was shorter than that. It seemed to move quicker once we were in Europe."

"Yes, it did." He chuckled. "We had to start staying in hotels then. We could not just park our car and camp out on the side of the road." They giggled.

"Oh!" She started to laugh harder. "Remember when the trailer separated from the car on the Autobahn?" Dara, having just taken a swig of his scotch, almost spat it out as he recollected the image. Both of them laughed hysterically.

"At first, I thought, which poor soul lost their trailer? Then I realized it was ours!" she cried out, tears streaming down her face as her body convulsed in fits of laughter.

"I was driving, and your mum and dad were both shouting! I don't know how I managed to drive alongside it and push it into the breakdown lane. We were lucky that no one else was in that lane." They finally settled into quiet smiles, lost in thoughts of their amazing trip.

They sat a while, in silence, reliving memories of that iconic trip, a different time. Dara's consciousness returned to their living room. His eyes scanned the space, noting all that was missing. Dust lines on the walls where pictures had once hung. His ears pinged from the quiet; the void of his children's presence suddenly hit him. The reality of what Silloo must have endured all these months overwhelmed him. An uncontrollable sob escaped from him, and he pushed the album aside and pulled her into his arms. Softly, he cried into her shoulder.

⬦ ⬦ ⬦

Chapter 20

As Silloo boarded a plane bound for Bombay, she turned to see Dara waving to her from the glass door at the terminal, the same glass door where she had stood months earlier waving goodbye to her children. Her body surged as the painful memory came flooding back.

She waved at Dara and blew him a kiss. Leaving him behind hadn't been her plan. She had hoped that they would board that plane together and leave Aden and the life it had stripped away from them behind, once and for all. Instead, she was leaving her husband, half of her life, behind, flying into an unknown story. The only consolation was that she would see her children in a few short hours. She would be able to hold them and kiss them and smell them. She would. She would hold them again.

Buckling her seatbelt and peering out the window, she watched Dara still standing in the doorway. He had become so thin in these past few months but was still so handsome. She watched him intently and thought it strange that she could see him so clearly, yet he was just looking at the body of a plane only knowing her presence in it. She blew him another kiss and settled her hands on her belly. Unbeknownst to her, the warmth of her hand transferred through her clothing, reaching her skin, and softly blanketed the unborn child growing within.

Tomorrow would be a new day, an opportunity for a new beginning, new dreams and hopes, and a chance to make new memories. They had survived. After all, she thought, what greater gift was there than that?

Epilogue

"In the blackest of your moments, wait with no fear."
—Rumi

November 14, 1976

As its wheels lifted from the tarmac, the Air India 707 jet rocked and shook as it leapt into the sky, transitioning into a gentle, ascending glide. It had been commissioned out of retirement to transport an especially valuable cargo and its escorts. Five Zoroastrian priests, along with Mr. Cowasjee-Dinshaw and a handful of crew members, were seated around a large metal box, chanting a prayer in unison: *Yatha ahu variyo, Atha ratush ashat chit hacha.* They paused briefly when they heard the muffled sound of the first rifle shot, followed by twenty more, their official send-off.

They had triumphed. What had seemed impossible and had been tenuous to the very last moment was now close to being a success. Captain Sam Pedder glanced at his co-pilot, almost in disbelief at what they had just accomplished, then signaled to him with his hand as he got up to check on the box and their select passengers. Making his way steadily into the reconfigured first-class cabin, he thought about how humbling it was to be a part of this mission: to move the holy fire from the fire temple in Aden back to India.

In preparation, the entire plane had been purified. Since its cleansing, it had only been touched by Zoroastrians. The whole endeavor had been quite remarkable. Sam watched as the priests, strapped into the customized seats that surrounded the *Atash Adaran*, continued to chant with intention. When all was said and done, this would be a ten-hour round trip. They had landed in Aden only forty minutes earlier, keeping their engines running while two of the priests raced to the temple with an urn specially designed to escort the holy fire to the plane. Once everyone had boarded the plane, the sacred urn was inserted snugly into a solid aluminum box that had been built into the 707's first-class cabin. The carrier was large enough to provide adequate oxygen for the fire to burn, and a small door at the top allowed the priests to maintain the fire with sandalwood. A tricky and dangerous task, given the circumstances.

Sam shuddered briefly, then made his way back to the cockpit. This mission would not be complete until the fire and its escorts were safely back on the ground.

One month earlier

"Good morning, prime minister's office, how may I help you?"

"Yes, hello, this is Mr. Cowasjee-Dinshaw calling from Bombay for Prime Minister Gandhi. I would like to speak to her regarding an important matter as it relates to the Parsi community."

"One moment please, Mr. Dinshaw," said the receptionist. The line clicked briefly and was quiet for a moment until a second click introduced a new voice, warm and rich.

"Good morning, Indira Gandhi here. Mr. Dinshaw, how are you today?"

"Madam Prime Minister, thank you for taking my call. I am well, by grace of God. I know you are very busy tending to the state of affairs here in India, but I have a grave situation that needs the immediate assistance of the top officials of the Indian government."

"Please tell me."

"As you may know, the Parsi community has an *agiary* in the port city of Aden, which was built by my grandfather in 1883. We have managed to keep it open and running for the past eight years after the British handed over power to the National Front. Our Parsi community in Aden has dwindled from more than thirteen hundred people ten years ago to just a small handful now. Unfortunately, with the Communist takeover in Aden, the temple is no longer safe. It is to be shut down by order of the government. We have one very big problem with this."

"Let me guess, the sacred fire? Correct me if I'm wrong, but isn't it that the fire in each *agiary* comes from the original fire, still burning, and is believed to have been lit by the Prophet?"

"Yes, indeed, madam. This is a fact. Each fire in every new *agiary* is consecrated with embers from the original fire, and my fear is that the sacred fire will burn out. It was my grandfather's dream to build the *agiary* and *dakhma* in Aden, transporting the fire from Bombay to Aden at that time. I just cannot leave the sacred fire there to simply be extinguished." He snuffed. "If there is any way that I can return the fire to Bombay, then I must at least try. It is my solemn duty." His voice softened.

"Mr. Dinshaw, I applaud your determination, but what is it that I can do? India has not had any jurisdiction over Aden for almost forty years. Outside of empathizing with you, I am not really sure what help I can be to you."

"Prime Minister Gandhi, I know that you have a very special connection to my people. And our Parsi community was so grateful for your assistance in getting the Barucha family out of Aden a few years back. So please bear with me as I suggest the only option available."

The prime minister signaled her aide for some tea, then settled into her easy chair and looked out her office window, focusing on her trusted old friends: the dominion columns. She listened intently.

Mr. Dinshaw explained that he and some other notable Parsis within the community had discussed moving the sacred fire to Iran, but the Zoroastrians of Iran had concerns about their government preventing the entry of the fire. A plan to move the fire to London was not feasible due to the sheer distance. So, the only real alternative was to move it back to India. Dinshaw had approached Field Marshall Sam Manekshaw, chief of the Army Staff of the Indian Army, to determine the best land route back to India, but this also posed several problems, the biggest being that the fire would need to pass through the Muslim holy cities of Mecca and Medina—again, not viable. There was no way that Saudi would allow it. The only possibility that they could conceive of was to fly the holy fire from Aden to Bombay.

"You say *fly* the holy fire? That seems like a wild idea, Mr. Dinshaw."

"Oh but, madam, let me explain. Air India has been contacted already, and they have first of all identified an all-Parsi captain and crew, and we are now working on a plan to secure a retired 707. What I need your assistance with is approaching the Yemeni government and requesting permission to remove the fire. You see, madam, you are our last hope. We have approached the Queen of the Commonwealth, Her Royal Highness Queen Elizabeth, but she has refused. We even went to the World Bank, but they also will not assist. Our only hope is the Indian government. Our only hope is you."

"I see." She paused, taking in all this information. "This plan of yours seems outrageous, not to mention quite dangerous. Are you prepared for all that can go wrong? Can you even take a live fire on a plane?" she said as her eyes again wrestled with the blur from the *jali*.

"Yes, madam. I understand the dangers, but as a devout Zoroastrian, what other choice do I have? Like I told you before, it is my solemn duty to explore every option. We have the best Parsi engineers in Bombay designing a solid steel box that will carry the fire safely back to India. I am very confident that we can remove the fire from Aden and bring it back home to India, where it belongs," Mr. Dinshaw said proudly.

"Let me think about this. I will speak with the deputy prime minister and get back to you. But before I go, let me ask you something, Mr. Dinshaw. Who is paying for all of this?"

"Why, of course *I* am paying for it, madam, and money is no object when it comes to our sacred *Atash*."

Prime Minister Gandhi hung up the phone, picked up her teacup, and swirled its contents, watching the tea spin around and around. The sacred fire of the Parsis was beckoning her for help. She sighed. How could she not assist?

⊹ ⊹ ⊹

Nestled in the Shamsan Mountain Range in Aden, the *agiary* overlooked the town of Crater. Within its walls, Dastoor Rumi Madivala tended to the fire slowly and deliberately. He was somber; this was their last night together in what had been a sanctuary to them both for many years. His life had been in its service, and it pained him that their time together was drawing to a close. Rumi had no doubt in his mind that the mission would be a success; the sacred fire had willed this all to happen, after all. How else could any of it be explained?

It had been his responsibility to care for the fire for the past few years, and even with all the unrest in Aden, he had never felt unsafe or at risk. Bombs had been detonated all around the grounds of the *agiary*, but never had one so much as chipped the paint of an exterior wall. He understood the immense power of the fire and its ability to protect him. This move was the right thing to do. And as sad as he was to bear witness to the end of this little paradise, he was ready to do whatever needed to be done to preserve the *Atash*. Nothing would stand in his way.

As the priest finished up his last offering and prayers to his loyal companion, he heard some impatient shuffling behind him. He turned around to see Mr. Mardden, the administrator of the *agiary*, looking anxious. "*Dastur-jee*, forgive me, but there was just a phone call from the commissioner of police. He will not allow the removal of the *Atash* without inspection." His voice cracked as he continued, "He said he will be here before midnight, along with the motorcade, to conduct the inspection." Mr. Mardden's eyes shifted nervously from the priest to the fire and then back to the priest.

Rumi could hear the pounding of his own heart. If a non-Zoroastrian laid eyes on the sacred fire, it would be contaminated, and then what would be the point of any of this? How could this be happening now? When would the end be in sight? All his confidence from just a minute before slid down his body through his *champals* and into the clean, cool concrete floor. He sensed Mr. Mardden's angst, and he understood exactly why this was a problem. Rumi composed himself. He could not seem rattled and had to think quickly.

"What did he say, exactly?" Rumi asked.

"Just that he would be here with the motorcade at midnight, and he will inspect everything to be sure that nothing is being smuggled out of the country," Mr. Mardden reported.

Rumi turned back to the *Atash*, begging longingly for some sign of reassurance. After a quiet reflection, he knew what he had to do. He quickly walked away from the fire to catch his breath. When he returned, he called on the other three priests.

"There is nothing we can do to stop the commissioner. We must just pray and have faith in the sacred fire and that *Ahura Mazda* will guide us through this. *Chalo avi-ja, fiker nathy.* Come on, come, don't worry." The group formed a prayer ring around the *Atash* and began chanting into the night.

Just before midnight, the rumbling of motorcycles and jeep tires approaching the gate of the temple could be heard, followed by the crunching of sandals on the sandy path to the *agiary* doors. The dreaded loud knock at the door had the priests and Mr. Mardden looking at one other in desperation but there was nothing more they could do. This was surely the commissioner. They had come so close to saving the *Atash* and getting it back to India to make history. Rumi's heart sank. The plan to save the fire had failed.

Mr. Mardden opened the door slowly, peering out through the crack to find a member of the Adeni *lugna* standing in front, with two Zoroastrian priests dressed in their white robes behind him. One of them was holding a large urn, a smile on his face as he gently dipped his head in greeting.

"Commissioner is not come, *iinah mayit.*"

Rumi stood up and hurried over, opening the door fully. "What did you say?" he asked.

"Commissioner is dead. He die this evening. Not coming. You go now," said the messenger impatiently in his broken English, then turned and walked hurriedly past the motorcade to return to his jeep at the end of the roadway.

The priests and Mr. Mardden stood for a moment in disbelief, watching as the vehicle disappeared in a cloud of dust, leaving behind the motorcade, two smiling priests, and a rather large urn.

Rumi quickly gathered his wits and got the attention of the other men. They had to prepare the fire. There was still a chance that this would happen. The plane was waiting on the airport tarmac just fifteen minutes away, engines running, ready to take off. There was no time to waste. They carefully transferred the fire into the urn, the embers burning calmly in their temporary home, then made their way to the motorcade.

In short time, they joined the three other priests waiting on board the plane, securing the urn within the metal box. Rumi's part was done. He bowed deeply, hands in prayer, to the other priests and Mr. Cowasjee Dinshaw before exiting the aircraft with Mr. Mardden.

The doors were shut swiftly in preparation for takeoff. As the plane began its ascent, a twenty-one-gun salute could be heard echoing through the Shamsan Mountains and across the port city of Aden, signaling the end of an era.

During the flight, as the priests prayed continuously, they

kept their eyes on the box, only leaving their seats periodically, one at a time, to feed the fire. Each time they opened the small door on the top of the box, there was a risk that the flame would ignite a fire in the pressurized cabin. The *Atash*, however, chose to burn gently, glowing softly throughout the flight.

Sam and his copilot brought the plane in for the landing at Santa Cruz airport in Bombay at 7:00 a.m. The airport was overflowing with Parsis who had traveled from all over India to welcome their sacred fire back home. Once the passengers had disembarked with the urn, the head priest, surrounded by a large group of Parsis, touched the ground before standing and uncovering the urn, allowing the flame to grow and rise to greet its visitors. But the fire's journey was far from over. The highway from Bombay to Pune was closed to all traffic to allow a specially outfitted bus to carry the sacred contents of the urn and its escorts to the Adenwalla Agiary in Lonavala, India, some sixty miles away. The priests continued to pray as the holy fire glowed.

The sacred fire from the *agiary* in Aden still burns brightly today in Lonavala—a testament to all who once called Aden their home and proof that with faith, love, and hope, the impossible is indeed possible.

The End

Silloo and Dara (aka Prochi and Rohin).

Silloo (aka Prochi) with the boys.

Silloo and Dara (aka Prochi and Rohin) at an award ceremony with Pierre and Valarie (aka Patrice and Joelle).

Silloo and Dara (aka Prochi and Rohin).

The Colonel's house boat.

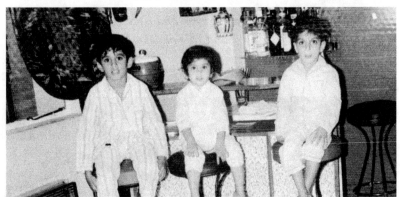

Rustom, Ana, and Aram (aka Sarosh, Arnie, and Sohrab).

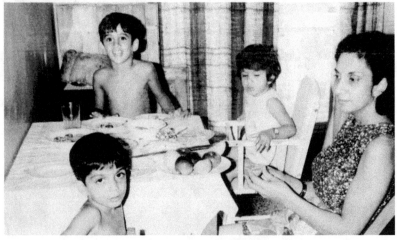

Silloo (aka Prochi) with the children in the apartment.

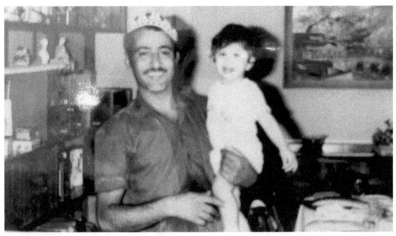

Ahmed and Ana (aka Arnie).

Traveling from Bombay to London in the Fiat.

*Steamerpoint Shopping District.
The stairs on the right led to Bhicajee Cowasjee.*

Dara and Silloo (aka Rohin and Prochi) at their wedding.

Acknowledgements

Some of my earliest childhood memories are of my siblings and me sitting with our mother as she retold "the Aden story." It was as much a part of our upbringing as chicken curry, or Lipton tea steeped with mint and lemongrass. Her accounts and the lessons from them, some that only came to me as I wrote this book, are now forever embedded in the essence of my being.

For years, we would all say how "someone" should document this slice of history. All of us recognizing how compelling the narrative was, but no one feeling worthy enough of the task. I still catch myself wondering if I have truly done this story its due justice. I hope that I have. I clearly remember the afternoon about five years ago when my mother handed me the old, tattered, brown legal-size envelope. We were, befittingly, sitting down to afternoon tea when she brought it to me. I had expressed interest in perhaps trying to document their story and she wasted no time in presenting me with her typed notes. Handing me the envelope, the corners held firmly in each hand, the way Japanese businesspeople hand you their business card. Holding it with an unfettered trust and faith that I would do something meaningful with her pages, the pages that she had kept with her, waiting for this moment for close to fifty years.

I took her envelope, unsure of what exactly I was going to do with it. It stayed, buried in my bedside drawer for over a year.

It was not until a move in 2018 that I pulled it out, began reading it, and then decided to try and tackle this monumental feat. After all, what did I know about writing a book? Would I write an account of what had happened or would I take some creative license and write it as a novel. Could I even do that?

In my writing of this book, I chose to take creative license where there were gaps and embellished where I felt it was needed. However, I have made every effort to accurately detail what happened from a historical perspective, especially, since this timeframe has not been widely documented. I relied heavily on what little is in print, but mostly from those still here to share.

And as everything must come to an end, so has this endeavor of mine. I now find myself at the point in the process where I can look back and reflect on all those that helped to bring this book to print. It is the precious moment where I get to press my palms firmly together at my heart and bow deeply to those that helped make this a reality. This book would not have come together without the contributions and support of these people.

I cannot say enough about everyone at Ten16 Press. Shannon Ishizaki and her delightful team worked tirelessly to bring the manuscript, cover and launch to fruition. I am so grateful to Lauren Blue and Emlyn Dornemann for their exceptional editing skills. Kaeley Dunteman for working with me tirelessly on the cover. Sean Malone for guiding me through the launch process so seamlessly.

Acknowledgements

To the writing community of the The Shit No One Tells You About Writing podcast. Between the weekly podcast and writing retreat, I learned so much in such a very short time. But most significantly the podcast led me to Ten16 Press, and Bianca Marais' wisdom and support of my process was what any debut author can only wish for.

Special thanks to my parents Rohinton Motiwalla and Prochi Motiwalla. My dad and I spent many hours together on FaceTime during Covid lockdown. He recounted the intricacies and horrors of this period of his life, for the first time since it happened. His memory for detail in his late eighties is impeccable. This book is his story, and it would not exist in any form without his dedication to its writing. What a gift it was to share this process with him and have him cheering me on the whole way.

My mother is the glue that binds this book together. Her endurance, resilience and sheer bravery is what saved these men and brought them to their eventual freedom, at no small cost to her mind or body. She is, and has always been, my inspiration. The timeline of this book is based on her meticulous diary entries, typed in the middle of the night on a broken typewriter that she kept hidden. I think she always knew in her heart that a book would someday exist. She is my constant reminder of the strength that we all possess if we choose it.

I have endless gratitude for Noel Brehony, chairman of the British Yemeni Society, Research Associate at the London Middle East Institute, author and diplomat. How fortunate

I am to have found him! Noel has had an extensive career as a diplomat in the Middle East. When we first came in contact with each other, we quickly realized that Noel, and his wife had known my parents and socialized with them in Aden. Noel advocated through the British Embassy to help release my father and the other men. When he heard from me through another Yemen historian nearly fifty years later, he wasted no time in getting in touch. And true to his nature he continued to help my family, this time in bringing our story to the world. His book, *Yemen Divided*, served as my go-to for historical accuracy and his keen eye combed the manuscript making sure that the timelines, people and details were in fact accurate.

To Joelle and Patrice Houette for sharing their time in Aden with me over oysters and wine in their beautiful home in Auray, France. My gratitude to them for everything that they did for my mother in those trying times is hard to articulate. They epitomize the meaning of true friendship.

To Shapur Rao, who was instrumental in reaching the right people at the right time, applying political pressure for my father's release. He graciously scheduled a FaceTime call with me at an inconvenient time in India, and proceeded to recount in detail the story as if it had just happened; I was awed. That day I was given insight to a side of the story so critical to how it ended, that I would have never known if it were not for him. This is a man who would stop at nothing to help his family and seek the truth.

Acknowledgements

To David Ferris and Shelley Singer for their professional eye. And to Heather Sangster, my editor, who has been a lifeline through the editing and publishing process. Her attention to every little detail was mind-blowing. I owe her much gratitude for getting this to where it needed to be so that it could be shared and am so grateful for the friendship that has spurned from this project. What an honor to have someone so seasoned in the industry believe so wholeheartedly in this book.

David Trabulsi, Max Trabulsi, Nylah Trabulsi and Shane Trabulsi, you all have lived this process alongside me for the last few years. Each of you have, at separate moments, picked me up, pushed me forward, and encouraged me to keep going. The four of you are the reason that I stuck with it and made it to the finish line. Thank you for always pushing me to be my best.

To Sarosh Motiwalla, Sohrab Motiwalla and Arnie Siberell, my siblings. This story is as much yours as it is mum and dad's. Sohrab and Arnie: thank you for your continuous encouragement and appreciation, for reading the earliest versions, and encouraging me to keep at it. It has come a long way since then. Sarosh, you left us far too soon. You endured so much as a child during this time and subsequently from this experience. I know you are watching from above and cheering me on. I have felt your encouragement throughout the process.

Thank you, Mahrukh Campbell, and Kashmira Motiwalla for finding and sharing a twenty-page, worn-and-torn letter that documented dates and details integral to the story.

Special thanks to Erin Krol, Jen Laman and Chris Babu. Erin you have been my sounding board since that Carnegie lecture we attended together, and how appropriate that you came up with the ultimate title for the book. Thank you for sharing this authoring journey with me. And Jen, thank you for being the first to ever read the manuscript start to finish, with all its typos and errors and gaps. Thank you for loving it, wholeheartedly pushing me to move forward and for introducing me to Chris Babu. I am so fortunate to have had a seasoned author give me real advice so early in the process.

Mrs. Johnson, my fifth-grade form teacher, for introducing me to the world of creative writing and encouraging me to find my inner writer.

Mr. Phil Moore, my high school English teacher, for teaching me how to find my voice, encouraging me to share that voice on paper and teaching me how to get it all out so that it made sense. It has taken many years, but I'm finally starting to get it.

Very special thanks to Anita Luria, Annelouise Norman, Aparna Verma, Beth Barry, Christi Feeney, Caitlin Weaver, Divya Krishnan, Jennifer Sullivan, Michelle Brockmann and Mya Poe for being my beta readers and the first to read the book as it is today.

To Humphrey, my four-legged furbaby, for never leaving my side while I wrote.

I would be nothing without the love and support from those closest to me, my dear friends and family who have cheered me

Acknowledgements

on since the beginning. Michelle Brockmann, Lisa Frackiewicz, Jennifer Sundeen, Jennifer Pinney, Donna Bennett, Charlotte Pride, Erin Krol, Jen Laman, Nancy Carter, Amee Chaudry, Kaik Barucha and Jan Mears.

And finally, to you. Thank you for picking this book up and giving it a chance. Thank you for traveling this journey with me. I hope that in sharing this story with you, you turn the final page feeling full.

About the Author

Roxana Motiwalla Trabulsi is the author of *Of Mud and Honey*. Born in London, United Kingdom, but raised in Dubai, Roxana now lives just outside of Boston in Massachusetts, where she writes and works as a freelance writer and graphic designer. A graduate of Northeastern University, she spent the first few years out of school purchasing mechanical parts for a local audio company. She and her husband moved to Tokyo soon after they were married and have lived there twice in the last twenty years. She currently sits on the board of the local farmer's market where she has not only contributed to creating a sustainable community but has also been able to bring new and diverse programs such as a self-sustainable seed library to her town. Ultimately, she revels most in her role as mum to her three children. She loves all things farmers market, travel, yoga, art and design, and of course, reading. She lives with her husband, her teenage son and their three-year-old cockapoo.